Jewish Lives, Jewish Learning

Jewish Lives, Jewish Learning

Adult Jewish Learning in Theory and Practice

Diane Tickton Schuster

UAHC Press · New York, New York

Library of Congress Cataloging-in-Publication Data

Schuster, Diane Tickton, 1944–
Jewish Lives, Jewish learning / Diane Tickton Schuster.
p. cm.
Includes bibliographical references and index
ISBN 0-8074-0788-7 (pbk. : alk. paper)
1. Jewish religious education of adults—United States—Case studies.   2.   Judaism—Study
and teaching (Continuing education)—United States.   I. Title.

BM75.S38 2003
296.6'8'084—dc21   2003054158

Contents

List of Exhibits

Acknowledgments

Jewish Lives, Jewish Learning is about adult Jewish growth, and my personal journey as a Jewish learner is part of the story of this book. That journey could not have been made without the support of scores of colleagues, teachers, friends, and loved ones who sustained me through this time of significant learning and change. My list of acknowledgments begins with my wonderful network of professionals in the field of Jewish education, most especially my colleagues at Hebrew Union College–Los Angeles: Isa Aron, Sara Lee, and Michael Zeldin. It includes the many learners I interviewed in preparation for this book, as well as dozens of rabbis, educators, and lay leaders in the Jewish community.

My gratitude extends to the adults I have taught at HUC and to the numerous professionals whom I have taught—and from whom I have learned—at gatherings of the Alliance for Adult Jewish Learning, the Central Conference of American Rabbis, Cleveland College of Jewish Studies, the Conference on Rabbinic Education, the Coalition for the Advancement of Jewish Education, the Experiment in Congregational Education, the Florence Melton Adult Mini-School, the Hadassah International Research Institute on Jewish Women, Me'ah, the National Association of Temple Educators, the Pacific Association of Reform Rabbis, the Union of American Hebrew Congregations' Department of Adult Jewish Growth, the Whizin Institute for Jewish Family Education, and at various synagogues, Federations, and bureaus of Jewish education.

Several individuals served as special sources of support through the learning journey that went into the production of this volume. Dr. Lisa Grant, my colleague and writing partner in the emerging field of adult Jewish learning, and Dr. Andrew Berner, my close friend and work associate for more than twenty-five years, sustained me through drafts and "second thoughts"—ever loyal, ever confident that this book would see the light of day.

Rabbi Suzanne Singer, first my student, then my "midwife-teacher," then my friend: every author should have an editor with the radar vision and clarity of mind that Suzanne brings to the task of refining another's work. Her editorial rigor challenged me to stay loyal to my task and to the "through lines" that gave this book its shape and cohesiveness.

Rabbi Hara Person and Kenneth Gesser of UAHC Press saw the need for this book from our first conversations. Their enthusiasm for my work never wavered, and I am grateful for their commitment to the field of adult Jewish learning. I would also like to thank the others at the UAHC Press who helped with this book, including Debra Hirsch Corman, Liane Broido, and Joel Eglash.

Above all, my mother, Reva Tickton, *z"l*, a stickler for "checking one's work," looked over my shoulder spiritually throughout the writing process. My father, Sidney G. Tickton, *z"l*, who loved a good story, continually championed the vision of *Jewish Lives, Jewish Learning*. From the moment I started interviewing learners in 1994 until his death in 2001, my father asked daily how my work was going and when the book would be done. This work is dedicated to his memory.

My daughers, Jordana and Ariana Schuster, not only nurtured me, but also were my ongoing role models for quality living and learning. I especially thank Jordi for her evaluative comments and editorial insights.

My husband, Jack Schuster, has been my greatest fan as I have evolved a career in adult Jewish education. His understanding of what it takes to stand before a new frontier, to develop a network in an evolving field, and to give voice to nascent ideas has emboldened me to move forward with steady step. He is my partner in Jewish life and Jewish learning, and I feel continually blessed by a loving marriage that is built on generosity, collaboration, and respect.

Others with whom I consulted who deserve special thanks:

Rabbi Judith Abrams	Rabbi Haim Dov Beliak
Dr. Karen Arnold	Rabbi Leslie Bergson
Judy Aronson	Rabbi William Berk
Rabbi Michael Balinsky	Irene Bolton
Dr. Adrianne Bank	Anne Brener
Dr. Karen Barth	Rabbi Yossi Carron
Rabbi Lewis Barth	Rabbi Jennifer Clayman

Reverend Emily Click
Rabbi David Cohen
Rabbi Norman Cohen
Dr. Steven M. Cohen
Rabbi Michael Cook
Rabbi William Cutter
Dr. Sandra Dashevsky
Dr. Aryeh Davidson
Judy Elkin
Rabbi Larry Englander
Rabbi Sally Finestone
Dr. Paul Flexner
Rabbi Karen Fox
Rabbi Elyse Goldstein
Rabbi Don Goor
Dru Greenwood
Rabbi Judith Halevy
Dr. Barbara Hammer
Lee Meyerhoff Hendler
Rabbi Eli Herscher
Dr. Bethamie Horowitz
Rabbi Talia Hyman
Rabbi Devorah Jacobson
Idit Jacques
Rabbi Samuel Joseph
Dr. Marshall Jung
Rabbi Earl Kaplan, *z"l*
Rabbi Patricia Karlin-
   Neumann
Dr. Judith Kates
Dr. Betsy Katz
Rabbi Jan Katzew
Rabbi Paul Kipnes
Rabbi Avi Levine

Dr. Elizabeth Wyner Mark
Rabbi Carole Meyers
Dr. Jonathan Mirvis
Dr. Wendy Mogel
Dr. Naomi Myrvaagnes
Rabbi David Nelson
Rabbi Ellen Nemhauser
Dr. Ruth Nemzoff
Rabbi Jan Offel
Rabbi Jonathan Omer-Man
Rabbi Lawrence Raphael
Dr. Joseph Reimer
Dr. Wendy Rosov
Rabbi Laurie Rutenberg
Dr. Jo Sanders
Rabbi Jeffrey Schein
Jane Shapiro
Barbara Shuman
Maida Solomon
Dr. Phyllis Sonnenschein
Rabbi David Starr
Dr. Bernard Steinberg
Joshua Stempel
Rabbi Lance Sussman
Dr. Linda Thal
Darcy Veber
Rabbi Pamela Wax
Linda Wimmer
Rabbi Laura Novak Winer
Dr. Ron Wolfson
Dr. Jonathan Woocher
Dr. Meredith Woocher
Dr. Lois Zachary
Rabbi Josh Zweiback

Introduction

Early in 1995, I picked up my weekly copy of the Los Angeles *Jewish Journal* and was intrigued to read about the rising number of baby boomers who were becoming interested in pursuing personal spiritual growth. The author reported on an interview with one of America's leading sociologists of religion, Wade Clark Roof, in which Roof indicated that American Jews were part of the explosion of adult interest and commitment to new religious engagement: "The 76 million people born to the generation that came of age during World War II now make up one-third of the nation's population. . . . All our institutions [will have] to adapt to this population and religious congregations [must] take seriously the culture of the boomers." Speaking of Jewish boomers, Roof continued, "I think a lot of them will be knocking on the rabbi's door, asking religious questions" (Eshman, 1995, p. 10).

In recent years, speculations by Roof and other social scientists (Wuthnow, 1994; Cohen and Davidson, 2001) have inspired leaders in the Jewish community to imagine that the increasing number of Jewish baby boomers now reaching midlife would lead to a dramatic upsurge of interest in Judaism and adult Jewish education. Lay leaders and Jewish professionals have hoped that the introduction of new adult learning opportunities would motivate Jewish adults of all ages not only to "knock on the rabbi's door" but, also, to "step across the thresholds" of Jewish communal or educational programs into active Jewish life.

And, in fact, despite a variety of reasons for alienation or disassociation with Judaism and Jewish life, more and more people are, as Wade Clark Roof anticipated, "knocking on the door" in search of Jewish learning opportunities. Not only are the numbers increasing, but the diversity of prospective Jewish adult learners is becoming more and more variegated.

For example, take the Florence Melton Adult Mini-School, a sophisticated two-year Jewish literacy program for adults. In 2001, when several hundred students and friends of the Mini-School gathered to celebrate the ninetieth birthday of the school's founder, it was announced that due to the increasing demand for quality Jewish adult education in the United States and abroad, the *sixtieth* Mini-School would soon open its door. School directors enthusiastically reported that enrollments were steady, curricula were being revised to help learners study beyond the initial two-year program, and a new faculty development program was being created to help teachers meet the needs of an increasingly diverse and intellectually demanding student population. Researchers studying the program reported that the faculty were especially gratified by their interactions with a vibrant constituency of lifelong learners. As one veteran Mini-School educator told them: "This is the most exciting teaching I've done in my entire life. . . . I see [this program] creating a community of learners. The students become my teachers while I teach them. I've worked with three different groups and am really looking forward to next year" (Grant, Schuster, Woocher, and Cohen, in press).

To be sure, Jewish adult learning programs have mushroomed during the past decade. Look at any issue of a Jewish community bulletin or of a national Jewish magazine and the announcements of adult courses, retreats, meditation sessions, and on-line study opportunities are in full view. Enrollments in Elderhostels on Jewish themes are fully booked. Boston's Me'ah program (a Federation-sponsored Jewish literacy initiative) has spread to Cleveland and Florida. Jewish Community Centers now reach out to young, unaffiliated adults through Derekh Torah, a twelve-week introductory course about Judaism. Law firms host early morning text study, and center-city programs such as New York's Skirball Center for Adult Jewish Learning offer after-work courses on topics ranging from "How Jews Read the Bible" to "Psychoanalysis and Rabbinic Literature" to "Friends and Lovers Engaging in Jewish Life." New community *kollels* (Jewish adult study programs) in cities such as New York, Toronto, Seattle, Phoenix, Milwaukee, and Atlanta feature classes by rabbis and scholars from across the Jewish spectrum. Jewish book festivals host overflow crowds. Attendance at the annual Jewish Renewal *kallah*, a five-day feast of Jewish learning, grew from 350 in 1985 to nearly 800 in 2001. When the University of Judaism in Los Angeles collaborated with five area synagogues and the local Federation to sponsor Yesod, a two-year adult learning program, eager registrants filled the 250 slots within days of the program's formation. And, while enrollments in travel-and-learn programs in Israel are uneven due to the unsteady political climate, surfing of Jewish Web sites and enrolling in on-line text study programs have become popular among thousands of Jews from all over the world.

The Call for Educated Jewish Adults

The proliferation of Jewish adult learning programs is a wonderful hallmark of an enlivened Jewish community, but this optimistic view has been tempered by the reality that a significant proportion—perhaps the majority—of contemporary Jews lack substantive Jewish knowledge and thus refrain from taking steps toward their own Jewish growth. Though successful and highly functional in other domains of adult life, these adults think of themselves as "underdeveloped" Jewishly and feel ill-prepared to function as "grown-ups" in Jewish roles and settings. Many have never had any affiliation with a Jewish organization or been part of an organized Jewish community and, as a consequence, feel uncertain how to join in. Others may have rebelled as adolescents against what they saw as constrictive Jewish families or institutions and now carry a child's view of Judaism that makes the religion seem irrelevant to adult life. Some were raised in comfortably assimilated Jewish families who provided the warmth of "ethnic Judaism" but did not equip them with intellectual content or a spiritual framework that could help them explain, to themselves or to others, why they were Jewish or what Judaism meant in their lives. Others grew up wishing to participate in meaningful Jewish life but were disenfranchised because of income status, divorce, gender, sexual orientation, or other conditions that led to exclusion; today these adults have considerable anger—which many disparagingly refer to as "Jewish baggage"—that makes them wary and defensive, cautious and self-protecting.

Concern about the high levels of Jewish "illiteracy" and alienation has caused many in the Jewish community to fear that Jewish continuity—sometimes perceived as "the ability to make Jewishly informed decisions that may be passed on to future generations"—may be compromised. The need to "grow" a population of dedicated Jewish adult learners and teachers has been articulated by a range of community leaders. In his 1997 Presidential Address to the Union of American Hebrew Congregations, Rabbi Eric Yoffie exhorted the Reform Movement to "lift up a whole generation of Reform Jews from a pervasive ignorance of Jewish people, texts, literature, and history, thus enabling them to become increasingly literate as

Jews." Outlining a five-point program in Jewish literacy, Yoffie urged Reform leaders to support initiatives for congregational Torah study, adult learning programs, and the cultivation of Torah readers and (by implication) new congregational teachers.

Similarly, when announcing plans for Me'ah, a large-scale Jewish literacy program designed for adults in the Boston Jewish community, Federation executive Barry Shrage (1996) called for learning opportunities that would help people to understand Judaism in a systematic and serious way:

> Establishing universal Jewish literacy as a communal norm . . . must be our highest priority. . . . We must . . . create a Jewish world that places the same value on understanding the basic works of Maimonides as on understanding the basic works of Shakespeare. The continuity of Jewish life requires knowledgeable adults who can understand and live Judaism in the context of community, with all its beauty, intellectual energy and spiritual and ethical values. Judaism cannot "skip a genera-tion." It requires adults who can be role models for their children and grandchildren. (p. 7)

While most communal leaders agree that Jewish continuity will be well served by helping Jewish adults to acquire Jewish literacy, there is little con-sensus about what propels people to engage in Jewish study in an active, ongoing manner; nor is much known about what actually motivates Jewish adults to proactively take on Jewish educational roles with their children, grandchildren, or other learners. A recent study of the impact of the Melton Mini-School on its learners (Grant, Schuster, Woocher, and Cohen, in press) provides the first "window" into the ways Jewish learning can affect adult meaning-making, connection to Judaism and other Jews, and behavior in the Jewish community. Additional studies are needed, especially those that can shed light on how Jewish lives are impacted *over time*. To date, there are no empirical longitudinal studies of continuity or change in Jewish adult learn-ers or, for that matter, of any other groups of adult Jews (Schuster, 1995).

And What About the Teachers?

Just as adult Jewish learners and Jewish communal leaders have particular concerns about the need for quality adult learning opportunities, so do pro-fessionals who teach Jewish adults express anxiety about the needs of this population. For many Jewish adult educators—rabbis, cantors, school directors, classroom teachers, family educators, informal educators, communal workers, and lay teachers—the concern stems from a lack of preparation for how to work effectively with adults. Numerous Jewish professionals have indicated that they know little about who Jewish adult learners are, what they bring to their learning experiences, what they find rewarding in their teachers, or what happens to them intellectually, spiritually, or behaviorally as a result of their learning. These de facto adult educators do not feel confident that they have a clear understanding of what constitutes effective adult learning practice or what Jewish adult learners need to thrive and grow. Unlike their counterparts in the Christian community who have dozens of books that guide teachers and learners alike, they have discovered that, as *a field of study*, Jewish adult religious education is in its infancy.

Of course, lifelong learning and the obligation to study have long been at the center of Jewish life. In the second century C.E., Y'hudah ben Tema offered a developmental educational timetable that prescribed engagement in learning throughout the life cycle:

> At five to scripture, ten to Mishnah, thirteen to religious duties, fifteen to Talmud, eighteen to wedding canopy, twenty to seek a livelihood, thirty to fullness of strength, forty to understanding, fifty to counsel, sixty to wisdom.... (*Pirkei Avot* 5:21)

Nonetheless, although the value of adult Jewish learning is still celebrated by scholars and laypersons alike, Ben Tema's model of what and when Jews are supposed to study has become largely irrelevant in the post-Enlightenment culture of the past two hundred years. Not only are the rhythms of modern Jewish life organized differently from the learning-centered sequence Ben Tema advocated, but most Jewish adults today come to learning with self-perceived learning "handicaps" (e.g., limited knowledge about Jewish texts or ritual, anxiety about acquiring Hebrew literacy, undeveloped analytical skills to bring to Jewish sources) that stop them from entering into substantive Jewish educational activities. Correspondingly, many Jewish professionals feel uncertain about how to meet—and genuinely serve—the learners who come to their doors.

Professional Development:
Responding to the Needs of Jewish Adult Educators

In 2000, I was invited to speak at a rabbinical conference about the characteristics of Jewish adult learners. There, I asked my audience to write down their most pressing questions about working with adults. When I looked through the responses, I found that the most frequently expressed concern was, ironically, *How can I get people to take the risk to try Jewish learning? What does it take to get Jewish adults in the door?*

Furthermore, when I taught a graduate seminar on Jewish education, I discerned a tone of wariness when prospective rabbis and educators described the adults they imagined *might* approach their doors. I was surprised to discover that some professionals in the Jewish community think of adults as "the enemy," a population characterized by resistance, defiance, or excessive demands. Comments I heard from my students, as well as from a group of Jewish family educators at a national meeting, included the following:

"I don't feel comfortable with adults. I don't like how they challenge my authority."

"It's tough teaching adults: they are so needy and insecure about their Jewish knowledge. They bring so much baggage into their learning. And they expect me to help them get over the past."

"Adults intimidate me. I know how to make learning fun for kids, but with adults it never feels like fun."

"I never know how to pace myself with adults, especially when there's someone who dominates the discussion and won't let the group move forward. Even worse are the people who come just to shmooze with their friends and could care less about what I had planned to teach them."

These comments reinforced my contention that before adult educators (and, by proxy, adult learning committees) begin to plan programs for adults—even before they start worrying about recruiting people to these programs—they need to understand more about adult development and learning in general, and Jewish adult development and learning in particular. Rather than starting exclusively with what a professional or lay leader thinks learners need to learn, adult educators need to begin by assessing who the learners are and what they seek as adults and as Jews. Moreover, rather than focusing on getting Jewish adults *to* the door, Jewish professionals need to critically assess what will happen once these learners step over the threshold and strive toward meaningful adult Jewish growth.

My Journey: Research Is Me-Search

This book would not have come about had I myself not stepped up to a rabbi's door— actually several doors—and begun a Jewish learning journey at midlife. I am a developmental psychologist and educator whose personal questions have always shaped my professional pursuits. When, as a graduate student in social work in the early 1970s, I was asked to write on an important issue of human development, I focused on women's transition to parenthood—certainly one of my own concerns during early adulthood. Later, when I was uncertain about the direction of my career, I acquired the skills of a career counselor and designed career and life planning workshops for young adults. In my early forties, when choosing a topic for a dissertation in human development and education while concurrently raising a family, I focused on "women's balance between work and family." Thus, it was no surprise that, in the early 1990s, at a time of significant personal transition (in a fifteen-month period, my mother died, my older daughter graduated from high school, I finished a book, and I turned fifty), I once again looked through the lens of my own experience to define a new area of professional inquiry. Like many other academics, my "me-search" became my research.

My journey to the study of Jewish adulthood actually had begun some years earlier when, anticipating my older daughter Jordana's bat mitzvah, I joined an adult *b'nei mitzvah* class to learn enough elementary Hebrew to be able to smoothly read the Torah blessings when called for an *aliyah*. The class turned out to be a highly alienating experience in which—after several months of sitting at long tables in a cold, poorly lit synagogue social hall, and being scolded by the rabbi for not having memorized Hebrew phrases for the group's upcoming "performance" in front of the whole congregation—I realized that I was reenacting some of my worst memories of "non-learning" and incompetence from childhood (which I experienced then on the athletic field). More and more, I realized that much of my non-learning manifested itself in a steady pattern of getting to class late, stumbling through my "turn" at recitation, and rushing out of the sessions feeling inept and ignorant. Between class meetings, I would "forget" to practice my Hebrew assignments and would avoid going to services, where I had begun to feel disturbingly self-conscious during prayers chanted in Hebrew. As the date of the adult *b'nei mitzvah* approached, I resisted shopping for a *tallit*; I felt inauthentic as a learner, I did not want to be part of a situation where I might embarrass myself, and I felt no ownership of an event that for me contradicted my inherent love of learning. Moreover, the rabbi had designed the format of the group *b'nei mitzvah*, choosing the Torah portion and assigning lines for me and my classmates to read. He took upon himself the task of commenting on the text, leaving only the responsibility for the "thank-you speech" and the *Oneg Shabbat* preparations to class members.

Although I ultimately did participate in the group *b'nei mitzvah* event, I had to confront the irony of the situation: here I was, a budding synagogue leader, as well as a seasoned professional who had herself spent several years teaching at the college level, yet I still felt insecure and uncomfortable about my ability as a learner. To my chagrin, I couldn't seem to find the words to talk to the rabbi about what was occurring; he had seemed so sure that all the students could become proficient with Hebrew and eventually would gain confidence by reading from the Torah. In his enthusiasm, however, he had failed to perceive individual student needs or to think about the values and attitudes different learners may bring into new learning endeavors.

Despite this unfortunate turnoff, my interest in "things Jewish" did not wane, and some years later I had two "corrective experiences" with Jewish learning that changed my sense of myself as someone who could get excited by texts and text study. First, in 1989, when my younger daughter was grappling with the personal relevance of her Torah portion *(B'shalach)*, a family friend, Rabbi Patricia Karlin-Neumann, offered to consult with her about views of Miriam in contemporary sources. When we called on Patty, she began pulling books off the shelf to show us different interpretations of the Torah portion. This was the first time in my life a rabbi had ever said, "Here's how to do this. If you want to understand Miriam and where this portion fits in, there are lots of things you can read so you can get perspective and form some opinions." When my daughter and I headed home carrying several volumes of commentary, I felt like I'd been given one of the greatest—and most unexpected—gifts of my life. As a former literature major, I was startled to realize that I had never thought of the Torah as a text for analysis and had not realized that biblical scholarship would capture my imagination. I was surprised by my naivete about Torah commentary and the feeling that "no one ever told me" that there might be relevance to my own life in the traditional sources.

A second "awakening" occurred in 1993 when I met Rabbi Judith Halevy, who expressed interest in my professional expertise on adult learning. Judith told me she had much to learn from me and asked if I would like to observe what she was doing in a class on midrash. I said that I would prefer to come to the class as a learner, with the promise that I would give her feedback later on. I was particularly struck by my *hunger* for a rabbi's invitation; Judith's welcome inspired me to travel weekly into Los Angeles from my home an hour away. In that class, I deepened my appreciation of the excitement of engaging text on different levels of interpretation, of exploring personal meaning in biblical stories, of partnering with *chevruta* to compare several translations of one work, and of writing my own response to a puzzling piece of Jewish literature. Additionally, over a period of months, I realized that as much as I was enthralled by the text "on the table," I was equally fascinated by the stories of the people "around the table." Having been trained as a clinical social worker, I found that I could not ignore the lives or concerns or growth experiences of my fellow learners. I was intrigued that each week these women and men would spend hours digesting what they had read, coming up with penetrating questions or novel explanations. They would return to class imbued with new insights, eager to share commentaries they had unearthed, ready to share poems or prayers they had written as they grappled with the personal significance of timeless ideas.

During a year with this group, I observed how the study of Jewish texts was affecting the way my classmates and I talked about our personal lives at that time, our work situations, and our desire for further Jewish study. I noted, too, the rising confidence many of my fellow learners brought to the analysis of the texts we were reading; even though most of us routinely turned to the teacher for her wisdom and explanations, gradually we became less and less inhibited about voicing our own views. One week, when Judith had laryngitis, I watched as she sat and beamed while class members threw themselves into discussion about a tale from the Chasidic rabbi Reb Nachman. Although individuals routinely turned to her for her nods and smiles—and an occasional head shaking over extreme interpretations—it was clear that the learning in this group had become far less "rabbinocentric" during our year of study together. I wondered, then, about the impact of that shift on Judith: how it felt to her to contract—to practice *tzimtzum*[1]—in order to make space for the learners to grow. At that time I realized that to study the experience of Jewish adult learners, I must study their teachers as well.

---

1. See chapter 7 for a discussion of how teachers practice *tzimtzum*.

Jewish Lives, Jewish Learning: Questions for Research

So began the research project that has engaged me in recent years. In 1994, I began to interview Jewish adult learners, asking one simple question: "Could you tell me about your life—your journey—Jewishly?" The responses to that question led me to broaden my inquiry: What prompts Jewish adults to begin to study Jewish texts? What matters to Jewish adult learners in the study experience? How does Jewish adult learning affect engagement with Judaism and Jewish life? What obstacles do Jewish adults need to overcome to feel safe and confident in their Jewish learning pursuits? These questions led, too, to inquiry about rabbis and educators: What do Jewish professionals need to know about human growth and development to be more sensitive to the needs of Jewish adult learners? What can they do to help adults overcome "pediatric Judaism" (a term widely used to describe learning that stops at bar mitzvah or never advances beyond a child's view of Jewish texts and holidays)? What characterizes effective teaching in Jewish adult education settings? What are some ways teachers of Jewish adult learners can themselves continue to learn and grow?

My questions about Jewish adult education extended my work of more than thirty years in the field of human development and education. Bringing to Jewish study what I have learned in other academic fields is a splendid example of the process of Jewish adult learning that philosopher Franz Rosenzweig described in his remarks in Frankfurt in 1920 at the opening of the Freies Jüdisches Lehrhaus, an institute for adult Jewish studies designed to provide assimilated German Jews with meaningful Jewish adult education. Commenting on the needs of learners and teachers in modern Jewish life, Rosenzweig (1950) said that, in a post-Emancipation environment, it is inevitable that Jewish adults will be shaped by their sense of distance and even alienation from Jewish life. He argued that rather than rejecting the lessons acquired in the larger world, Jewish adults could find meaning in their journeys from "the periphery" back to the center of Jewish life, from "life to Torah." He further commented that for those of us for whom "Judaism . . . being a Jew, has become the pivot of our lives," we need not "give up anything" but rather should find meaningful ways to bring what we know from the world outside to our experiences in the Jewish community. In that sense, the chapters that follow constitute landmarks— selected souvenirs—from my own journey as a Jewish adult and Jewish adult learner.

From Stories to Theory to Practice:
Studying Texts of Jewish Lives

As a scholar who studies the dynamics of Jewish lives and Jewish learning, I have discovered that there is much to be "mined" from the personal reflections of adults who are involved in systematic Jewish study activities. In this book are stories of a number of Jewish adults who have "knocked on a door" to enter into Jewish learning and, in the process, have grown and changed as adults, as Jews, and as Jewish adults. Each story is a composite, based on my interviews with Jewish learners and their teachers. Many of the quotes are taken from interviews, but all identifying characteristics have been altered to protect the privacy of my informants. (Chapter 7, which presents the verbatim comments of a number of outstanding Jewish adult educators, is an exception and refers to these individuals by their real names.)

My approach is that of a phenomenologist: someone who *starts* with people's experiences and later moves to thinking about hypotheses or categories or ways of explaining data. Phenomenologists generally care less about statistics than we do about the intricacies of what happens in people's lives. We ask for—and like to hear—people's stories. It is in the stories that we look for patterns, analyze issues, pose questions, interpret findings in light of other people's theories or come up with theories of our own, and then consider ways to alter specific situations or improve practice.

When I set about gathering Jewish adult learning journey stories, I did not have a fixed set of theoretical assumptions, although my training in the field of human development had predisposed me to assumptions about stages and tasks of development, the processes of socialization and human attachment, and what helps adults adapt to times of change. As a developmental psychologist, I hoped that I might find some instructive intersections between Jewish lives and existing scholarship on adulthood. As an educator, I was especially interested in what people said had "made a difference" in their journeys as learners. I didn't begin my inquiry with a hypothesis about what Jewish adulthood might look like. I decided to talk to a lot of people to see what they had to say.

Accordingly, in this book I invite the reader to approach stories of Jewish adult life using some of the methods and analytical tools that inform my work. In the chapters that follow are case studies of Jewish adults who have embarked on Jewish adult learning journeys. These stories are presented for several purposes. First, each story is discussed in terms of psychological and educational theory and research that can help to explain Jewish adult development and learning. Such theoretical perspectives typically were not included in the professional training most Jewish professionals received; accordingly, this material is offered as a new paradigm for thinking about adult growth and change.

Second, the stories are presented as text documents appropriate for group analysis and discussion—for "text study." Rabbis, cantors, educators, lay leaders, and Jewish adult learners themselves are invited to share these stories and use them to explore salient concerns in contemporary Jewish life. The stories, which are based on actual interviews but are composites edited for coherence and readability, are designed to prompt dialogue and to encourage personal meaning-making. They are meant to be "triggers" for new insight and consciousness about the challenges and needs that confront Jewish adult learners and their teachers today.

Third, the stories are offered to encourage Jewish adults—both lay and professional—to tell their own stories to one another. As Rabbi Laura Geller (1997) has eloquently described, each year when, as a community, Jews stand together to "receive Torah," they are actually rediscovering the power of interpersonal ties and the holiness of Jewish communal stories.

> On Yom Kippur morning we stand again at Sinai. . . . The Torah portion begins with us standing together in community, a community that includes each one of us. It brings us back to Sinai [and] empowers us to write the Torah of our lives. We fashion our own stories out of our vows and promises, tying our lives to other people in our families. But that is only the beginning. Our personal stories become the story of community, of responsibility to other people who need our help. Our stories are linked to the larger Jewish story of *tikkun olam,* the challenge to repair what is broken in the world. That's what it means to choose life, for ourselves and our descendants. (pp. 263–264)

Beyond the stories, the book contains suggestions for effective practice, drawing extensively on insights from the fields of adult development, adult learning, adult religious education, and the sociology of American Jewry. And, while most of the stories are about *learners,* each one also highlights the practices of key *teachers.* These practices—both successful and not—form the basis for discussion about what practitioners do that *makes a difference* in the fostering of adult Jewish growth.

Overview of Contents

In chapter 1, we meet Ben, a forty-six-year-old doctor who, like Moses at the Burning Bush, had a wake-up call that propelled him into the kinds of learning activities and insights typical of contemporary Jewish adults. We look at Ben's learning journey in terms of the kinds of life transitions and relationships that mark the lives of many Jewish adult learners.

We learn in chapter 2 about Danielle, a recently retired magazine executive who, for the first time, is exploring her Jewish identity and overcoming her "fear and trembling" as she takes first steps to become Jewishly literate. Danielle's shift from apprehension to "doing and listening" provides the basis for discussion of my "Ten R's That Foster Adult Jewish Growth," an abbreviated road map to helping adults to become knowledgeable, self-affirming Jews.

In chapter 3, the story of Fern provides the basis for a discussion on the nature of contemporary Jewish identity. Like other midlife seekers who want to move "from the wilderness to the Promised Land," Fern has explored a number of spiritual and political communities in her quest for an authentic adult Jewish self. Her journey reveals the importance of relationships for Jewish adults who are revising the narrative of their lives.

The learning-and-teaching journey of thirty-eight-year-old Allison is presented in chapter 4. Allison's intellectual growth and her desire to transmit what she has learned to others demonstrate that, like other educated Jewish adults, this woman wants to do more than just "stand" at Sinai. We consider in this chapter how recent feminist scholarship can provide perspective on the growth and development of learners as they "come to voice."

In chapter 5, the experience of Phil, a fifty-two-year-old information technology expert, is showcased. Like Jacob, Phil has "wrestled with angels" as he has tried to find answers to some of life's tough questions. His adult Jewish learning experiences illustrate some key theories about how adults "make meaning" when they find that old beliefs and assumptions no longer make sense.

We shift in chapter 6 from learners to teachers, to focus on the challenges facing Jewish professionals when they encounter the diversity of today's adult Jewish learning population. Through the story of the efforts of Rabbi Ariel Jordan, who wishes to better understand the learners "before whom she stands," we are introduced to some findings about the motivations and learning styles of adults, as well as some basic principles about adult learners.

In chapter 7, the insights of several outstanding Jewish educators are shared. Selected interview material from these teachers highlights how Jewish professionals can most effectively practice *tzimtzum*—contracting and making space for one's learners rather than always filling up the learning environment with only one's own energy and inspiration.

In chapter 8, the story of a scholar-in-residence who has much to learn about working well with adult learners provides the framework for presenting some nuts-and-bolts suggestions—some *tachlis*—that can help Jewish professionals to become more effective in their work. This chapter features "how-to" exhibits and reading suggestions that anyone interested in the field of adult Jewish learning will find useful.

The epilogue raises an under-addressed issue in the Jewish community: what kind of professional development opportunities do rabbis, cantors, educators, and Jewish communal workers need to remain vital and dynamic in their work with adults? Like their students, Jewish adult educators are also learners who need to grow. Some starting points for such growth and enrichment are identified.

1

Hineini: Showing Up as a Jewish Adult

Now, Moses was tending the flock of his father-in-law Yitro . . . and came to Horeb, the mountain of God. . . . He gazed, and there was a bush all aflame, yet the bush was not consumed. Moses said, "I must turn aside to look at this marvelous sight. . . ." When Adonai *saw that he had turned aside to look, God called to him out of the bush: "Moses, Moses!" He answered, "*Hineini *[Here I am]."*

—*Exodus 3:1–4*

When and why do Jewish adults show up, knock on the door, and say, "Here I am. I am ready to learn"? What causes people to embark on the journey of adult Jewish growth, to take steps toward finding new meaning in Jewish life and Jewish learning? How do adults describe what might be called "*Hineini* moments," times in their lives when, like Moses encountering the Burning Bush, they have felt prepared—even compelled—to open themselves to some kind of dialogue with Judaism, God, or their identities as Jews?

According to Rabbi Amy Eilberg (2000, p. 1) a *Hineini* moment involves "saying 'yes' to relationships, to life, to the Divine." When Jewish adults say yes in these ways, they make a leap into the unknown, often taking significant intellectual and spiritual risks as they explore Judaism on new terms or interact with the Jewish community in new ways. For many, their success as Jewish learners will reflect their willingness to respond "with trust, with humility, with openness to learning and surprise" (Eilberg, 2000, p. 1). Their growth will be enhanced particularly by how Jewish professionals respond and help them to find new meaning and direction in Jewish life.

In order to understand the *Hineini* experiences of contemporary Jewish adults, I conducted interviews and discussion groups with a wide range of people, asking them to describe their experiences of involvement with Jewish life and learning. I was especially interested in what had sparked their

adult Jewish growth and how rabbis, educators, and other Jewish professionals had assisted them in their Jewish learning journeys.

Jewish Lives, Jewish Learning: Mapping Jewish Journeys

A valuable consciousness-raising opportunity presented itself when a synagogue invited me to speak about my work on Jewish lives and learning. As
part of my presentation, I asked members of the audience to tell me—and
one another—about their growth and development as Jews, and, particularly, what got them started on their Jewish journey. To facilitate the conversations, I devised a fifteen minute self-reflection activity that could be accom-
plished in one of two ways: participants could either make notes about
themselves and their lives (dates, places, people, key moments) on a
preprinted Jewish Journey Map Map (see Exhibit 1-1), or take a piece of
blank newsprint and draw their life story in whatever creative way they
wished. Most people chose to use the preprinted form, although some were
delighted to spread paper out on the floor and draft more abstract and individualistic expressions of the accumulated experiences of their lives.

After the reflection and drawing period, I instructed the participants to
"code" their maps with four symbolic labels. "First," I announced, "put an 'A'
at the place or places on your map or picture that indicate *when you became
an adult.*" (This statement brought some laughter, especially from people
who said that despite their age, they weren't sure they could be considered
adults.) Next I said, "Now put a 'JA' for when you became a Jewish adult—
whatever that means to you." Then I requested, "Put 'JC' at all the places
where you had a significant (meaning either positive or negative) interaction with a Jewish community and 'JL' at places where you had good or bad
encounters with Jewish learning." After everyone had completed these tasks,
I invited them to hang their maps and drawings up on the walls so that we
could all visit the congregation's new "gallery of Jewish life stories." Once we
had all had a chance to look over the extraordinary range of Jewish journey
pictures that emerges in any group of Jewish adults, our discussion of Jewish
lives and Jewish learning could authentically begin.

Building a Shared Vocabulary Through Sharing Experiences

As with any new topic of discussion, the map-drawing activity generated a
vocabulary that group members could use to talk about the beginning of

EXHIBIT 1-1

Jewish Journey Map

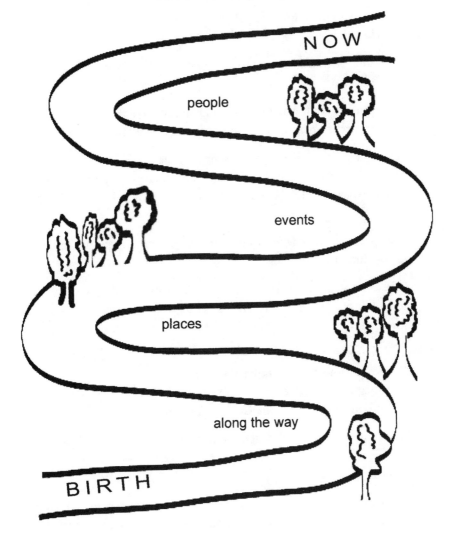

All theology is autobiography. As we tell our own stories we often discover the divinity that is present in our lives. And if we listen carefully, we hear our stories as part of the cosmic Jewish stories.

Rabbi Laura Geller, 1997

Jewish adulthood and related experiences. In this group (and others I have conducted since that time), I found that, for most people, "adulthood" is associated with the *assumption of responsibility* and *being responsible for the consequences of one's choices.* Typically, people recalled times when they had to separate themselves from old patterns or take on new roles. Sample comments included:

> "I became an adult when I moved out of my parents' house and had to pay the bills."

> "I became an adult when I had a child and realized it was now up to me to make decisions about what kind of life I wanted her to have."

> "I became an adult when I was twenty and was promoted to head counselor at a summer camp. Suddenly I was the one telling people what to do and what wouldn't be tolerated. It was awful: I couldn't be one of the guys anymore."

> "I became an adult when I was thirty-eight and bought life insurance for the first time!"

> "I became an adult when I was seven and my parents divorced and were squabbling all the time. I was the go-between and had to figure out when to tell them things and how to keep the peace. I grew up in a hurry."

The recollections of "becoming a Jewish adult" tended to be about milestone events in Jewish settings. The participants specified events that marked the time they *had entered a "Jewish environment" on new terms.*

> "I became a Jewish adult when I was in college and went to Hillel without anyone telling me to go. I didn't go often, but when I did, *I* was in the driver's seat—not my mother!"

> "I became a Jewish adult when I went to Israel and considered making *aliyah.* It was the first time I really felt like a Jew. I liked how I felt when I was there."

> "I became a Jewish adult when my parents came to *my* house for seder. My wife and I used all my mother's recipes and I asked my father to conduct the service, but it was on my turf and I was the one who hid the *afikoman* for the kids to find."

"I became a Jewish adult when I joined a temple. It happened because my grandson was going to Sunday school and asked me to go to a "Bring a *Bubbe*" event on Mother's Day. I myself had never belonged to a temple before; my late husband wasn't interested. But, that day, in the sanctuary, when all the children stood up and sang to the *bubbes*, that was the day I said, 'It's time for me to be official here.'"

For many Jewish adults, feeling "grown up" as a Jew involves renegotiating one's concept of whose "agenda" is at the fore. It also involves recognizing that one can make an independent choice about whether to sustain (or develop) a Jewish identity or not. As contemporary sociologists like to point out, today most American Jews are "Jews by choice." I have found that comments about claiming one's Jewish adulthood typically express the dynamics of conscious decision making—celebrating the occasion when a person chose to say, "Yes, I am a Jew."

Barriers to Hineini

The Jewish Community

In the discussion about "JC's"—Jewish communal experiences—I observed that once people began talking about their many Jewish "communities"—families, neighborhoods, synagogues, camps, college groups (Hillel, fraternities), volunteer and charitable organizations, clubs (including country clubs), and other places where Jews come together—the comments were rarely "neutral." For some people, Jewish community had been a positive force throughout their lives, and they recalled consistently feeling "at home" with other Jews. For others, joining Jewish groups in adulthood had given them a "sense of belonging" that they were able to build on as they settled into adult life. More often than not, however, people recalled occasions of feeling alienated or disenfranchised by a Jewish group or organization. They described "old baggage" they were carrying around about the Jewish community:

"Where I grew up, if you didn't have the right clothes and didn't live in a certain part of town, you never felt "good enough" as a Jew. I remember going to *shul* and feeling so out of place. My mother felt that way too: the women were incredibly cliquey and snobbish."

"I got to college and was excited about going to things at Hillel. I figured it was a good place to meet some girls. But at the very first Rosh

Hashanah I realized that as a Reform Jew, I was an outsider at the services. I didn't know many of the prayers, a lot of the melodies were different, and I hadn't read any Hebrew since my bar mitzvah. I sat there feeling miserable for a few hours and left. I never went back to Hillel after that."

"My parents got divorced when I was eleven. In those days, nobody in our community got divorced. It was a scandal. After that, my parents' friends, all of whom were Jewish, 'took sides.' A lot of people stopped inviting us over. I especially remember one Chanukah when we didn't get asked to a latke party. What had felt like a loving and stable Jewish community just disappeared."

"When our kids were small, we moved to a small town where there were only a few Jewish families. Neither my husband nor I had grown up with Jewish observance in the home, so I didn't really know what was expected of me—what I was supposed to do. Everyone was very friendly, but then one of my children had a birthday party and I served nonkosher hot dogs. The mothers wouldn't let the kids eat them. It was one of the most embarrassing moments of my life. I *never* felt accepted by the community after that."

"After my business got going, I was asked to make a contribution to the local Federation. I said fine and wrote a check for $150. The next week I got a call from the chair of the campaign, who laid this guilt trip on me and made me feel like a nothing. Worse than nothing. I didn't know that they were expecting $500. I probably could have afforded the $500, but I couldn't stand the feeling that people were talking and that I was being judged by other Jews."

Jewish Learning

Finally, when I asked people to shift the conversation and talk about the "JL's"—their experiences of Jewish learning—the mood in the room became more tentative. Rather than giving direct answers, people began to ask me questions:

"What do you mean by Jewish learning?"

"If I learned Bible stories from my grandfather but never went to Sunday school, is that considered Jewish learning?"

"I was bar mitzvah, but I never learned anything. Is that a time of significant Jewish learning or *nonlearning?*"

"I grew up as a Lutheran and remember hearing sermons filled with anti-Semitic remarks. Would you call that Jewish learning?"

"When I think of Jewish learning moments, I think of Hebrew school and the same drills over and over. Nothing dynamic. Nothing relevant. Stuff I learned by rote and never used again."

Even among people who had participated in Jewish adult learning programs, many statements revealed how many people in the group were products of what is frequently described as "pediatric Judaism"—Jewish learning that is child-centered and assumes that no real intellectual Jewish growth continues after early adolescence. Despite feeling comfortable as adults and as Jewish adults, and regardless of their level of Jewish communal affiliation, the majority of people in this audience (and others I met with later on), expressed a strong "disconnect" between their Jewish lives and meaningful Jewish learning. On the whole, their perception of past Jewish learning moments lacked the vitality and spirit that might provide a basis for meaningful learning in the adult years. Thus, Jewish professionals are faced with the challenge of helping adults to discover the excitement of Jewish learning; they cannot assume that there is a base of favorable past experiences on which to build. Accordingly, they need to become more familiar with what adult learners need—what makes a difference to them—when they start new learning journeys. Insights to these needs can be found in the stories of Jewish adults who themselves have embarked on such journeys.

Ben's Story: Meeting a Hineini Adult

One evening I was meeting with a Jewish Community Center group that had invited me to talk about Jewish adulthood. During a break, a doctor named Ben Kleinman approached me and said, "If you're interested, I'd like to tell you more about my story. I've become something of a Jewish learning junkie. And it's really changing my life."

What music to my researcher ears! Shortly thereafter, Ben and I met for the first of several interviews. As with other learners I'd been studying, I began by asking him my "Jewish journey" question: "Could you tell me about your life—your journey—Jewishly?" And like most of my interviewees, Ben sat back, raised his eyes to the ceiling, and said, "No one ever asked me that question before." And then he said, "You know, ever since we met I've been thinking about when I became a Jewish adult. And the answer is: I became a Jewish adult five years ago when my mother died and my father remarried—to a non-Jewish woman. That was when it hit me: I had to grow up because I didn't have a Jewish home to go home to anymore."

Like other stories in this book, Ben's story is set off as a "text" for study, analysis, and commentary. Like other Jewish texts, the story can be read and discussed on several levels: What kind of person is Ben Kleinman? What caused him to say *"Hineini"*? What are the lessons from his experience? How is his story like stories of other contemporary Jewish adult learners? If we were going to speculate on the "end" of this story, what would be some key issues to keep in mind? How does his story touch us and provide insight to our own Jewish lives and Jewish learning?

For me, Ben's story prompts two levels of analysis. First, looking at the story from the perspective of adult developmental psychology, I find a number of themes that may explain some of the dynamics of Ben's adult Jewish growth. And then, looking at the story in terms of possible implications for Jewish professionals, I see a number of issues that practitioners should bear in mind when they encounter *Hineini* stories in Jewish adults.

❧ Story 1 ☙

BEN

Ben Kleinman was born in 1952 in upstate New York. His grandparents migrated to the United States early in the twentieth century. According to Ben, his Judaism was marked by the contrast between his grandfather's commitment to traditional observance and his parents' tenuous relationship to Jewish practice:

> My grandparents came over from Lithuania, the Ukraine. My grandfather never learned to speak English very well. Judaism was his whole life. The synagogue was modern Orthodox: very traditional, individual davening, all in Hebrew. That was his whole life— his Judaism. He was a chicken farmer.
>
> I went through Reform; to my parents, it was very important that we keep up appearances. So I went to Hebrew school and got bar

mitzvahed. I had a fairly charismatic rabbi, some cousins who were Jewishly involved, and it was all kind of fun. But there was no Jewish life at home. Outside of the grandparents, there were no Sabbath candles, no blessings. There was nothing Jewish. I don't even remember if there was a mezuzah on the door.

Although Ben's family did not engage in Jewish practices in their home, they attended seders, which Ben described as "mainly social events." Sometimes they didn't go to seders, however, because "if Passover coincided with hockey playoffs and there were conflicts about how to spend the evening, hockey always won."

Ben's "Jewish life" ended when he went to college. He did not affiliate with any Jewish groups and preferred to date gentile women. His fiancée converted to Judaism prior to their marriage, but the conversion was perfunctory: "It involved some study on Maureen's part, but it wasn't a big or deep spiritual experience." After Ben completed medical school, he and Maureen moved to the western United States, where he affiliated with a Catholic hospital and family practice medical group. The couple had four children in six years and moved several times. In one community they enrolled the children in a Jewish preschool, and in another they joined a Reform congregation for two years. Ben worked extremely long hours and looked to weekly hockey games for recreational pleasure.

In the late 1980s, Ben experienced a crisis in his medical practice that had "some Jewish overtones, which involved some prominent member of the Jewish community." Wanting to "do the right thing" from a Jewish point of view, Ben consulted with a local rabbi about Jewish ethical practices. The rabbi recommended that Ben go consult a *beit din*, a rabbinic court, about ways to resolve the dispute. Furthermore, the rabbi counseled Ben that he could not be Jewish "in just part of your life."

Ben's reaction was strong: "I thought, 'This guy's crazy, it's ridiculous. This is a thoroughly legal issue, and there's no way I'm gonna let a bunch of old rabbis sit around telling me what to do.'" Nonetheless, he subsequently found himself recalling the rabbi's comments: "I remembered that line: 'You can't be Jewish in just part of your life.'"

In 1991, a confluence of circumstances prompted Ben to think about his Jewish identity. First, his mother died and his father remarried to a woman who was not Jewish. Ben found that even though he liked the woman his father chose, his sense of "home" had changed. He also found that he was becoming nostalgic about his grandfather:

> Passover was coming, and even though I'd never gone home for Jewish holidays, I suddenly minded that I didn't have a Jewish home to go home to anymore. There's nothing Jewish in my father's house. I started missing my grandfather. There was something very powerful about my grandfather and his Jewish life. I couldn't relate to it then and I can't relate to it now, but there was something very centered and satisfying about him. I wanted to catch a glimpse of what that was.

Then Ben went through a "kind of an emotional crisis" involving interpersonal communication problems at work and home. When he decided to seek professional help, he felt he "had to see a Jewish therapist." He was startled to discover that the psychologist seemed instantly familiar to him: "At that time, I had a beard and a mustache. And I walked into the room, and he had a beard and a mustache. And there was this instant connection." The therapist suggested that Ben might want to think about his behavior and concerns in a Jewish context: "He suggested to me—in just one of his throwaway comments—that maybe I should be looking more at what I'm doing Jewishly, to sort of get my life more in balance. And that kind of 'clicked in.'"

Shortly thereafter, Ben and his family moved to a house around the corner from a college Hillel. From a flyer, he learned that a Talmud class at the Hillel was open to community members. Without knowing anything about Talmud, Ben decided to check out the class. He immediately found himself engaged by the discussions. He was drawn to what he saw as "otherworldly" qualities of the discourse:

> You know, I spend all the other time in my life doing stuff that is very pragmatic and has moment-to-moment effects. And this was totally outside of the realm of what I was doing. We spent *weeks* discussing when you could blow out candles on Shabbat. I mean, I didn't even *light* Shabbat candles, and here I was spending weeks discussing the fine points of this. It was so removed . . . and in foreign languages with people I'd never even heard of.

About this time, Ben was injured in a hockey game and had to have knee surgery. He realized that, at thirty-nine, he couldn't play hockey any more. Even though his life was already overextended, the loss of hockey games represented a major blow to Ben's sense of well-being:

> I had to give up the hockey. And I have four children, all of whom need lots of time, and a very wonderful wife who needs lots of time too, and I want to spend it with her. And a very, very busy practice and I do all kinds of things outside. I work with sexually abused children and I consult to psychiatric hospitals and I speak and I teach at the medical school. I'm doing all these other things, and time is at a premium. So when I gave up the hockey, which I felt was *my* thing that I was doing, I replaced it with Talmud. I used to practice hockey on Monday nights, but I stopped practicing hockey and went to Talmud.

As Ben got more involved in Talmud study, he began to think about studying other Jewish texts as well. Over time, he decided that he should "learn some of the prayer stuff too." He began attending services at a Conservative synagogue and participated in classes on Jewish philosophy, meditation, and literature at various adult education programs. He enrolled his children in religious school and volunteered to serve as physician at a Jewish summer camp. He noted that "you have to teach your children by what you say, you have to teach your children by what you do" and said that if he wanted his children to "grow up Jewish," then he had to "grow up Jewish too."

The more Ben studied, the more he began to see how his Jewish learning was permeating his personal and professional lives. He found that he was bringing home "the stories, the little midrashes," although he felt cautious about imposing his values on his wife and children: "I can't impose my view on the rest of the family if they're not at that same point. If they don't share my enthusiasm for some of this stuff, I can't be shoving it down their throats."

At work, however, Ben began to notice that his patients were hungry for guidance beyond their immediate medical needs. He found that sometimes he played "the role of father, of religious leader" because his patients had "no one else to ask." Working with a primarily non-Jewish clientele, Ben incorporated his own learning into patient education, often telling his patients "little Chasidic stories." He shared with patients aspects of his own religious journey, citing proverbs and psalms that he himself had found helpful. He found that he was comfortable quoting Jewish texts rather than "Sartre or Camus or Dostoevsky" to deliver the message that "you're not alone; someone else has been here; somebody else has described this circumstance."

When interviewed at age forty-three about his Jewish learning journey, Ben described the breadth of his studies: Talmud, Kabbalah, the autobiographies of Maimonides and Isaac Luria, the stories of Reb Nachman of Bratzlav, and the essays of Rabbi Lawrence Kushner. Although he described himself as a self-directed learner, he said he greatly enjoyed having the opportunity to study with others:

> When I began the Talmud study, I didn't know what I was getting into. It involves me with very high caliber people whom I would probably never have contact with otherwise, who come from very different perspectives. There's a mix of young students and older people, people who come from very different life experiences and bring their own values and judgments. But we're all studying the same text. It's just fabulous in that regard.

He noted that learning about Talmud was turning him into a life-long learner:

> The reality of it is that a lot of it is extraordinarily relevant (though some of it's ridiculous: some of the numerology stuff is just silly). But I feel so comfortable now that I can look at it and say, "These guys are silly." Or, "this is a very chauvinistic point of view." Or, "this would never fly today." You know, the Rabbis could have their commentaries on commentaries, and I can make commentaries on commentaries on commentaries. And if somebody thinks they're worthwhile, they'll put 'em in the margins; and if they don't, they won't. I feel very comfortable with that kind of intellectual freedom. It's all so unlimited. It's something that never stops. You could spend your whole life and never "get it."

Ben also indicated that he valued the mentoring role that his Talmud teacher assumed in his life:

> She would ask me questions that would put me on the spot. I had to answer from my heart, totally honestly. I haven't had that feeling, outside of the marriage with my wife and with my kids—someone

who wasn't my family—that kind of intimacy about wanting to know what I'm *really* thinking. That was an incredible feeling. So, she pushed me, she got me started, kept saying stuff and giving me resources and helping me with material. I finally said, "Why didn't I hear any of this before? Why am I just learning this now? Why didn't I learn it when I was a kid?" And she said, "You weren't ready to hear it then. Your ears weren't open to hear it then."

Although Ben's reading extended beyond exclusively Jewish sources, he indicated how much he relished becoming familiar with thinkers from his own tradition:

This is to go back and find something very old. It's of tremendous value not to have to reinvent the wheel, to find that other people have been struggling with the same issues for thousands and thousands of years. And to see how this survived, all the interpretations of this. I mean, I learn a lot from Dostoevsky, but the people who wrote 1,800 or 3,800 years before him had very worthwhile things to say too. And it's kind of more interesting to look at something centuries old. And this is a heritage that was passed on to me.

Deeply mindful of his heritage, throughout the interview Ben mentioned his grandfather's legacy. He said that he wanted to obtain more knowledge about Judaism so that he could extend Jewish tradition to his own children:

I do feel this link, this sense. You see, I want my kids to be Jewish because it's a good way to be. You know, my dad did what he thought he had to do in his way, and I've got to do what I think I've got to do in my way to keep it going. I see that connection and I've got to make that link. And I can't make it just to make it—with bagels and cream cheese. I'm that link, what goes from my *zayde* to them.

Ben's Story: A Developmentalist's Perspective

Ben Kleinman's story contains four elements that are found in many *Hineini* stories:

- A history of insecure or ambivalent attachment to the Jewish community that at some point in adulthood becomes the source of significant

personal dissonance
* A time of transition in which claiming or reclaiming "something Jewish" becomes psychologically, intellectually, or spiritually meaningful
* A passion to initiate and explore new Jewish learning opportunities
* A deep appreciation for mentors who support learners on the Jewish journey

Insecure Attachment to Jewish Life

In developmental psychology, theories of *attachment* have given rise to numerous studies of what characterizes effective parent-child dynamics. Attachment scholars explore how children and parents send messages to one another that establish interpersonal trust and reliability, help the bonding process, and ultimately give children the sense of security they need to cope with separations. In the 1960s, psychologist Mary Ainsworth (1973) studied mothers and infants in their homes and described three types of attachment patterns: *securely attached* children, whose mothers were "sensitive and promptly responsive to their babies' cries and other signals"; *insecure-avoidant* children, whose mothers' responses were "relatively insensitive, interfering, and rejecting"; and *insecure-ambivalent* children, whose mothers tended to be inconsistent, that is, erratically warm and cold responses. When these three types of infants were observed in situations where they had been separated from and then reunited with their mothers, Ainsworth found different reactions in the children. The secure children, accustomed to their mothers' warmth and responsiveness, greeted their mothers affectionately when reunited and gradually were able to resume their own play activities; by contrast, the children whose mothers were insensitive and rejecting tended to ignore their mothers (at both the point of separation and of reuniting), avoided close contact, and seemed prematurely "independent." The *insecure-ambivalent* children tended to cling to their mothers at the time of separation and displayed ambivalent behaviors, both clinging and pushing away when the mothers returned.

Looking at how these three types of children functioned in social environments later on, Ainsworth and subsequent researchers found that the *securely attached* children are much more able than the *insecure-ambivalent* children to explore their surroundings and develop healthy interpersonal connections. In school, the securely attached children tend to be more curious, more persistent in play, more empathic toward other children, more independent, and higher in self-esteem. The *avoidant* and *ambivalent* children have poorer interpersonal skills: they don't know how to "read" social cues and give off signals that cause other children to keep their distance. In adolescence and adulthood, people with histories of avoidant attachment are likely to have problems with forming close ties with others. Those who have a history of ambivalent attachment often have problems with overdependence and may show anger or impatience toward the people or institutions on whom they feel they must rely. Fortunately, even though people raised by avoidant and ambivalent mothers may suffer long-term negative consequences of their early socialization, they can also be helped later on by caring teachers, counselors, and others to develop social skills, self-confidence, and the ability to take healthy risks in their lives.

Although most research about attachment has focused on the way children respond and interact, recent scholarship has sought to apply attachment theory to the experiences of other populations. When thinking about the *Jewish attachment* patterns of contemporary Jewish adults, some of the issues Ainsworth raised become pertinent. Adults who have grown up feeling unresponded to or emotionally disconnected from a Jewish community (whether it is the community of family or synagogue or neighborhood) can be expected to have many of the reactions to Jewish life that Ben Kleinman initially exhibited. Ben's parents provided little secure attachment to anything that felt authentically Jewish to him; he did not form close ties with Jewish friends in college, his wife's conversion did nothing to bring him in closer to his own Judaism; and his work in a non-Jewish environment enabled him to separate himself from his Jewish roots. His reaction to the rabbi's suggestion that he consult with a *beit din* about a Jewish issue provoked an angry response—he wasn't going to let "a bunch of old rabbis" tell him what to do—and even though his children attended a Jewish preschool, he had no sense of personal connection to their experiences there.

However, as an adult, Ben Kleinman began to find that his avoidant/ambivalent relationship to Judaism and Jewish life didn't feel comfortable—that old ways of resisting "things Jewish" no longer felt right to him. He was challenged by the rabbi's admonition that he couldn't be Jewish in just one part of his life and, later, when struggling with some personal issues, felt he should be seeing a Jewish therapist. He discovered that he wanted to come in closer to his Judaism—to renegotiate his relationship to his Jewish identity and, it turned out, to honor the Jewish values his grandfather had modeled to him. Ben's widowed father's marriage to a non-Jewish woman caused him to realize that the responsibility for "securing" his attachment to Judaism (having a Jewish home to go home to) was now up to him.

With the benefit of helpful counselors and rabbis and a variety of positive learning experiences, Ben began to reframe his understanding of Jewish history, politics, law, and literature. Over a several-year period, his Jewish attachment pattern shifted dramatically, and he had several *Hineini* moments of saying "I am here, I am ready, I am prepared." These occurred when he began to actively explore Jewish life and learning, to reflect on his Jewish values, to develop ties with other Jews, and to feel more competent as a Jewish adult. His adult Jewish growth was significantly abetted by the willingness of his teachers to help him examine his Jewish identity in a thoughtful and consistent way. On his Jewish learning journey, he was welcomed and challenged by Jewish professionals who helped him to think about and resolve his sense of alienation and provided a base of support while he diversified his experiences as a Jewish adult.

Transitions and Jewish Identity

When do adults like Ben generally begin reframing their lives? And do these patterns of change apply to the issue of reframing Jewish lives? The field of adult development psychology has blossomed since the 1970s, with increasing attention being paid to patterns of adult growth and change. Whereas earlier theory about adulthood was predicated on the assumption that life patterns would pretty much be "set" by the time an adult reached his or her forties, later scholarship revealed both the diversity of adult life choices and the numerous instances in which adults find themselves shifting gears, redefining purpose, and making new meaning of their life experiences. Thus, a major issue in the study of adulthood is about how people respond to change when transitions do occur.

The work of Daniel Levinson and his associates provides a framework for understanding the psychological impact of transitions in adult life. Levinson et al. studied the "seasons" of adulthood and concluded that, over time, people cycle through periods of stability and periods of considerable change. Levinson argued that, at times of major transition, individuals find that their old views—of themselves, of their relationships, of their work, of what gives meaning to their lives—no longer fit. At these times, the individual goes through a psychological process of giving up the old way of seeing the self and, as a result, may feel quite disoriented or displaced for quite a while. Although Levinson believed that these transition periods were age-linked—and thus could be expected by everybody at certain ages—other psychologists have concluded that the timing of adult life transitions is quite random; we never know when someone is going to enter into a period of significant growth. Likewise, there is randomness in what triggers a transition: certain life events (e.g., reentry to college or retirement) may *cause* a transition or may, for some people, be the *result* of a transitional time in their lives.

Transitions expert Nancy Schlossberg has observed that while our lives are filled with transitions, not all are alike. Schlossberg notes that some transitions are anticipated (e.g., children's entry into school, the onset of puberty, getting married, empty nest). Other transitions are not so predictable (e.g., accidents, illness, sudden job loss or promotion, changes in the stock market—both up and down), and some are what Schlossberg called "non-event transitions": when something that you thought would happen just doesn't occur (e.g., becoming pregnant, getting a hoped-for promotion, having grandchildren). There are also "sleeper transitions": shifts that subtly creep up into a person's consciousness over time (e.g., the acknowledgment of an increasingly unhealthy physical condition, the gradual awareness of having outgrown a relationship or job).

Regardless of the type or cause of the transition, psychologists consistently note that the process of adjustment to any life transition takes longer than most people expect. In that sense, the adaptation to transition is also idiosyncratic; one cannot predict how long it will take to give up old assumptions, develop new ways of thinking, and find new meanings in one's life. Becoming a "different" person takes time.

Recent research on contemporary Jewish adult life patterns similarly found that transitions in and out of Jewish life are neither predictable nor age-linked. In a study of more than 1,500 Jewish adults, social psychologist Bethamie Horowitz found that "Jewish identity is not something static that a person either has or does not have. Rather, identity can evolve and change, ebb and flow, in relation to all sorts of influences, internal and external. A person may be much less connected to Judaism at one point in his/her lifetime and more deeply identified at another" (Horowitz, 2000b, pp. 188–189). This fluidity means that not only are Jewish life patterns unpredictable and full of change, but also the timing of *Hineini* moments will be unscheduled and prompted by highly diverse "trigger events." Thus, one Jewish adult may be moved to rethink her Jewish life on the occasion of a child's bar mitzvah, while another may begin a transition at the time of retirement. Some will transition abruptly, sparked by a moment of new consciousness or insight, while others will make a shift over a long period of time during which they sensed that some things "just didn't feel right."

As Horowitz notes, because of this variability in the timing of and triggers for Jewish adult transitions, the Jewish community needs to promote an "open-door" policy that encourages people to come in *when they are ready* instead of making them feel guilty or less than adequate when they are not ready. The community also needs to provide an array of learning opportunities, since people are coming at different times and for different reasons. And Jewish professionals need to be attuned to the needs of adults who are in transition—people who are trying to understand themselves and their lives in a new way and who may wish for a Jewish perspective to help them in the process. They need to be prepared, as well, for people who are going through a transition that they may associate with "being Jewish" (e.g., a birth or death) and thus might benefit from the insights provided by Jewish texts or tradition.

A number of significant transitions occurred in Ben Kleinman's life when he was in his early forties—transitions that Ben ultimately associated with his life as a Jew. First, he went through a period of change in health status—culminating in his third knee injury—and this transition caused him to rethink how he was spending his time. While he didn't go "looking" for a Jewish activity to fill his Monday nights, he clearly was open to this experience when it came along. In that sense, the trigger event that led to his engagement in Jewish learning was unanticipated and serendipitous. But Ben's receptivity to Judaism at this time of change was not random. Being in transition likely made him more open to reflection about his life and to thinking about his experiences from a Jewish point of view.

A second transition had to do with Ben's emotional status. In the interview, he didn't give much detail about the communication problems that took him into therapy, but clearly when he was in this transition, he found himself seeking Jewish support. Moreover, when the therapist suggested that he pay closer attention to what he was doing in his Jewish life, he took this as a positive suggestion. It's unclear whether the transition caused the Jewish interest or whether a longing for a Jewish connection precipitated the transition. However, it remains clear that at times of personal vulnerability Jewish adults are likely to be open to meaningful Jewish experiences.

A third transition occurred in Ben's Jewish family life. As he became more and more involved in Jewish study, he realized that his wife and children were not as enthusiastic about Jewish learning or observance as he was becoming. As he faced a widening gap between himself and family members, he had to work through what it would mean to pursue a Jewish journey independent of those closest to him. Ben's transition as a Jewish adult therefore threatened to prompt other transitions in his life, leading him to even deeper questioning and potential upheaval in his family system.

Passion for New Jewish Learning

In *A Generation of Seekers,* a study of baby boomers and spirituality, sociologist Wade Clark Roof (1992) describes a group of people who are deeply involved in personal quests:

> For them, life is a journey, an adventure that leads to new discoveries, and to insights that can flow only from experience and autobiography. Journey implies a hope for the unity of things, for combining thought and feeling, doing and being, the inner and outer worlds. Journey conveys the notion of ongoing movement or . . . living, moving, experiencing, feeling, deepening, growing search. (p. 79)

Roof's group of "highly active seekers" share many characteristics of *Hineini* adults—individuals who have come to some kind of "crossroad" in adult life and have made a decision to explore and learn about Judaism and Jewish life. Their journeys are marked by the "travelers'" passion for Jewish study and by their vibrant motivation to learn everything they can about a Jewish topic—and then to learn more. Like "self-actualizers" described by Abraham Maslow (1970) in his work on human motivation, *Hineini* adults "perceive things . . . freshly, naively, and as they really are. They can look at any painting—or any tree, bird, or baby—as if seeing it for the first time; they can find miraculous beauty where others see nothing but the common object" (Crain, 1992, p. 391). The vitality, determination, and intensity of *Hineini* adults reflect the urgency many of them feel as they hurry to "catch up" and acquire an authentic Jewish education. They place high demands on themselves and their teachers, ever eager to find "maps" that will guide their learning experiences and new tools (such as Hebrew and textual analysis) that will contribute to their Jewish literacy and overall Jewish growth. Their excitement is palpable: having overcome whatever "roadblocks" previously impeded their Jewish journey, they now want to maintain momentum, find fellow travelers, discover new places (of knowledge) to visit, and even become guides to others by sharing their new knowledge and related wisdom.

Ben Kleinman's *Hineini* story is rich with examples of how contemporary Jewish adults move, in the words of Franz Rosenzweig, "from life to Torah." Indeed, Ben's journey began when, in *his* words, he went from "hockey to Talmud" on Monday nights! From the very first time that he walked into a Talmud class and began debating Jewish texts with other Jews, Ben sensed that he had "come home" to an essential part of his identity and well-being. His thirst for Jewish learning was unquenchable, and his energy for exploring multiple avenues of learning (while also sustaining a family and highly demanding career) was daunting. Nonetheless, the more Ben studied, the greater his energy for learning seemed to become.

Mentoring on the Jewish Journey

In *Mentor: Guiding the Journey of Adult Learners,* Laurent Daloz (1999) celebrates the many ways a teacher or other learning guide can influence the growth of an adult learner. Citing the work of Carl Jung, Daloz explains that, archetypally, mentors represent "knowledge, reflection, insight, wisdom, cleverness, and intuition" and come into our lives when we need understanding, good advice, and support that we cannot muster from within. He describes why mentors are especially important to adults who are embarking on new learning experiences and describes what the mentor's role is in supporting adult growth:

> The mentor is concerned with the transmission of wisdom . . . they take us on a journey. In this aspect of their work, *mentors are guides.* They lead us along the journey of our lives. We trust them because they have been there before. They embody our hopes, cast light on the way ahead, interpret arcane signs, warn us of lurking dangers, and point out unexpected delights along the way. (p. 18)

Leona English, who writes extensively on adult religious education, points out that most discussions about mentors are centered in the literature on adult career development and tend to focus on how mentors help initiates to learn to "play the game" in the workplace. In adult religious education, however, the goals of the mentor need to be somewhat different. Although mentors play the roles of teacher, sponsor, encourager, and counselor, they must also play the additional role of *friend*. English (1998) writes:

> [A] strong relational component . . . captures the essential mutual respect and honor that should characterize a religious education mentoring relationship. . . . Educational researcher Nathalie Gehrke uses the metaphor of mentorship as gift exchange, capturing the notion of mutual self-giving in the mentor-mentee exchange. Gehrke further develops this metaphor by using Martin Buber's classical "I-Thou/I-It" distinction to show that regarding the other as "it" in a functional sense is what defines a helping relationship, not a mentoring one. An I-Thou relationship facilitates mentor and mentee personal and professional development, the "stretching to be more because someone believes in your potential." (p. 7)

Befriending as a mentor involves offering support, patience, respect, and what Abraham Maslow would describe as a sense of "belongingness." Developmentally, for Jewish adults who have never felt supported or valued—or who have never felt they "belonged" in Jewish settings—the care and respect offered by mentors are crucial components of personal and spiritual growth. Indeed, adults who feel Jewishly "stunted" often talk about how much it meant to them that a Jewish professional was willing to meet them "where they were at" and were able to relate to them "as a friend" (that is, as more than just a teacher or counselor or other busy professional). Leona English says that the goal of befriending is not to create lifelong friendships between "equals" but rather to create an ongoing climate of support and meaningful dialogue that helps the mentee to feel less alone wherever he or she is on the learning journey.

Although some learners develop without a guide, it is, in the view of Kathleen Taylor, Catherine Marienau, and Morris Fiddler (2000), "a much lonelier and more difficult process . . . more prone to missteps, injury and losing one's way" than the mentored experience. Taylor, Marienau, and Fiddler note that the workplace has long encouraged mentoring of employees and that it is now time for mentoring to occur in adult education:

[Mentors] know the ropes, see the bigger picture, and understand the culture of the organization. They care about their proteges' progress and sometimes intend that their proteges succeed to their place at some future time. Educational mentors . . . are seasoned in the ways of educational environments and expectations. They understand the culture of learning and care about their learners' progress. They may also hope that their learners will take their place at some future time, not necessarily in their roles as educators, but in their roles as facilitators of others' development and growth. (pp. 128–129)

Throughout Jewish history, the importance of teaching and mentoring the young has been acknowledged in texts on education. In Proverbs we find instructions for teachers who guide young people about how to lead their lives. A Jewish model for mentoring is found in the role of the Chasidic rebbe, whose role is to give seekers advice about practical matters and religious concerns. In modern times, educational leaders have written about the need for new Jewish professionals to receive mentoring from more senior practitioners (Zeldin and Lee, 1995). To date, however, little has been written about the mentoring relationship that should occur between Jewish educators and their learners.

In Ben Kleinman's experience, having mentors who reached out to him and stretched him to be Jewishly "more" than he initially expected proved especially significant in his *Hineini* experience. Although Ben's first reaction to the rabbi who recommended consulting with a *beit din* was negative, ultimately he perceived that rabbi as someone attuned to his needs for integration as a Jew. Ben carried the rabbi's words with him for several years, using them as a guide when he finally was ready to begin taking his Judaism more seriously.

Later, when Ben was grappling with personal conflicts in his life, he intuited that he needed perspective from a Jewish therapist. As it turned out, the Jewish therapist provided an important *mirror* for Ben, both in terms of physical appearance (beards and mustaches) and with respect to the inherent value of Jewish adults coming to terms with their Jewish identity when they seek to get their lives "in balance." The therapist served as a transitional mentor when Ben was beginning to see himself on a Jewish journey.

Ben's most significant—and highly cherished—mentor was the Talmud teacher. This mentor took him "beyond Talmud" by asking penetrating questions, providing intellectual resources, giving technical help, and communicating that Ben's growth had true value and meaning. Because he felt valued and cared for by a Jewish professional, Ben was able to envision a longer pathway of adult Jewish growth. Ben described this mentor in highly exuberant ways, indicating that this was the first person since his grandfather who made him want to "connect" Jewishly and to ensure connections for his own children in the future.

From Theory to Practice: Working with Hineini *Adults*

Jewish adulthood is filled with "teachable moments"—*Hineini* experiences when people suddenly find themselves called to action and to a changing relationship with Judaism and their understanding of themselves as Jews. At such moments of heightened readiness, they are open to the guidance and support of Jewish professionals who can authentically "hear" them and respond in meaningful ways.

Ben Kleinman's story points to several things that Jewish professionals can do to meet Jewish adults at times of significant growth and change. Jewish professionals should:

1. Be on the lookout for Jewish adults who may be in transition and offer to give them a Jewish perspective on changes in their lives. Recognize that these transitions may prompt a hunger for Jewish learning and provide study opportunities that are responsive to immediate concerns (e.g., programs about Jewish mourning practices for midlife adults; courses on Jewish ethics at times when a community is in an economic crisis).

2. Remember, as well, that as Jewish adults begin to study, their new learning may lead them to new questioning and unanticipated changes in their views of self and world. Offer to sustain people through these times of upheaval by providing a steady Jewish presence in their lives.

3. Provide "learning moments" for those who are not yet at the *Hineini* place. Offer "getting acquainted" opportunities that place no pressure or shame on Jewish adults who may not be ready for Jewish involvement. Invite prospective learners to programs that demystify Judaism and assure "easy access" (e.g., programs in public places such as book-

stores, museums, and the workplace). Extend personal invitations to study one-on-one with new learners, selecting content that is relevant to their interests and needs.

4. Respond to Jewish adults on their own terms by letting them know that you understand they may have ambivalent or resistant feelings toward Judaism, Jewish learning or practice, Jewish community, and themselves as Jews. Help them to identify and talk about their negative *and* positive Jewish attachments. Offer to be a nonjudgmental sounding board as they work through the complexities of what it means for them to come in close to Jewish life.

5. Become a mentor to Jewish adult learners. This requires purposeful preparation and informed understanding of the mentor's role and responsibilities (cf. Daloz, 1999; Zachary, 2000; Zeldin and Lee, 1995). Recognize that in today's society, adults look to guides and coaches (not to mention personal trainers!) in all domains of their personal and professional lives. Mentoring a Jewish adult in a way that challenges and supports Jewish growth and learning can be an immensely enriching experience for both the teacher and the learner.

2

Beyond Fear and Trembling: Supporting Adult Jewish Growth

> . . . As morning dawned, there was thunder, and lightning, and a
> dense cloud upon the mountain, and a very large blast of the horn;
> and all the people who were in the camp trembled. . . . Now Mount
> Sinai was all in smoke, for Adonai had come down upon it in fire
> . . . and the whole mountain trembled violently . . . and when the
> people saw it, they fell back and stood at a distance. . . . Moses went
> and repeated to the people all the commands of Adonai and all the
> rules. . . . Then he took the record of the covenant and read aloud
> to the people. And they said, "All that Adonai has spoken we will
> do and we will listen."
>
> —Exodus 19:16, 18; 20:15; 24:3, 7

It's one thing for a Jewish adult to "show up" at the rabbi's door, but quite another for that person to cross the threshold of a Jewish institution and take the "leap of faith" that will bring him or her in close to Jewish life and new Jewish understanding. The Israelites, in the face of receiving the Ten Commandments, had to shift from a stance of "fear and trembling" to a more proactive, faith-filled attitude of "doing and listening" (naaseh v'nishma) in order to confirm their covenant with God. So, too, contemporary adults must overcome their apprehensions, taking risks that will help them to fully "connect" to Judaism and to their Jewish identities.

For Jewish professionals, there is an ongoing challenge regarding how best to support these individuals who come toward the door of Jewish learning but often pull back in the face of new learning challenges. Many Jewish adult educators are surprised by what seems to be a resistive, negative, and fearful attitude on the part of individuals who appear successful and competent in other life domains. Indeed, it is often the very person who, in the "real world," delivers cogent legal arguments in a contentious courtroom or insightfully counsels traumatized clients in a therapy session, or skillfully "multitasks" the coordination of big fund-raising events in the community, who now comes across as vulnerable, insecure, demanding, or defensive in a Jewish worship or learning setting.

When we listen to what some people have to say about the Jewish baggage they have been carrying since childhood, the negative (or ambivalent) cast of their later attitude toward Judaism and the Jewish community is understandable. Embedded in their accounts are messages of alienation, mistrust, disenfranchisement, and inferiority. Even adults who grew up with a love of Judaism and a sense of belonging and efficacy in Jewish social or cultural milieus may report feeling illiterate and/or inauthentic as Jews. Many say that they feel blocked from pursuing adult Jewish growth because of stressful memories of being undereducated or turned off or silenced or discouraged from active participation in previous Jewish learning endeavors. Others describe "fear and trembling" associated with the anxiety of being exposed for lack of knowledge or embarrassed when called on to function as a "competent" Jewish adult.

Consider, for example, the recollections of Lee Meyerhoff Hendler (1998), a nationally known Jewish Federation lay leader. In her book *The Year Mom Got Religion*, Hendler describes how she got to a point when she could no longer tolerate her Jewish "illiteracy":

> I [realized I] was a fraud. I'd known it all along. I just hadn't wanted to admit it because if I did that I just might have to *do* something about it. . . . I knew that something huge was missing from the equation "Volunteer work + Contribution + Israel + Holocaust + nostalgia + 2 candles once a week = a Jew." I claimed that I was living a life based on convictions, and that the anchor for most of these convictions was Judaism. Yet, when I probed what I truly knew about Judaism, and examined how I lived my convictions *as a Jew*, I found neither substance nor dependability. My anchor actually rested in sand. (p. 38)

Hendler, like many of the people I interviewed, had to admit to herself that her illiteracy was undermining her effectiveness as a Jewish leader and parent. In her book, she confesses that she had avoided attending synagogue services because others might notice her awkwardness. A proud and highly independent woman, Hendler recalls how hard it was to take the first steps of worshiping in public: "Suddenly I was a gawky teenager all over again, wondering what tiny misstep would reveal to everyone that I didn't belong in this place. . . . I knew about as much as an average ten-year-old" (p. 45).

Overcoming Pediatric Judaism: First Steps

Lee Meyerhoff Hendler's depiction of her "childlike" level of Jewish knowledge—naive, immature, inadequate—recalls what leaders in the Jewish community have long described as both the cause and the consequence of "pediatric Judaism." Forty years ago, Rabbi Alfred Jospe of Brandeis University's Hillel Foundation despaired over the limited Jewish knowledge of incoming students: "Thousands of students enter our universities every year with what I call a "pediatric Judaism"—religious notions which were arrested on the sixth or eighth grade level of intellectual development . . . " (Kahn, 1980, p. 9). Jospe urged the Jewish community to think about the risks associated with neglecting the learning needs of Jewish adults. By the mid-1990s, it was widely acknowledged that most parents were "religiously" dropping their children off "at the doors of impressive synagogue education buildings" while simultaneously failing to think of Judaism as an activity for themselves (Cowan, 1994). In 1996, Rabbi Lawrence Hoffman, a leader of the progressive Synagogue 2000 initiative, cautioned that pediatric Judaism had become one of the "sins" of modern synagogue life: "We have planned for children only. . . . In our understandable anxiety to pass on Judaism as their heritage, we [have] neglected its spiritual resources for adults, leaving ourselves with no adequate notion of how we too might draw sustenance from our faith as we grow up and grow older." Exhorting the Jewish community to confront the negative consequences of pediatric Judaism, Rabbi Hoffman urged synagogue leaders to help Jewish adults see Judaism as "an adult faith, with adult consciousness, adult intellect, and answers to the challenges of adult life" (pp. 20–21).

Overcoming pediatric Judaism begins with Jewish professionals (1) encouraging adults to acknowledge their learning concerns, fears, and uncertainties, (2) showing them that Jewish learning is accessible and non-threatening, and (3) helping them to identify what they *want to learn* and what they *need to learn*. These basic socialization strategies often get ignored by rabbis, educators, and adult education committees eager to create Jewish adult learning programs without sufficiently determining who the prospective learners are, what their apprehensions are, and what might best support their growth. If asked, Jewish adults can identify the gaps in their previous

Jewish education and the areas of Jewish knowledge in which they feel incompetent. Once they are assured that their "fear and trembling" is understandable, most adults will disclose what makes new learning feel awkward and will genuinely appreciate proffered guidance and support. Moreover, when adults are helped to figure out their Jewish learning needs and take small steps toward becoming more Jewishly informed, they become more confident about their capacity for Jewish learning and their ability to overcome obstacles to acquiring competence as a Jewish adult.

The Quest for Competence

For insight into how people gain confidence and competence, we turn first to general psychological theories. Child development experts have been analyzing the antecedents of competence and self-esteem for decades. Forty years ago, in a classic essay on what drives human behavior, psychologist Robert White (1959) argued that human beings are characterized by a basic motivation to be competent and to interact successfully with their environments. His views were supported subsequently in analyses of socialization by John Clausen (1993) and Albert Bandura (1994), who said that, in the quest for competence, people seek to acquire both "a sense of potency, activity, and efficacy" (that is, a sense of effectiveness) and "a favorable self-evaluation" (that is, positive self-esteem). In other words, to achieve competence, a person has to do well and also has to like his or her choices and behaviors in the process.

In studies of manifestations of children's competence at school, White (1959) found that the more capable children perceived themselves to be, the more motivated they were to try new things. Studies of children and adults have found that competence is associated with confidence: the greater number of successful new experiences people have, the more self-trusting they will feel the next time they are asked to take a risk with something new. Conversely, when people don't feel successful, their self-esteem is threatened, and if they feel insecure or inferior, they are less likely to try again.

In Erik Erikson's (1963) view of human development, a significant developmental task also involves competence. Erikson designated this task as *industry:* learning to become an effective worker in society. Traditionally, age six to twelve is the time when children acquire the "tools and rules" of society, including learning how to read, write, compute, and function as a member of a team. It is also a time when children learn to "stay on task" and finish what they begin. Children who aren't successful at industry are at risk for developing a sense of *inferiority*. Such children tend to feel outdistanced by age mates and may get messages from teachers, parents, and even peers that they just don't have "what it takes" to master new challenges. In this age group, feelings of inferiority can also occur in specific areas of competence and may be in response to a variety of experiences: failure to learn how to work with fractions, being the last one chosen for a game, being left off a birthday party invitation list, not managing emotions well with bullies or teasers, and so on.

Experiences that lead to feelings of inferiority are not limited to the years of childhood, however. At any age, a person may attempt new learning and, confronted with new challenges, may feel a sense of failure or incompetence. Moreover, most adults carry some scars from inferiority episodes that inhibit their willingness to take risks in unfamiliar domains later in life. Erikson argues that healthy psychological functioning involves learning that one is not always all-knowing or perfectly informed. Maintaining a balance between *industry* and *inferiority* is part of what motivates us to keep on learning.

Competence and Jewish Learners

Just as kids can feel incompetent when it comes to playing basketball or learning to do mathematical calculations, so do many kids feel incompetent in Jewish learning—and all the more so when they become adults. What of Jewish children—and adults—who never achieve a sense of competence about themselves as knowledgeable Jews? What of people who receive no formal Jewish education and thus are unable to develop confidence about themselves as Jewish knowers? What about people whose Jewish education stops before they acquire a mature understanding of Judaism and later feel "fraudulent" about their Jewish knowledge base? And what about individuals who at one point or another are made to feel unacceptable or inadequate as Jewish learners—reflective children whose questions about God or prayer are dismissed as impertinent, girls in Hebrew classes who are told they have no place on the *bimah*, bored children who can't sit still and lose interest, learning disabled children who can't process the Hebrew alphabet, disengaged children whose parents will not or cannot validate the Jewish learning experience, and so on?

The voices of individuals who have suffered a lack of competence—and a corresponding lack of confidence—in Jewish learning endeavors have resounded in my work with Jewish adults (see Exhibit 2-1). Though these people may be "grown up" chronologically, as learners they often sound (and feel) like children. Their stories show that, from an Eriksonian perspective, they have not resolved the task of industry and are continually struggling to overcome feelings of inferiority as knowledgeable Jewish adults. While they see themselves as capable and competent in other domains, they are hesitant and unsure when it comes to Jewish study. They carry so much baggage about their Jewish ignorance that they exaggerate the demands of Jewish learning and assume they will feel diminished if they take steps to learn. Because they don't have a "map" or "guidebook" for Jewish study, they are convinced they will be "lost" even before they begin the learning journey. Ashamed of their ignorance, they worry that others will be judgmental and impatient with their questions and lack of skill.

The irony of this mind-set is made especially evident when these same people are asked to describe recent "new learning" activities in their lives. When I meet with Jewish adults to talk about my research, I make a point of asking them: "What is something new you learned in the past year? Why did you learn it? What helped you understand the new information? What got in your way or frustrated you in the learning experience?" Invariably, the responses include animated accounts of how people figured out how to program a handheld computer or how to gather information about a threatening medical condition. Years of research about adult learners has shown that when adults are motivated to learn, they become highly self-directed, focused, and efficient; they transfer the learning skills they have developed elsewhere and readily apply them to the challenge at hand. Moreover, according to adult learning authority K. Patricia Cross (1981), the more adults learn, the more they are motivated to increase their learning. Once adults begin new learning projects, they tend to enlarge their scope of interest, deepen their knowledge about topics of personal interest, and look for ways to share their knowledge with others.

Danielle's Story: Getting Past Fear and Trembling

So what does it take to get Jewish adults to *want* to learn Jewish things, to overcome their fears and develop the motivation to move beyond pediatric

EXHIBIT 2-1

Feeling Jewishly Illiterate

Sara, attorney, age 38
I know so little about basic traditions. In college I got some history and philosophy, but I don't even know which way the mezuzah is supposed to point on the door. And I can't read Hebrew, and I don't know any of the prayers. I get invited to my partners' kids' bar mitzvahs and I always hope no one I know will take the seat next to me. My mother-in-law says I should take a class at the JCC, but unless there's someone to go with, I doubt I'll get there.

Andrew, city planner, age 42
Like many people in my generation, I did not learn very much about Judaism. I have always found it hard to see where my Jewish background gave me anything specific that would help me as I moved along whatever path I was moving forward on. That's why I think so many people have been drawn to the simpler and more accessible Eastern religions—the *Jew in the Lotus* stuff—which I think is far less intellectual and requires far less knowledge. My generation was not trained very well about Jewish things. Maybe we knew a few stories, but there was no way for us to see the richness. There were no teachers, no one who could "peel back the onion."

Ruth, teacher, age 47
Last year, I was seeing a Jewish man, and he said, "Let's go hear this talk about midrash." And I didn't even know what midrash was. There were all of these stories that people did not exactly make up but could be interpreted and reinterpreted and applied to life. Even though I teach English, I did not know that you could do things like that in Judaism. So that got me curious, and I started studying Jewish text. I was stunned—kept finding there was more I wanted to know. But I always feel like I can never catch up. I never got any Jewish tools growing up.

Ari, engineer, age 53
I went to Hebrew school until my bar mitzvah, and mostly I remember asking a lot of questions and not getting answers. The teachers were part-time do-gooders who had no skills. I wasn't a troublemaker, but I wasn't listening and nobody ever challenged me. So I started going sideways and drifted away. I would say, educationally, what I got was very typical of people educated in the fifties and sixties: it was minimal. My education is still sorely deficient in any understanding of the history. Once you get out of the Five Books, what's the history?

Martha, realtor, age 62
I'm studying now. It's very hard for me, the Hebrew. I have never studied Hebrew. This is like from scratch. It's very difficult for someone who has not had to be in this position of being a third grader, swallowing my ego when I have to stumble, word by word. Here I am, the temple president, and I'm just learning the *alef-bet*.

Morris, businessman, age 70
I grew up in a semi-Orthodox environment. I went to *cheder*. And went to a Jewish religious school after public school, which was a very unsatisfactory kind of experience, as I look back on it, because there was no learning involved. It was typical, "This is what you are supposed to do and this is what you're supposed to believe and this is what you're supposed to say, and don't question it." So I got significantly turned off for about fifty years.

Judaism toward a more mature, informed, and positive relationship with Jewish heritage and tradition? What helps Jewish adults to grow—and what is the role of the Jewish professional in fostering that growth? The experience of Danielle Salomon, a retired magazine executive whom I met while traveling on a flight to Israel, provides insight to our understanding of the Jewish adult learning journey.

ᘓᔕ Story 2 ᔑᔭ

DANIELLE

Danielle Salomon was born in Morocco in 1935. In her early years, Danielle received no formal Jewish education. Her father occasionally took her with him to *shul,* and there were always special treats at Chanukah, but her family's participation in Jewish life was more communal than religious.

In 1939, Mr. Salomon arranged for his wife and young daughter to relocate to Panama. However, before he could join them, Danielle's father suffered a fatal stroke. Five years later, Mrs. Salomon married another refugee, and when Danielle was twelve, the family relocated to Detroit.

Danielle's stepfather discouraged any Jewish identification or observance. An emotionally restrained agnostic, he tended to mock anyone who took religion seriously. Danielle learned early on that, at home, it was better not to initiate discussions about Judaism or her Jewish heritage. For most of her adolescence and early adulthood, Danielle adhered to her stepfather's code of silence about Judaism and assimilated into the non-Jewish community.

By the time Danielle finished college and started a long career in magazine publishing, her identification with Judaism was deeply buried. In her mid-thirties, however, she became romantically involved with Marcy, a Jewish woman from Chicago. Thus began a long relationship that included the celebration of Jewish holidays with Marcy's large and very ethnically Jewish family. When she participated in these family gatherings, Danielle found herself recalling pleasurable Jewish holiday times from her early childhood. She was pleased when Marcy's mother gave her a Star of David pendant. Marcy introduced

Danielle to Jewish women's diaries and autobiographies, and Danielle began to assemble a library of books on Jewish themes. In honor of Marcy's fiftieth birthday, Danielle arranged for them to go on a tour of Jewish sites in Spain and North Africa. She was profoundly moved by the trip—by learning for the first time about her Sephardic heritage—and said that this new understanding transformed her self-image as a Jew.

Marcy was diagnosed with advanced breast cancer at age fifty-three. In the months following Marcy's death, Danielle realized that she wanted to better understand Judaism and its views of mourning. She felt a strong need to be part of a spiritual community that could help her feel less alone in her grief. With considerable trepidation, she approached Dov Benjamin, the rabbi of a congregation known to be friendly to gays and lesbians. The rabbi welcomed her with great sensitivity and urged her to come to services and say *Kaddish* for Marcy. He assured her that she if she came to services, he would make sure she did not feel awkward or out of place. Later Danielle recalled the things that stood out for her as she took her first steps into worship and learning:

> Rabbi Benjamin ran, essentially, a learner's service. He had all the main things transliterated on six or seven pages. He had them in Hebrew, he had them transliterated, he had them in English, so you knew what to do. And if he called on you, which was always unexpected, and you said, "Well, I don't know how," he said, "Well, that's all right, we'll talk you through it." And they did. They all made me feel a part of things.

Over several months, Danielle found herself looking forward to attending services. She struck up a friendship with another mourner, a widow named Andi, and the two of them decided to take a beginning Hebrew class taught by the synagogue's cantor. Her experience was eye-opening:

> The class wasn't "hard," but I felt incredibly stupid when I couldn't remember things from week to week. I would stumble again and again when we tried to read aloud, and I kept putting pressure on myself to learn things quickly and get it right. Finally, I had to realize that learning a language like Hebrew when you're in your late

fifties just isn't going to be easy. You have to be willing to make mistakes and then try again, to say "I don't know that," and to ask for help.

Danielle appreciated the support she received from Rinana Sandlar, the cantor, who urged the students "to take things slowly and to see each class as an opportunity for review." Cantor Sandlar not only encouraged the students, she recommended that they work collaboratively.

> She suggested that Andi and I become study partners—that we call each other every evening and read aloud for twenty minutes. We got into the habit of doing this, and when we messed up, we'd quote Cantor Sandlar to one another. I have to say: I learned more than Hebrew from Cantor Sandlar. I learned *an attitude toward learning.*

A turning point in Danielle's learning came when she began to make connections between what she was studying with Cantor Sandlar and her own sense of authority as a Jewish "knower":

> You know: little things can make such a difference when you're just beginning. For me, a wonderful moment came one Friday night at services. Andi and I had been learning prayer-book Hebrew, but we were still very slow with it. That night, I noticed how both Andi and I were tracking the words of the *Sim Shalom* with our fingers. Cantor Sandlar was singing the prayer and we were keeping up, word by word. I caught Andi's eye when we reached the *amen*, and we both started giggling—like little kids. We were so excited. We were so proud of ourselves!

Reinforced by the positive experiences with learning and worship, Danielle was pleased when Rabbi Benjamin invited her to begin to study Judaism in a systematic way. His Introduction to Judaism class provided Danielle an important opportunity to think about her Jewish identity:

> There were so many things I didn't understand. Having been brought up in such an assimilated family, I didn't know anything. I knew I was a Jew, but that was about it—and nothing about it had ever seemed very positive.

So, I took the rabbi's class, which opened up a lot of questions. First there were his questions, to answer at home. I saw that if I wanted to answer them honestly, I really had to think about them. So I did. And it was helpful to me to see which of my answers fit in with being Jewish—and which ones didn't! And, too, the rabbi told us it was important that we think critically about what we were learning, not to take things as gospel just because he said them.

The class also provided an opportunity for Danielle to begin to articulate her own questions and to get what she called "authentic and grounded" Jewish answers:

I knew very little about being Jewish, but I had a lot of questions. Questions about what is a Jew, questions about God, what and where. Questions about why do we do this or that festival, why do we even keep it? Questions about the law and interpretations of the law. Even questions about Jewish etiquette: What's the right kind of gift to give to a child at a bar mitzvah? When do we give charity? I wanted to fill in the holes, to stop operating on what I call "haphazard knowledge."

Over time, Danielle decided to study Torah on a regular basis.

Once my appetite got whetted, there was no turning back. I joined a women's study group that was led by a retired professor. Studying Torah became an extremely important part of my life: studying with the group during the week, rereading the text on Saturday mornings, learning about translation, finding different interpretations—including interpretations that sometimes make more sense for today rather than four thousand years ago. Professor Aharon really stretched me and showed me the value of consulting different sources to increase my understanding. Gradually, I began to "read" on a whole new level.

The study group members regularly observed Rosh Chodesh and used these monthly occasions to celebrate special moments in group members' lives. On the occasion of Danielle's sixtieth birthday, several women created a Rosh Chodesh ceremony in her honor. They gave her a *yad* to symbolize how far she had come in reading and understanding Hebrew.

The Rosh Chodesh celebration was the first truly *Jewish* spiritual moment of my life. When the other students gathered around me to give me their blessing, I felt that the *Shechinah* had entered into the room. It was so powerful—as if all the pieces of my life had finally come together.

When interviewed at age sixty-three, Danielle said that a crucially important dimension of her learning journey was her experience with supportive, responsive teachers who taught her about the importance of *questions* in Jewish learning. Thinking back on the teachers who had "made a difference," she offered her personal "prescription" for the best kind of Jewish adult educator:

> The kind of teacher I am looking for does have to be someone kind of special. The person can be either male or female—I don't care. I have to feel not only that they know a lot—that's one thing—but also that I can ask questions, any question, and not be laughed at. Any questions—and nobody says, "How come you don't know that?" Even if that question is something that maybe a thirteen-year-old asks: when I was thirteen I couldn't ask it, so I'm asking it now.
>
> I want a teacher who, if he or she can't provide an answer, then provides me with details about where I can go to look it up. That's good enough. Nobody has to know everything. I want somebody like Cantor Sandlar, who will start a class saying, "Let's review what we learned last time so everyone can be on the same page." And, I want somebody like Professor Aharon who can suggest "Let's read this and this" or "Let's study that and that." Somebody who doesn't mind going off on tangents. And somebody like Rabbi Benjamin— somebody who listens well.
>
> And, most of all, I want somebody who opens my mind to different ways of looking at things. I don't want anybody saying, "This is what God is" or "Here's *the* answer." I want a teacher who says, "Here are some ways to think about things. Here are some ways Jews struggle with these questions."

Danielle's Story: A Developmentalist's Perspective

Danielle Salomon's story typifies the developmental needs and growth experience of many Jewish adult learners. It is a story of a well-educated, intellectually sophisticated woman who grew up increasingly disconnected from her Jewish roots. As a child in Morocco, Danielle had a "secure" attachment to her Jewish family, although she received no Jewish education. Later, after emigrating first to Panama and then to Detroit, Danielle learned to "hide" her Jewish questions and became alienated from her Jewish past. Her involvement as an adult with a Jewish partner, Marcy, and Marcy's warm Jewish family, prompted Danielle to begin to reframe her self-perception as a Jew. Her interest in her Jewish identity was further sparked by a tour of the Jewish sites of Spain and North Africa and then, tragically, by Marcy's struggle with cancer. When Marcy died, Danielle realized that she wanted a more grounded understanding of Jewish mourning rituals. A rabbi made prayer, worship, and Jewish learning experiences safe and nonthreatening for her and helped her to acquire some basic Jewish literacy, kindling a zest for pursuing additional learning. Although Danielle did not begin her "formal" Jewish education until she was in her mid-fifties, within several years she had moved from a position of childlike "fear and trembling" to a position of competence and confidence as a Jewish adult learner.

Like the other adults whose voices we read earlier in this chapter, Danielle's adult Jewish growth occurred when her *developmental needs as a learner* were met. Exhibit 2-2 identifies a number of those needs. These "Ten R's That Foster Adult Jewish Growth" have emerged in my analysis of interviews about "what matters" to Jewish adult learners who are moving from a place of "fear and trembling" to a position of increased personal authority as a Jewish adult. While every learner brings particular learning needs and values to Jewish learning venues, on balance Danielle's experience as a learner is representative of the "success stories" I have consistently heard in my research.

The 10 R's and Danielle's Adult Jewish Growth

Recognition

Like many contemporary Jewish adults, when Danielle was growing up, she was discouraged from being "seen" as a Jew—by herself or by others. As an adolescent, she hid her Jewish identity and was not given a chance to develop self-respect as a Jew. When her partner's family welcomed her and Marcy's mother gave her a Star of David to wear, Danielle experienced her first adult moments of pride in her Jewish identity. Later, Rabbi Benjamin's graciousness affirmed that Danielle could be accepted in a Jewish setting

EXHIBIT 2-2

Beyond Reading, 'Riting, and 'Rithmetic:
Ten R's That Foster Adult Jewish Growth

1. **Recognition**   Being seen, welcomed, and respected as a learner; being treated as an adult who values options and independence

2. **Resocialization**   Being helped to learn/relearn Jewish tradition and practice by facilitative teachers who encourage and empower learners to become self-directing

3. **Reinforcement**   Being rewarded for engaging actively in Jewish learning; being affirmed for having questions, insights, doubts, and skills for self-direction and deeper learning

4. **Repetition**   Being encouraged to review and revisit material

5. **Rigor**   Being challenged to grapple with substantive material; being shown how to access such material

6. **Relevance**   Being helped to discover connections between traditional teachings and contemporary experiences

7. **Relationships**   Being encouraged to find a community of learning that includes partners for dialogue, mentors, and facilitators; being invited to become collaborative in the teaching-learning-teaching process

8. **Reverence**   Being affirmed in the pursuit of a relationship with God or in the cultivation of meaningful spiritual experiences

9. **Retreat**   Being given opportunities to separate from the ordinary; being offered sanctuary within Jewish settings

10. **Ritualized rejoicing**   Being honored in ways that joyfully support the learner's adult Jewish growth (e.g., celebrations of learning)

and that her learning and worship needs would be respected. He understood that she needed to feel comfortable in a Jewish learning environment because she did not want to be humiliated for her lack of knowledge. Because she was treated "like an adult" by Rabbi Benjamin and other teachers, Danielle developed a new sense of herself and her ability to learn Jewish things. These professionals demonstrated respect for what Danielle brought to her learning from her experiences in the larger world, and they helped her to recognize her own competence and authenticity as a Jewish learner.

Resocialization

In sociological terms, socialization is the process by which a newcomer (e.g., an infant, immigrant, or new employee) is helped to learn the "rules, values, and customs" of the new "society" into which he or she has entered. Danielle's earliest socialization as a Jew likely was warm and family-centered, but her stepfather's messages overrode any earlier positive feelings. As a teenager, Danielle was socialized to deny and avoid her Judaism.

Consequently, when she wanted, as an adult, to learn about Judaism and herself as a Jew, she needed teachers who were encouraging and willing to help her feel more and more authentic as a Jewish person. Her teachers' willingness to teach her both the *content* and how to *study* the content made a lasting impression on Danielle. Eventually she was able to internalize the values and love of learning modeled by other, more experienced members of the Jewish community.

Reinforcement

While adults tend to be more intrinsically motivated when it comes to new learning than children (who typically take on new learning because there are promised "rewards"), Jewish adults who are new to learning or observance generally look to others for encouragement and reinforcement for their participation. For most of these learners, the experience of being taken seriously and valued by a Jewish teacher is new and unusual. Because these adults do not think of themselves as ready for a substantive "Jewish conversation," the more they are validated and affirmed in the Jewish learning process, the more confident they will become to take learning risks, explore new modes of inquiry, and reinforce themselves as learners. Danielle's teachers consistently zeroed in on her learning needs and helped her shape her learning journey. The more they rewarded her commitment to learning, the more independent Danielle became as a self-directed Jewish adult learner.

Repetition

Research about adult intellectual capacity conclusively shows that, barring physical impairment, adults are able to learn new things throughout their lives. In later life, however, the brain does not process new information quite as quickly as before, and sometimes recent learning does not get adequately "encoded" for easy retrieval. In addition, when learners are stressed, their ability to take in and retain new information may be disrupted. As a result, adult learners sometimes feel that, because they can't remember things as efficiently, they must be losing "control" over new ideas or recently acquired skills. They are critical of themselves when they can't master material quickly and apprehensive when they can't recall specific details. Self-criticism, impatience, and anxiety can interfere with adult learning, but repetition and review can help people to regain their sense of mastery and familiarity. Learning aids that can help adults to "stay on top" of information enable these learners to feel competent and "adult."

These general findings about adult learners are especially relevant to the experience of Jewish adults who are newcomers to Jewish learning. Frequently, Jewish adults bring to the learning situation a level of anxiety and tension that interferes with how they process new information. Many believe that they are too old to learn Hebrew or that because they didn't learn the basics as children, they will never be able to "catch up" and become Jewishly literate. They don't have familiarity with traditional texts and assume that they cannot be "authentic" Jews unless they devote themselves to study and an observant lifestyle. When they do engage in learning, many are self-demanding and easily frustrated, sometimes doubting that small gains will eventually accrue with time and practice. They forget that Jewish learning is—and always has been—a lifelong process that assumes that people will revisit content again and again (consider, for example, the Torah cycle, Passover seder rituals, prayers). Once Jewish adult learners become comfortable with the idea of repetition, they discover the benefits of ongoing practice and review. Teachers who incorporate systems for review into the learning process send learners the message that repetition is *normative* in Jewish learning. Review sessions that reinforce earlier learning and "level the playing field" help Jewish adults to feel that they are participants in an ongoing learning conversation.

Repetition and review were particularly important to Danielle when she undertook the study of Hebrew. The cantor's suggestion that she and her friend, Andi, become study and review partners gave Danielle a way of approaching learning that was highly satisfying. Specifically, Cantor Sandlar's commitment to reviewing material at the beginning of each class session also helped Danielle to feel more in control of course material.

Rigor

Over the past fifty years, the educational attainment level of American Jews has been significantly higher than the national average for other adults. Since most Jewish adults today have completed at least a bachelor's degree, the capacity for serious learning in this population is correspondingly high. While not all Jewish adults seek rigorous Jewish learning experiences, many find that once they begin to study, they are impatient with anything less than substantive content, thoughtful analysis, and a commitment to ongoing inquiry. Jewish adult learners are respectful of brilliant teachers and appreciate learning situations in which their own assumptions are challenged or new ways of seeing material are presented. For Danielle, the "rigor" of the questions posed by Rabbi Benjamin in the Introduction to Judaism class challenged her to probe more deeply into her Jewish identity and to commit more thoughtfully to subsequent Jewish learning activities.

Relevance

Jewish adults who are intimidated by Jewish learning rarely understand that the lessons found in traditional Jewish texts or in Jewish history, law, and philosophy can be profoundly relevant to their contemporary experience. Typically they hold a naïve or limited view of the contents of the Bible and have no familiarity with the tradition of text interpretation. When helped to see that they can "join the conversation" of Jewish discourse, find personal meaning in texts, and even create their own commentaries, these learners tend to be startled and surprised. Their "fear and trembling" shifts to *naaseh v'nishma*, and through "doing and understanding" they become more firmly engaged in Jewish "meaning-making." In this shift, they are especially appreciative of opportunities for dialogue with knowledgeable teachers and contact with other learners who share their enthusiasm for learning. They value discovering relevance for themselves and seeing how others are similarly impacted.

Danielle's participation in a variety of Jewish adult learning activities heightened her awareness of her many questions about Judaism. The more her questions were addressed, the more she was able to find relevance and a sense of personal meaning in the material she was studying.

Relationships

For most adults, the rabbinic wisdom of "Get yourself a teacher, find yourself a friend" (*Pirkei Avot* 1:6) lies at the heart of successful Jewish learning. Although many people are satisfied to *access* information independently, the true joy of learning comes when ideas are exchanged, different perspectives are offered, and thoughtful questions are introduced. A core element of the successful adult learning experience is a *democratic spirit* where competition is minimized, learners are supported in their efforts toward mastery by both teachers and fellow learners, and everyone is accorded respect. Adult learners prize their teacher-learner and learner-learner relationships and frequently describe how important it was "not to feel alone" on the learning journey. Recent scholarship about collaborative learning and learning communities has shown that when learners come together and grapple with challenging material, everyone benefits from the interactive discourse.

The story of Danielle's learning journey is about both her *and* her relationships. As a child, her inquiry about Judaism and her Jewish heritage was shut off by her stepfather; for many years, this relationship shaped Danielle's attitude toward Judaism and herself as a Jew. Her relationship with Marcy and her Jewish family provided Danielle with a positive, affirming context in which to begin to rethink her Jewish identity. When Marcy died, Danielle wanted to better understand Jewish mourning practices and was grateful to be invited into a synagogue community where her learning needs would be treated with respect. From the time she became involved with Rabbi Benjamin's congregation, she was encouraged to form authentic attachments with her teachers and with other learners. These increasingly "secure" Jewish attachments provided Danielle with an important base for her ongoing adult Jewish growth.

Reverence

One area that causes fear and trembling in Jewish adults is the concept of God. Many Jewish adults are uncomfortable discussing God. They worry that pursuing adult Jewish education will mean needing to have a clear idea of God. Alternatively, they may not believe in a traditional view of God and worry that this will label them as outcasts. At the same time, they are looking to fill a spiritual gap in their lives.

In *A Generation of Seekers*, Wade Clark Roof (1993) describes how contemporary American adults are looking for meaningful spiritual experiences but lack the vocabulary to describe what they are seeking. Quoting from an interview with a Jewish neurologist, Roof notes that this man, like others interviewed, differentiates between being "religious" and being "spiritual":

> I'm certainly not religious, in the sense that I don't believe in God and I don't subscribe to standard religious doctrine; but I think I'm spiritual, in the sense that I have a very deep sense of world realities. . . . I feel extremely strong about the importance of right action for others, being fair to others. . . . Another part of being spiritual to me is sort of this sense of reverence about the world, which I think religious people attribute to God or their relationship to God; for me, it's much more abstract. . . . [I'm sensitive] to reap[ing] the beauty of the world and history and life and how moving it is to wake up in the morning and see the flowers coming up and the clouds in the sky. . . . (pp. 77–78)

The neurologist's effort to articulate how he understands the place of God and reverence in his life has an urgency about it: he wants to assign a "label" to the awe and wonder he associates with the divine, but he doesn't have a vocabulary that quite fits his actual experience. Like the men and women described by Steven M. Cohen and Arnold Eisen in *The Jew Within* (2000), this man has a conception of "reverence" for something larger than himself, but he does not expect to find God in "standard religious doctrine" or, by extension, in synagogues or other places associated with Jewish life. This gap between "spirituality" and "Jewish experience" was mentioned by many of the Jewish adult learners I interviewed. However, few of the people I interviewed mentioned having conversations about God with a rabbi or teacher. Danielle was one of the few who even referred to God in her reflections about her Jewish journey; her comments about the presence of the *Shechinah* in her Rosh Chodesh celebrations suggested that, through her study with other women, Danielle had begun to think about God and to find a vocabulary for talking about the spiritual dimensions of her adult Jewish growth.

Curiously, while Danielle looked to her teachers for explanations of the Jewish view of God, she did not talk about her spiritual development as a direct outcome of her Jewish learning. Rather, her spiritual growth seemed to be enriched by her teachers' collective message that Jews grapple with spiritual questions through questioning and study. Moreover, she valued her teachers' lack of dogmatism; consistently they showed her that there are many ways to conceive of God and that no one path fits all people.

Retreat

One way for Jewish adults to come in the door of Jewish learning is through a retreat where they can congregate with other like-minded Jews. For the people I interviewed and many other Jewish adults, retreat has become associated with the idea of "getting away from it all"—finding special activities that enable one to separate oneself from the ordinary. Common retreat activities are weekends that focus on spiritual growth, summer Jewish learning programs, meditation sessions, and trips to meaningful Jewish sites (including Israel). Because so many contemporary adults lead highly complex and busy lives, the idea of retreat is highly appealing. Especially valued are opportunities that help people to reduce the stress in their lives and give them structures for reflection and new meaning-making. To be successful, a Jewish retreat must offer adults a sense of sanctuary, a "safe place" in which one will be accepted and nurtured rather than pressured or pushed.[2] Ironically, most Jews do not find that sense of sanctuary within the walls of Jewish institutions. Many see synagogues as places that re-create the stresses of the outside world and organizations as groups that require conformity and prescribed behaviors.

Danielle did not attend any structured retreats, but she certainly found "safe spaces" for her learning journey in Rabbi Benjamin's synagogue and her various classes. Her descriptions of her experiences in these settings evoked images of warmth, joy, and secure attachment.

Ritualized Rejoicing

Historically, Jews have honored learners on special occasions, acknowledging their contributions publicly and according them special status as teachers to the community. The adult bar/bat mitzvah has become a popular vehicle through which many contemporary Jewish adults are recognized for their studies, but it is not (and should not be) the only mechanism for celebrating learners' growth. Nor should it be seen as the end, as it often is, even for adults. Just as learners of Talmud are acknowledged when they complete

---

2. The Union of American Hebrew Congregations' *Live Together, Learn Together: A Congregational Kallah/Retreat Manual* (New York: UAHC Department of Adult Jewish Growth, 2000) offers excellent suggestions for planning retreats for adults.

a tractate, so too should the important milestones of modern learners be treated with some kind of ritualized rejoicing.

For Danielle, the celebration created by her classmates in honor of her sixtieth birthday was an occasion of immense joy. She regarded the gift of a *yad* as a powerful symbolic statement by her Jewish community that she had, at last, become an authentic Jewish adult. While this celebration was by no means the culmination of Danielle's adult Jewish growth, it provided a tangible "marker" on her journey and affirmed the distance she had come.

In the end, we should remember the insights of Erik Erikson described at the beginning of this chapter. Becoming an educated Jew does not mean knowing everything. Becoming competent as a Jewish adult is a developmental process, through which one can overcome feelings of self-doubt and acquire a new sense of personal authority or authenticity. Jewish professionals can do a great deal to allay the fears of Jewish adults by helping them to move beyond fear and trembling into ongoing experiences of discovery and learning in adult Jewish life.

From Theory to Practice: Helping Adults to Move Beyond Fear and Trembling

The "Ten R's That Foster Adult Jewish Growth" suggest a number of strategies that Jewish professionals should keep in mind when they welcome Jewish adults into Jewish institutions, learning experiences, and communal gatherings. These strategies are grounded in the belief that the Jewish professional can play a crucial transformative role in helping learners to move from "fear and trembling" to active and sustained Jewish growth. Jewish professionals should:

1. Take a "developmental" stance toward prospective adult Jewish learners, recognizing that although people may be "grown up" in most arenas, Jewishly they have more "growing up" to do. Without infantilizing these individuals, offer them Jewish learning activities that feel safe and supportive. At the same time, provide them with a vision for their development, showing them a roadmap for Jewish learning and some of the "small steps" they can take to move forward on the journey of Jewish growth.

2. Show learners that you are a learner as well as a teacher. Invite people to join you in a study project or to read a book you are interested in.

Offer to show learners what tools you use when you need to learn new materials. Consult with people about *their* expertise and let them teach you what they know.

3. Assume that learners who come to your door need validation and reinforcement. Even those learners who have made Jewish study a part of their lives appreciate being acknowledged by the "official" Jews in their community. When you offer your enthusiastic endorsement of their learning and express interest in what they are learning, you "send a message" that you care about both the learner *and* what is being learned.

4. Challenge learners to build their level of Jewish literacy and help them to diversify their knowledge base and repertoire of skills. For example, help them to find a personally meaningful psalm *and* suggest that they incorporate favorite lines or images into an ethical will; share with them the various ways to translate a text *and* show them how to write a commentary on that text; invite them to rewrite prayers in their own words *and* encourage them to set the prayer to a liturgical melody; suggest that they engage in independent study about a Jewish topic using Internet resources and then ask them to teach you about the mysteries of Jewish cyberspace. By challenging Jewish adult learners to "do, and then do more," you help them to move beyond their fear and "listen" in new ways. By supporting them in their growth, you demonstrate that you are a traveling companion in their learning journey.

5. Create opportunities for learners to celebrate their learning—to show that they have moved beyond their fear and are now able to share what they have understood with others. When you establish a precedent of public acclaim for learners, such as inviting people to give a *d'var Torah* or to speak about their learning experiences or to share something they have created as a result of their Jewish learning (such as a poem, a piece of stitchery, or a family tree), you begin to build a community of learners who associate learning with communal ritual and affirmation.

3

From the Wilderness to the Promised Land: Journeys toward Jewish Identity

Prepare to cross the Jordan... into the land.... Be strong and resolute; do not be terrified or dismayed, for Adonai *your God is with you wherever you go.*

—Joshua 1:2, 9

The language of journey and travel is at the heart of the "meta-story" of the Jewish people. From Abraham's departure for unknown destinations to Joseph's journey to Egypt, to the Israelites crossing of the Sea of Reeds, to generation upon generation of migrations around the world—the departures and arrivals, itineraries and landmarks, baggage and paraphernalia of "Jews on the journey" frame our thinking about Jewish growth and change. Such language is similarly found in work about adult development. Indeed, in the introduction to an excellent college text called *The Journey of Adulthood*, Professor Helen Bee (2000) tells her students:

> Some of you reading this are just beginning the journey of your own adult life; some of you are part way along the road.... Whatever your age, you *are* traveling, moving through the years and through the changes and transformations that come with the years.... Every journey is unique. No two adult lives are exactly alike. Still, there have to be some common themes or there would be no reason for a book on adult development. Amidst the variability, there are some typical itineraries, some commonly shared experiences, some shared lessons or tasks. [This book addresses] both the uniqueness and the common ground of adult lives. (p. 3)

Like many other developmental psychologists, Bee grounds much of her discussion of adult growth in the commonalities of adult change—physical and cognitive changes, the growth (and loss) of work and family roles, and

shifts in how individuals come to understand the continuities and disconti-
nuities in their life experiences. Like most writers about adulthood, Bee
assumes that when an individual embarks on the journey of adulthood, he
or she will be well on the way to completing important developmental tasks
usually associated with adolescence. In her book, Bee reviews Erik Erikson's
classic timetable for healthy psychosocial development, which names the
task of "identity versus role confusion" as the primary preoccupation of
adolescents:

> The teenager (or young adult) must achieve a sense of identity—both
> who he or she is and what he or she will be—in several areas, including
> occupation, gender role, politics, and religion. (p. 36)

Bee tells us that when Erikson first developed his developmental theory,
he hypothesized that if young people did not explore their options and
make decisions about personal and vocational commitments during adolescence, they would spend their adult years confused about their values and
unable to become contributing members of society.

As Erikson's biographer Lawrence J. Friedman (1999) notes, however,
Erikson later broadened his theory and acknowledged that identity is rarely
"achieved" or fixed by the end of adolescence. In his later years, as his own
identity (a complex identity shaped by his Jewish-Danish-German-
American life experiences) evolved, Erikson speculated that the formation
of one's identity is a lifelong process filled with twists and turns, role
changes and value shifts, transitions that require ongoing assessments of
interactions between "the self" and one's "society." Indeed, post-Eriksonian
theorists have pointed out that while human beings tend to have relatively
consistent personality traits over the life cycle, growth in adulthood pushes
people to reframe old meanings, adapt to changes, and develop multiple
selves appropriate to different situations and circumstances. In other words,
during the adult years, most people do "change" and, in that sense, identity
formation—how each of us comes to define ourselves and the things that
matter to us—is a continuing phenomenon.

Erikson's theory of identity formation (1963) provides an important
starting point for discussing Jewish identity formation, because his theory
raises some important issues relevant to the authentic development of many
Jewish adults today. First, if identity formation is an ongoing process, so too
is the evolution of Jewish identity over the life cycle. Likewise, if (as Erikson

argues) exploring one's commitments and belief systems (including one's religious values) typically begins during adolescence, and if a Jewish adult has come of age without having "done the work" of Jewish identity formation, then exploration about the personal meaning of Judaism in one's life will have to occur during the adult years. Such journeys typically begin when a Jewish adult realizes that he or she has never grown beyond the pediatric Judaism of childhood or early adolescence. Under the best circumstances, this discovery leads to a process of thoughtful and self-conscious consideration of one's willingness to actively learn about and make a commitment to Jewish values, beliefs, and practices.

Unlike journeys that have clear or predetermined destinations or predictable timetables, the Jewish journey typically evolves slowly and takes a long time (even, perhaps, forty years of wandering in the wilderness!). For most Jewish adults today, venturing into a journey of Jewish identity formation includes (1) investigating alternative paths (e.g., Reform, Conservative, Reconstructionist, Orthodox, Renewal, Humanist, Meditation, Kabbalah, Chabad, EcoJudaism—the list goes on and on); (2) utilizing various "way stations" or other checkpoints at which to "get directions" and learn "the lay of the land" (e.g., study programs, synagogues, community organizations, cultural activities, social groups); (3) locating fellow travelers with whom to share the journey, who will provide validation, modeling, and support; and (4) creating time for rest, reflection, and other types of personal synthesis or integration.

This type of developmental journey is reminiscent of what adolescents go through when they struggle to figure out who they are and what matters to them regarding career and lifestyle. In the pages that follow, I frame the journey of Jewish identity formation in terms of points made by prominent developmental theorists as well as several social scientists who have been studying Jewish identity in contemporary times. Before we move to theory or research, though, let's begin with a story.

Fern's Story

At a regional conference of the Women of Reform Judaism (WRJ, formerly the Reform Movement's National Federation of Temple Sisterhoods), I conversed with a vendor of beautiful, handwoven *tallitot* named Fern Hoffman. This intense, articulate baby boomer told me she had traveled a long journey since her social protest days of the 1960s. Raised in an assimilated family, Fern's engagement in Jewish life and learning had begun in her late thirties when she found herself wanting to understand the Passover seder and wondering how best to explain Jewish practices and traditions to her non-Jewish friends. Now in her early fifties, Fern had recently divorced, relocated, and become actively involved in women's activities at a synagogue in her new community; she said that amidst all the changes, she was "searching" for herself and was in the "process of integrating *several* identities" (as a newly divorced woman, an artist, a Jewish feminist, and a member of a synagogue community). The story of Fern Hoffman's learning journey provides insight into how Jewish adults who are growing and changing personally during times of broad social change negotiate a "restorying" of their lives and their sense of themselves as Jews.

❧ Story 3 ❧

FERN

Fern Hoffman was born in 1945 in Oakland, California, to professional parents who had little use for the "hokum" of traditional Judaism. Her father was a law professor, and her mother served on the board of several child welfare organizations. Their social world was almost exclusively Jewish. Membership in a large "classical Reform" synagogue was de rigueur, but the family only attended services when Fern's maternal grandmother visited from New Jersey. Early on, Fern developed an antipathy to pro forma religion:

> As a child, going to services, I had a very strong visceral reaction against what I called "stand up and sit down" religion. I really reacted very negatively to being told what to say. And I simply refused to say blessings and prayers in the congregation. I'd stand up, because I didn't want to embarrass my grandmother by not standing up, but I felt really compelled to pick and choose from the prayer book and say things my own way.

When Fern was in high school, she noticed that her father took particular pleasure in "breaking rules," by "eating bacon and eggs on Yom Kippur." However, despite their disdain for religious observance, both of Fern's parents championed Jewish causes and regularly modeled social responsibility. Her father represented farmworkers who challenged unfair labor practices in California orchards; her mother picketed realtors who maintained discriminatory policies toward Jews and other ethnic minorities. Fern's parents taught her to stand up for her beliefs, even if those beliefs were unpopular. By the time she was in high school, Fern had joined the NAACP and had cultivated a relationship with a black boyfriend. She saw herself as a romantic rebel and enjoyed challenging the status quo. After reading Leon Uris's novel *Exodus,* she imagined moving to Israel, living on a kibbutz, and digging for Dead Sea Scrolls. This dream notwithstanding, when she wanted to apply to Brandeis University to study "art and archeology," her mother refused to let her move so far away from home. Instead, Fern attended San Francisco State University "just before all hell broke loose" and became quickly "radicalized" by the political events of the early 1960s. By her second year in college she was leading "an intensely antireligious and secular life." Although Fern "never ceased being Jewish," she perceived having a Jewish identity as "something that didn't matter . . . it wasn't something to *act on.*"

After college, Fern moved to the East Coast and began to assume leadership roles in organizations committed to building international peace. She became a political fund-raiser and visited the Middle East to speak out against Israeli treatment of Palestinian and other Arab populations. She gradually developed a strong antipathy toward Jewish organizations that, in her view, held "materialistic and imperialistic values." Although she didn't deny her Jewish heritage, she found herself frequently apologizing to others for any behavior that might be considered "an expression of Jewish arrogance." Her public stance was a source of embarrassment to her parents, and she imagined that she was perceived as a "traitor" by fellow American Jews. Despite her self-imposed "outsider status," Fern found that she wasn't completely comfortable being isolated from other Jews. She had a "sense of longing" that was intensified one Rosh HaShanah when she had been riding a city bus to do an errand and, as she got off, found herself witnessing the departure of hundreds of Jews from a synagogue service. Her reaction was strong:

> I had this incredible reaction, feeling alone, and I felt that if somebody had bombed all the Jews who had gone to temple on Rosh

HaShanah that year, I wouldn't have been counted. It bothered me—not that I wasn't in temple, but that I was out on the street. . . . It wasn't guilt, but more a sense of not being where I belonged. It was important to be counted among the Jewish people, even if I wasn't doing anything Jewish.

Some months thereafter, Fern met and married Jerry, a graduate student in public policy. Jerry, who had grown up in a secular Jewish family in New York, shared Fern's humanitarian concerns but little of her ambivalence about "coming in close" to the Jewish community. For him, being Jewish was "bagels and lox and attending occasional seders." They were married in a park by a "long-haired rabbi" who led the wedding guests in exuberant horas and line dances. At the time, Fern viewed her wedding celebration as one of the peak Jewish experiences of her life. When she and Jerry had been married for three years, they had a daughter. Fern discovered then that honoring her child's Jewish heritage mattered to her more than she had anticipated:

> When the midwife handed me Jessica's birth certificate to sign, to give her a name, I found myself looking for the place where it says "religion." I wanted to fill something in—kind of like saying, "Okay, it's official." But they don't ask for that on birth certificates. I knew then that it wasn't simply a matter of filling in blanks. I realized that, for me, "Jewish" was definitely, unalterably, part of the picture.

Shortly after Jessica's arrival, Jerry accepted a teaching position at a small college in Maine. For Fern, the move represented a chance to withdraw from political work that had become consuming. The family moved to a rural area—"definitely 'the *galut*' "—and Fern decided to revitalize her "artsy self." She joined a local weavers' guild and began to make shawls that could be sold at crafts shows. Through the guild, she met two Jewish women who said they were interested in creating a family *chavurah* and sharing responsibilities for their children's basic Jewish education. Fern offered to create a family-oriented Passover seder and said she would consult *The Jewish Catalog* to learn what was appropriate for the occasion. One of her antiwar colleagues sent her a "xeroxed freedom seder Haggadah" and a feminist friend told her about a "women's Haggadah." Excited by the notion of "creating one's own Jewish experience," Fern decided to try her hand at assembling a

Haggadah tailored to the needs of her *chavurah* community. Working on that project started her on a Jewish learning journey. In subsequent years, she revised her Haggadah many times and shared Passover with diverse groups. She especially enjoyed introducing seder rituals and symbols to non-Jewish friends and noted that teaching gentiles about Judaism was "almost a religious experience" that gave her a sense of genuine Jewish connection:

> I really loved being a bridge for my Christian friends, helping them come into contact with a Jewish person and to know a little bit about what it is to be Jewish. When I explained things to them, I actually, for the first time as an adult, felt legitimate, felt as good as anyone as a Jew.

Over the next fifteen years, Fern continued to host seders. She used her weaving skills to make and sell *tallitot*. In 1990, after Jessica began college, she and Jerry ended their marriage. Fern moved to Philadelphia to take a position as a fund-raiser for a human rights organization. As part of her job, she regularly attended Quaker meetings with her coworkers. She thoroughly enjoyed the silence of the meetings and realized that she identified with many Quaker values. However, Fern increasingly became aware that she didn't want to "join" the Friends Meeting, that it was now time for her to "claim" her Jewish identity by affiliating formally with a Jewish community. She began "synagogue shopping":

> Many people tried to persuade me that I should be "joining" the Friends Meeting, but it just was not possible. I'm *not Quaker*. I consider myself Jewish, as irrevocably Jewish as I am female. I realized that joining a temple was kind of like subscribing to a magazine: it's affirming something that I already am and choosing a community in which to be that. All of a sudden, my "anti-Jewish institutions" fangs retracted, and joining wasn't such a monumental decision.

After sampling services and adult education classes in several synagogues, Fern found a congregation where she thought she would be "at home." She even imagined preparing for an adult bat mitzvah:

> The first night I went to services, when Rabbi Shalev took the Torah out of the ark and held it in his arms like a baby, in a manner that

seemed embracing and relaxed, as opposed to stiff and awestruck by this thing, it knocked my socks off. . . . There was something about how that rabbi held the Torah and the way he used his hands and his eyes to communicate to the congregation—I just knew this place might be a possible niche. When I drove home that night, I had this fantasy that someday I would be bat mitzvahed at that temple.

Once Fern joined the congregation, she enrolled in a class on prayer-book Hebrew. The study experience motivated her to reflect on her own learning needs and desires. She also realized that she wanted to meet Jews who were "serious about God":

> I really like the Quakers' attitude toward God. I am completely comfortable with the notion that there are mysteries in the world that defy explanation. It's not really important to me to come to some finished, clear polished description or definition. But being with people—with Jews—who wrestle with God, people for whom the issues around God are important—this was very important to me: to be among people who struggle around these issues.

In the next few years, Fern helped form a study group for people who wanted to "reframe" the meaning of Judaism in their lives. She also began to attend services and participate in communal ritual activities. A number of events confirmed her sense of belonging in the synagogue community. First, she discovered the depth of Rabbi Shalev's commitment to peace and social justice, thereby finding her own values "mirrored" by someone she valued in the Jewish community:

> We were doing a study session one night, and the issue came up of sending the troops into battle. And the rabbi said some things, and then he said, "I don't know why I'm saying I would do that. I'm a pacifist." And I raised my hand and I said, "Would you repeat that?" And I went up to him afterwards and I said, "You know, I feel so blessed, so fortunate to have found this congregation and this Jewish place in my life and to have found you—because you do so much and I respect what you do. But I never dreamed, I never even considered the possibility of having a rabbi who called himself a pacifist. It makes my heart sing." And he said, "I love that language: it makes my heart sing. It makes mine sing, too."

And, on another occasion, she found the kind of fellowship and joy with other Jews that she had experienced when dancing at her wedding:

> One of the best moments was on a Saturday morning during Purim when I helped decorate the sanctuary for the Purim carnival. It was this incredibly foolish and relaxed time of filling the ark with helium balloons that would fly out when the ark doors were open and tying helium balloons to every fixture in the sanctuary. It was fun and community-building. It was profane. It was making light. It was taking some of the sacredness out of that sanctuary and being able to play.

Eventually, Fern's involvement in congregational activities led to an invitation to serve first as program chair for the temple's Sisterhood and later as treasurer for the whole congregation. She considered, but ultimately rejected, enrolling in an adult bat mitzvah program. Speaking of her "adult Jewish growth," she said that, over time, she had come to feel she no longer needed to "prove" herself Jewishly and that her priority was to "create lasting Jewish social justice programs." She wanted to help local teens to build an interfaith coalition and thought she might do some writing about her experiences to share with non-Jews who didn't know much about Jews or Jewish life. In reflecting on her Jewish identity, Fern stated:

> I don't need to do a bat mitzvah any more. Today I see that the difference between me now and me ten years ago is that I'm a Jew, I'm a legitimate Jew. I'm here. I don't need to "do" something. It's like couples who've lived together for twenty years and say "I don't need to get married. I am married." I no longer feel any need to be confirmed as a Jew. This is who I am: *I am a Jew.*

Fern's Story: A Developmentalist's Perspective

Fern's journey is a Jewish identity formation story that highlights three themes found in the developmental literature on identity formation:

- Identity formation is *ongoing throughout life* and involves *exploration of options*. At times of personal upheaval and change, the individual typically reassesses what constitutes his or her identity and then may reframe personal commitments and priorities. One's identity is never fully "achieved" but, rather, is formed and re-formed.

- Although identity formation is an internal psychological process, *one's identity is shaped by external forces* as well. Role models, mentors, peers, and other social contacts affect how people define themselves, perceive options, and decide about commitments. For women especially, identity achievement is often described in terms of relationships with significant others.

- Consciousness of one's identity can be enhanced by the creation of *a personal narrative*—a "reinvention" of the self through the crafting of one's developmental journey. Rather than serving to create a "false identity," the narrative may help provide cohesion and meaning to an individual's evolving sense of self.

Identity Formation Is a Lifelong Process

In the 1980s, a disciple of Erikson, James Marcia, expanded on the concept of identity "statuses" and proposed that, in order to achieve a clear sense of self, a person must undergo a period of searching. In Marcia's view (1980), healthy identity formation requires this period of "moratorium" in order to sufficiently struggle with uncertainties and clarify personal choices. During moratorium, the individual does the "work" of identity formation by considering alternatives, testing out ideas and roles, and experiencing the "crisis" of dealing with the unknown. By sustaining the challenges of moratorium (M), the person becomes better equipped to assert an "achieved identity" (A). Over time, however, one's achieved identity is likely to again come into question—people outgrow old definitions of the self or are challenged to take on new roles or attitudes. They then appropriately return to moratorium status, move to a new achieved identity status, only to go sometime later into moratorium again. Marcia labels this process "MAMA" and urges adults to recognize the dynamics of the developmental process.

Marcia also points out that some people spend years in a state of moratorium, unable to make choices and move toward an achieved identity; these are people who never quite "commit" and thus fail to develop adult roles that "take root" in society. There are also individuals who, early in life, avoid the uncertainty of moratorium by making premature decisions about career, gender roles, politics, or religion. Such people never consider options—"My father was a doctor, I'll be a doctor"—and may adopt uncritically the values or ideological systems of others. While such a "foreclosed identity" may offer a sense of psychological safety for many years, it is not uncommon for people who haven't "done the work" of identity formation to wake up later and ask, "But what did *I* really want to do? What is it that *I* believe?" Marcia cautions that "foreclosing" identity too early robs people of the sense of personal authenticity and confidence that comes with the struggle of exploring, questioning, and "finding" one's self and personal belief system.

The fluid process of identity formation described by both Erikson and Marcia conforms to recent findings by social psychologist Bethamie Horowitz (2000b) in *Connections and Journeys*, a study of Jewish identity in 1,500 Jewish adults. In her research, Horowitz examines what being Jewish "means to people." Using interviews and surveys, she asks questions about "where, if at all, being Jewish fits into people's lives today and . . . how a person's relationship to being Jewish evolves over the course of his or her lifetime." Her results show that Jewish identity is "much more fluid" than what past studies found (which measured such things as candle lighting and seder attendance). Horowitz concludes: "Although we may take a snapshot of where people are at a point in time, we now know that Jewish identity is dynamic and Jewishness changes in relation to other aspects in individuals' lives" (Horowitz, 2000a, p. 18).

In *The Jew Within* (2000), a study of American Jews who are "moderately affiliated" (that is, neither marginally nor deeply involved) with Conservative and Reform synagogues, Steven M. Cohen and Arnold Eisen also conclude that the majority of contemporary Jews have a dynamic, fluid sense of their Jewishness. According to Cohen and Eisen, many Jewish adults of the baby boom generation see themselves as continually engaged in Jewish journeys in which they "change Jewish direction, and change again, at many points in life" (Cohen and Eisen, 2000, p. 38). They are "explorers in Judaism" who take it as a given that they will be in "perpetual quest of Jewish meaning." Rather than assuming or settling into a fixed Jewish identity, these adults *expect* from time to time to revisit the meaning of Judaism in their lives and how they define themselves as Jews.

Moreover, at least among Jews affiliated with synagogues and other mainstream Jewish organizations, the ongoing "fashioning" of a Jewish self is deeply significant. "Our subjects," Cohen and Eisen write, "reported a strong desire to find a sense of direction and ultimate purpose, and they wish to find it largely or entirely in the framework of Jewish practices and beliefs" (p. 8). In other words, while Jewish identity may ebb and flow, when these Jewish adults do pursue the work of identity formation, they want to be able to do so within the frame of Judaism and Jewish tradition.

At the same time, Cohen and Eisen observe that, in their quest for Jewish identity, contemporary Jewish adults insist on a Judaism they can see as personally meaningful, rather than being focused on the needs or expectations of a Jewish community (a synagogue or city or "the Jewish people"). These authors conclude that Jewish adults today seek a personalized Judaism that can be individually crafted and reinvented according to one's own choosing and timetable.

The fluidity, persistence, and self-determining aspects of Fern's Jewish identity formation are seen throughout her life story. From it we learn that, even as a child, Fern had strong convictions about Jewish observance and values. Early on, she challenged the meaning of "stand up and sit down" practices in her family's Reform synagogue and yearned for a more "activist" Jewish identity. As an adolescent, she did not achieve a solid sense of her Jewish self but, rather, became more and more alienated from the Jewish community. Nonetheless, by the time Fern was in her late twenties, the salience of her Jewish identity—the awareness that it *mattered* to her—became increasingly clear to her. Crucial turning points on her journey occurred (1) when she realized how much she wanted to be "counted" among the Jewish people and (2) when she wanted to "identify" her daughter as Jewish. These early adult moments of "Jewish consciousness raising" started Fern on a gradual but persistent journey toward a mature Jewish identity.

As a young parent, Fern began to widen the net of her Jewish community and took steps toward gaining some basic Jewish literacy. Creating a family Haggadah, hosting seders, and using her skills as a weaver to create *tallitot* served as important steps to expressing her Judaism in ways that had personal meaning for her. Over many years, Fern strengthened her sense of Jewish identity but did not actively deepen ties to the Jewish community. At midlife, following a divorce and relocation, Fern's journey toward a more defined Jewish identity took a sharp turn. In moving to a new community and new stage of her life, Fern began to explore options for herself as a Jew. She tried out various religious settings and began to evaluate where she would feel most at home. She selected a synagogue whose rabbi had values consonant with her own and, once there, took on the challenges of Jewish learning. Over time, she took on various leadership roles, both by forming a study group and by participating in synagogue governance. Her active participation in Jewish communal life helped her to see herself as having achieved a "legitimate" Jewish identity.

External Influences: Relationships Impact Identity

A person's identity does not develop in a vacuum. Identity theorists have asserted consistently that to understand how an individual evolves a sense of self, we must look carefully at the social contexts that have supported and challenged the person's growth. Erik Erikson (1963) posits that the peer group provides a critical arena in which the adolescent can "rehearse" adult roles and try out different personae. Ultimately, however, in Erikson's model of "psychosocial development," the growth of a "self" requires that a person become more and more *separate* from others. In other words, to be a mature person, one must view oneself as a differentiated and autonomous being rather than as engaged and interdependent with others.

Peter Blos (1962) offers a contrasting view about the role of peers in shaping adolescent identity, placing greater emphasis on the potential impact of interpersonal dynamics on the adolescent's emerging sense of self. Blos proposes that teenagers who are engaged in "finding themselves" rely heavily on "mirroring," reinforcement, and support from age peers whose feedback helps them clarify their individuality. Extensive studies of adolescent peer groups confirm that such groups offer important social milieus in which to try out new competencies and obtain critical assessment about one's behavior and values (Buhrmester and Furman, 1987). When a person of any age is going through major life changes—or changes in identity—having social support and friendship is crucial for sustaining a sense of personal continuity and maintaining psychological well-being (Antonucci, 1990).

During the past twenty years, scholars who have studied women's identity formation have offered yet another perspective about the likely impact of relationships on identity formation. Psychologist Jean Baker Miller (1991) theorizes that, especially for women, healthy identity may derive from an individual's ability to feel intimately connected with others. Describing this identity as a "self-in-relation," Miller says that a person's well-being and self-esteem are enhanced by the knowledge that she or he is part of vibrant and sustained interpersonal systems.

Additionally, in the view of Miller and other feminist psychologists (Jordan et al., 1991), it is through key relationships that people experience "mutuality." In a mutual exchange, each individual affects and is affected by the other person: "One extends oneself out to the other and is also receptive to the impact of the other. There is both receptivity and active initiative toward the other" (Jordan, 1991, p. 82). This mutuality leads to a sense of self that is attuned to the needs and desires of others without a loss of one's own sense of self. Indeed, rather than losing one's self in the other person, the "self-in-relation" achieves a strong sense of personal worth and is able to appreciate differences among people. In a cogent discussion of mutuality, theorist Judith Jordan (1991) describes the ultimate benefits of mutuality for a person's identity:

> When empathy and concern flow both ways, there is an intense affirmation of the self, and paradoxically, a transcendence of the self, a sense of the self as part of a larger relational unit. The interaction allows for a relaxation of the sense of separateness; the other's well-being becomes as important as one's own. This does not imply merging, which suggests a blurring or a lost of distinctness of self. (p. 82)

The importance of opportunities for mutuality in interpersonal relationships among Jewish adults has been noted by a number of scholars who study Jewish identity formation. A quarter century ago, in an analysis of American Jewish identity, social psychologist Simon Herman (1989) pointed out that Jewish identity is shaped significantly by a person's social interactions and described how positive Jewish "reference groups" could help people to overcome feelings of alienation and ambivalence about their Jewish identity. In work on Jewish "identity education," educators Perry London and Barry Chazan (1990) encouraged Jewish educators to help learners participate in group experiences that reinforce a positive sense of Jewish peoplehood. They also noted that Jewish professionals function as crucial Jewish identity role models; often their lives serve as dynamic "texts" that others study and learn from. More recently, researcher Bethamie Horowitz (2000a) found that Jewish interpersonal experiences tend to have a lasting impact on the development of a positive Jewish identity:

> Jewish identity can be powerfully influenced by significant relationships—with grandparents, rabbis, teachers, and other individuals to whom Jewishness is important. Often interactions with these people are powerful because they are seen as authentically Jewish and come to represent a "lived" Jewish life. These individuals . . . act like "beacons" in

that they represent something meaningful. . . . They often represent something authentic, and people look back on them (or toward them) in constructing their own Jewish lives. (p. 191)

While it may appear obvious that what Jewish adults need in order to develop their Jewish identities is simply contact with other Jews, the reality is that many contemporary Jews distance themselves from relationships with Jews and Jewish communities and, as a consequence, cannot develop the kind of mutuality that contributes to healthy Jewish identity formation. In an open society in which Jews are free to "choose" their adult identities, some Jews actively remove themselves from the Jewish networks that might reinforce a positive Jewish sense of self. Moreover, if a person feels "Jewishly insecure," he or she is unlikely to reach out to other Jews for support or affirmation. On the other hand, when Jewish groups and communal leaders are open to and inclusive of individuals who previously have felt marginal in the Jewish community, the results can be startlingly positive.

The story of Fern's Jewish identity formation is studded with examples of how external influences—social contacts, group experiences, interactions with significant Jewish individuals—had a positive impact on her acquisition of a vibrant Jewish identity. Whereas her early family influences did little to confirm Fern's Jewish sense of self, from the time she moved to the small college town in Maine, she interacted with people with whom she felt connected and "seen" in a mutually affirming way. Her experiences of creating seders and haggadot with peers helped her to overcome feelings of otherness among Jews; her skills as an artist and a communicator enabled her to share her Judaism with non-Jews in a personally authentic way. Later, when Fern relocated to Philadelphia, her encounters with Jews (in the synagogue) and non-Jews (in Quaker meetings) helped her to differentiate herself as a Jew and to see her Jewish self "in relation" with others. Increasingly she realized how much she longed for relationships with Jewish people whose values mirrored her own.

At Rabbi Shalev's congregation, she found the spiritual connections she had been seeking, as well as a learning community in which she could learn important basics and "practice" her Judaism among peers. Rabbi Shalev served as a "beacon," modeling Jewish observance and social values that had particular meaning for Fern. When she found people with whom to "play"—people who could act foolish and light in preparing for Purim activities—she acquired a broadened sense of herself as a Jew and as a member of the Jewish community.

The external influences on Fern's Jewish identity—peer relationships, encounters with role models, and participation in a mutually supportive community—all contributed to her adult Jewish growth. Ultimately, she discovered that she did not feel the need for a *public* affirmation of her Jewishness, which might have taken the form of an adult bat mitzvah. Rather, as Fern pointed out, she no longer needed to prove her Jewishness to others. At the same time, her personal goal was to develop social action programs that would bring synagogue members into contact with other faith groups. She could see herself facilitating an interfaith network for teens and she planned to write about being a "peace and justice Jew" for a non-Jewish readership. In this sense, as Fern consolidated her Jewish identity, she imagined a "possible self" that would help others to gain insight to how Jewish values are consistent with the pursuit of tolerance and peace in the world.

Personal Narrative and the Construction of Jewish Identity

Developing an autobiographical narrative is, in the words of anthropologist Kirin Narayan (1991), "a means of making sense of one's own and others' experience." Through narrative, a person arranges a "progression of events [that] captures the dimension of time in lived experience." By organizing "the flux and welter of experience" in a narrative form, Narayan writes, we are helped to "make sense of our pasts, plan for our futures, and comprehend the lives of others" (pp. 113–114). In the process of constructing one's narrative—and especially one's Jewish narrative—Jewish adults are encouraged to reframe their Jewish identities and to look more broadly at how Judaism has informed their lives and development. In constructing their Jewish narratives, they are afforded the opportunity to reconfigure how the past fits into the present and envision how current choices and actions can shape what some psychologists call "possible selves" (Markus and Nurius, 1986) and others label "imagined futures" (Hinchman and Hinchman, 1997).

Lewis and Sandra Hinchman (1997) note that narrative theories of identity "have the virtue of making the self seem a 'work in progress' that can be 'revised' as circumstances require." In other words, when someone crafts his or her story, he or she can become the ongoing "author of [the] story, an active shaper of outcomes rather than a passive object acted upon by external or internal forces." The more an adult feels a sense of such self-authorship (and corresponding self-determination), the greater will be his or her sense of identity and willingness to develop that identity over time. For the Jewish adult—especially if he or she has not consciously reflected on his or her Jewish story before—the construction of a personal Jewish history helps the person to see Jewish identity more clearly. In like fashion, when the storyteller extends the story beyond the present, a personal visioning of one's "Jewish future" can spark optimism about multiple ways to explore Judaism and deepen one's Jewish sense of self.

To begin crafting a personal narrative, many adults need encouragement to tell their stories; they need to be persuaded that communicating details of their lives to others will be beneficial to both the storyteller and the "story listener." William Randall, an adult education theorist, writes that when people "restory" their lives, they are transformed not only by the experience of pulling all the pieces together, but also by the experience of communicating their new understanding of themselves to another person. Randall (1996) suggests that educators who invite adults to tell their stories often become part of the storyteller's story, both by serving as a "keeper" of the story and by helping the teller to think about the meaning and possible outcomes of the story in new ways. Thus an educator can play a positive, even formative, role in the storyteller's identity development.

Randall's points have significant implications for the Jewish professional who invites a Jewish adult to reflect on the narrative of his or her Jewish identity. When such a narrative is developed and shared, both the teller and the listener are likely to have considerable "investment" in how the story turns out. The Jewish professional may be called on to assist in the outcome of the story or may be asked for assurance that the narrative is Jewishly "acceptable." As a "representative" of the Jewish community, the Jewish professional may be asked to "keep" or "bless" the story. Or he or she may be consulted about how to "edit" or reframe the story to make it conform with Jewish values or halachah. And, because of the healthy interdependence that can develop between the storyteller and the story listener, the Jewish professional may find that his or her *own* Jewish story is being affected by the story that is being told.

For Fern, the conscious construction of her Jewish narrative—and her increasing reflection about her Jewish identity—had begun before we met at the WRJ conference. Like many of the people I interviewed, however, she said that our conversations provided a forum for more deliberately sorting out the "flux and welter" of the Jewish journey she had been pursuing. She said that she found that each time she told me her story, it helped her to see the outlines of her past and to appreciate why certain turning points had had such profound impact on her sense of self and of her Jewish self. She acknowledged that although in many ways she felt she had "arrived" as a Jew, she also knew that she would continue to explore and reinvent her Jewish identity.

I interviewed Fern over a period of several years, eager to hear about her synagogue leadership experiences and her new areas of interest in Jewish learning. In these conversations, I began to hear more and more details of her vision for the future—her broadening sense of herself as a Jewish adult and leader in her community. At the same time, when I spoke to her after the tragedies of September 11, 2001, she indicated that, in the face of terrorism, she was renewing her commitment to the peace movement and would likely direct some of her volunteer energy toward organizations outside the Jewish community. Nonetheless, she assured me, she saw her goal as one to "heighten consciousness among Jews" about the need for interfaith and cross-cultural dialogue, and she was excited that she would now bring to the table what felt like an "authentic" Jewish perspective.

During our fall 2001 interview, Fern told me how she hoped I would keep in touch because she found that our conversations helped her to appreciate "the big picture" of her Jewish journey: "When we talk," Fern mused, "I remember the 'me' that used to be and also get a fuller sense of the 'me' I've become." In this respect, I realized that, to some degree, Fern's Jewish identity is now being constructed and reconstructed "in relation" with me: that with each interview, I, as a Jewish professional, have become part of her emerging Jewish story and am influencing her evolving Jewish identity. And, when I share her story, I am affirming—and thus blessing—her continuing Jewish identity formation.

From Theory to Practice: Helping Jewish Adults Through the Wilderness

In their insightful proposal for a Jewish identity curriculum, Perry London and Barry Chazan (1990) state that the lifelong process of Jewish identity formation will best develop in "nurturing and sensitive environments" where Jews of all ages can explore their beliefs and options as Jews. They urge Jewish professionals to acknowledge the many paths that Jewish adults travel toward Jewish identity and to create meaningful opportunities in which Jews will be able to express and celebrate their emerging sense of self.

Jewish professionals can be vital, proactive catalysts for Jewish adult identity formation. To help with this crucially important work, Jewish professionals should:

1. Help people to understand that Jewish identity formation is an ongoing process that involves times of uncertainty, questioning, and doubt followed by times of integration and heightened Jewish meaning. Assure them that their "wandering" can lead to a "promised land" of Jewish identity, though each person's journey and timetable are idiosyncratic.

2. Help people who are searching for a Jewish identity to find other Jews who are "fellow travelers" on the journey of identity formation. Encourage people who are exploring new and possible Jewish selves to connect with peers who can provide feedback, support, companionship, and mutuality. Offer educational and social activities in which people can find others with whom to discuss and "try on, try out" aspects of Judaism and Jewish life.

3. Invite Jewish adults to begin to construct their Jewish narratives. Tell them how the creation of a Jewish narrative affirms a person's sense of self-authorship and the lifelong dynamism of Jewish identity development. Share your own Jewish story, and make yourself available to listen as they "restory" their Jewish lives. Let Jews who are on the journey of Jewish identity formation "include" their rabbis, cantors, and educators in their evolving Jewish sense of self.

4. Introduce Jewish adults to learning opportunities where they will meet other Jewish adults who are seeking to better define their Jewish identities. Beyond formal classes, Jewish adults can find like-minded peers in Jewish book discussion groups, Jewish environmental and political action projects, Rosh Chodesh and women's seder activities, Jewish music and art programs and festivals, Jewish genealogy groups (both on-line and in person), Jewish travel programs, and other recreational activities that focus on Jewish experience.

4

More than Just "Standing" at Sinai: Jewish Adults as Learners and Teachers

Moses received the Torah from Sinai, and he handed it down to Joshua, who handed it over to the elders, who handed it over to the prophets, who in turn handed it over to the members of the Great Assembly.

—Pirkei Avot *1:1*

The opening mishnah of the *Pirkei Avot* quoted above provides a time-honored image of the passing of Jewish knowledge from one generation of learners to the next. The "educational model" inherent in this mishnah implies an approach to Jewish continuity that rabbis and teachers have followed for centuries. It suggests that Jewish learning begins with revelation "at the top." But it also assumes that when information is passed along from one set of authorities to the next, learners will share what they have learned with others. In other words, Jewish tradition long has taken as a given that learners will do more than just *receive* information. Although the faithful might come to learning passively and without questioning, the fully responsible Jewish person must engage in study *and* help others to learn as well. And, as Rabbi David Hartman (1985) points out, standing and receiving the Torah at Sinai is not the end of the story of Jewish learning: "The Sinai moment of revelation . . . invites one and all to acquire the competence to explore the terrain and extend the road" (p. 8).

Moreover, according to Israel Goldman (1975), a scholar of Jewish education, Jews are obligated to be *lifelong* learners who never stop learning and teaching about the tradition. In Goldman's view, "From the very beginning . . . the Jewish ideal has been to enlighten and inform the mind of every Jew at every stage of his life in the teachings and observances of his religious culture" (p. 7). Goldman contrasts Judaism with other religions that, throughout history, were committed to keeping people "in ignorance and darkness." Conversely, in Judaism, "the revelations of God . . . were made the possession of the whole people," and the obligation to study and teach consistently assured the transmission of ideas from generation to generation.

Despite Judaism's tradition of lifelong learning, a significant proportion of Jewish adults today are illiterate about Judaism and Jewish tradition. Communal leaders have called for new educational models that can help people to acquire Jewish knowledge and can support their quest for connection to Judaism and other Jews. Because minimal scholarship about Jewish adult learners is yet available, scholars are turning to research about other groups of learners for frameworks that may explain the shifts that occur among people who achieve new intellectual maturity. As we will see below, studies of intellectual development in female college students (and particularly in "reentry" women who pursue college degrees during adulthood) provide a useful starting point for thinking about the growth of Jewish adults who are finding their way into substantive Jewish learning.

From Silence to Voice: Insights from Research on Women as Knowers

Since the publication in 1986 of *Women's Ways of Knowing*—a landmark book about what fosters intellectual development of college women of all ages—adult educators have been enriched by the insights of Mary Belenky, Blythe Clinchy, Nancy Goldberger, and Jill Tarule. In their work, Belenky and her colleagues describe how, in their roles as educators, they have observed how women students frequently speak of "problems and gaps in their learning" and show signs of "doubt [about] their intellectual competence" (1986, p. 4). Through their research, this team wanted to understand why, for many female students, the " 'real' and valued lessons [of higher education] did not necessarily grow out of their academic work but in relationships with friends and teachers" (p. 4). They also wanted to discern what helps people to acquire a sense of self as a *constructed knower*—someone who recognizes that all knowledge is developed in a changing social context and who feels capable not only of formulating ideas but also of sharing knowledge with others.

Using in-depth interviews, the researchers investigated how different groups of women perceived themselves as knowers; they were particularly interested in what shapes a learner's readiness to construct knowledge and what kinds of environments support the learner as she "comes to voice," that is, as she becomes comfortable sharing her views with other people. Belenky et al. found that when some women enter learning environments, they view their position as one of *silence:* they see themselves as "voiceless in relationships with whomever they perceive as authorities." Often these women can't imagine themselves as capable of learning or that teachers will want to help them "find voice." Other women are (to use Belenky's terminology) *received knowers,* who conceive of themselves as able to "receive and reproduce knowledge from authorities" but don't see themselves as capable of independently "creating" knowledge. These women have a strong sense of themselves as "learners" but prefer to be "mimetic" in their knowing: they will listen to the teacher and repeat back what is heard rather than process ideas on their own. *Subjective knowers* tend to believe that what they know is true and are not inclined to explore alternative points of view; they like to learn but gravitate to ideas that confirm their previously held worldviews. *Procedural knowers* are "invested in learning and applying objective procedures for obtaining and communicating knowledge" (1986, p. 15); they enjoy gathering information, probing sources, analyzing ideas, and comparing different points of view. Procedural knowers particularly value teachers who can model the "procedures" of knowledge construction: how to construct an argument, how to find supporting evidence, how to interpret differing opinions, and so on. *Constructed knowers* see all knowledge as "contextual"—they understand that ideas change depending on when they are developed and the social context in which they are explored. Constructed knowers experience themselves and others as "capable of creating knowledge" and have a sense of their own intellectual authority. They enjoy conveying ideas to others (Tarule, 1988, p. 22).

Since its publication, *Women's Ways of Knowing* has sparked considerable debate among educators, especially concerning the question, do women learn differently from men? In my work in Jewish adult education, I have come to the conclusion that the issue of gender and Jewish learners is less significant than the larger question of the authority of the knower. When adults feel disenfranchised from learning or have never been helped to engage in intellectual discourse about certain ideas or traditions, they perceive themselves as "silent." Thus they avoid situations in which their underdeveloped intellect will put them at risk for embarrassment or other discomfort. They do not see themselves as capable of "joining the conversation," even though they may be fully conversant in other aspects of their lives.

Many of us find that we are silent knowers every time we call a plumber to clean out the blocked drainage system in our home. When the plumber describes how "roots and sewer lines" are the cause of the problem, we don't fully understand his terminology, aren't sure what questions to ask, don't know how to judge repair recommendations, and fear being ripped off due to our vulnerability and ignorance. The older we get, the more resistant we may become to learning how to deal with what feels like a "marginal" part of our lives—so we remain silent and relatively uninformed. On the other hand, with respect to medical issues, many adults shift from being silent, received, or subjective knowers. Thanks to the media, we have become aware that we *must* become knowledgeable and inquire beyond what a particular doctor tells us or what we subjectively believe to be "reality" about certain medical options. Many of us have become proficient at researching medical conditions and treatments and have built up the confidence to challenge authority. We now ask and evaluate additional opinions. While few of us aspire to become medical professionals, as "knowers" we have become more initiating and participatory in medical decision making. Thus, with experience and practice, we have shifted from being silent knowers to procedural knowers on medical issues.

In their research, Belenky et al. found that shifts in knowing are more likely to occur when a person has (1) an internal desire to "find voice" and (2) encouragement from teachers who can coach the learner on how to speak up and explore options. In other words, intellectual growth likely requires both a "need to know" and the availability of people who can show the learner how to become a more confident and inquiring knower.

My Own Experience as a Jewish Knower

As I discussed in the introduction, my growth as a Jewish learner began when I "connected" with some rabbis who showed me how to study textual interpretations and apply them to my own life. Until that time, I was very much a *received knower* in the Jewish community: I attended adult education classes, went to lectures, created Passover seders in much the way my parents had done. I remember once attending a Torah study group at my congregation—and "fleeing" after forty-five minutes because I didn't know how to talk about the weekly *parashah* (something from Leviticus no doubt!) and feeling intimidated by the debates others seemed so ready to engage in.

A turning point in my development as a Jewish "knower" occurred in 1994, shortly after I had begun to interview Jewish adults about their study experiences. I was invited to "teach" the Book of Ruth at a *Tikkun Leil Shavuot* and reacted with a wave of insecurity: How could *I* presume to do such a thing? What did I know? How could I interpret this story? When I explained my dismay to my daughter, she responded impatiently, "Mom, you teach "text" in college classes all the time. What makes you think you can't teach a Jewish text? Just go to the library and read about Ruth." Sheepishly I replied, "If I get some books, will you help me understand what they're saying?" My daughter rolled her eyes: "Read first, Mom. Then we'll talk."

So much I have learned from my children! My daughter's challenge—her insistence that I become a *procedural knower* by gathering information and beginning to sort it out for myself—was an important part of my becoming an "adult" in the Jewish learning process. At the same time, her willingness to talk about my reading with me—to help me articulate my thoughts and even to "make meaning" of things that were puzzling—had a hugely motivating impact on my desire to learn. Ultimately she and I planned and conducted a program about Ruth and Naomi together, and with her support I took some "first steps" in sharing my new learning with others.

The Role of Connected Teachers

My growth as a knower mirrored what Belenky and her colleagues found in the students they interviewed. Once I entered into the learning process, my learning was enhanced by the availability of a challenging and supportive "teacher." Belenky et al. refer to such educators as connected teachers and describe how they are "midwives" to fragile, emerging knowers. They explain that connected teachers avoid what Brazilian educator Paolo Freire (1971) called the "banking" model of education:

> Midwife-teachers are the opposite of banker-teachers. While the bankers deposit knowledge in the learner's head, the midwives draw it out. They assist the students in giving birth to their own ideas, in making their own tacit knowledge explicit and elaborating it. (Belenky et al., 1986, p. 217)

Unlike banker-teachers, who "anesthetize" learners and fail to challenge them to become connected with the learning process, connected teachers "assist in the emergence of consciousness [and] encourage . . . students to speak in their own active voices" (p. 218). They recognize that, at the outset, adult learners tend to feel vulnerable and tentative—hesitant to assert ideas or to reveal gaps in knowledge. But connected teachers believe that, with focused support, these learners can be helped to stretch beyond their self-imposed limitations. Their job is to support the evolution of the learner's thinking and to focus not on the "[teacher's] knowledge (as the lecturer does), but on the students' knowledge" (p. 218). This focus shifts the responsibility for knowledge construction to the learner and helps the teacher to function in a facilitative role rather than that of "the expert."

Belenky and her colleagues theorize that adult learners are most apt to thrive in learning situations that are *democratic*—where the educator doesn't operate from the assumption that he or she is the only expert in the room or from the notion that the role of the teacher is to retain a superior position to the learner.[3] Connected teachers place the *growth of the learner* as the central objective of the educational process:

> Midwife-teachers help students to deliver their words to the world, and they use their own knowledge to put the students into conversation with other voices—past and present—in the culture. (p. 219)

Connected teachers place a high value on *posing questions* that help learners to see what they already know, what their experiences have taught them, and what they still need to learn. They encourage learners to make connections between what they are learning and their own lives. Such teachers conscientiously provide safe opportunities for the learner to "test out" new ideas and express opinions. They come in close to the learner—sharing their own experiences, questions, and strategies for learning—in order to help the learner feel less alone in the learning process. Connected teachers recognize that learners often need a "holding environment" from which to embark on new ways of knowing. Rather than concerning themselves about students becoming too dependent, they assume that once learners have been supported and affirmed, they will be emboldened to take steps into a larger

---

3. This view is further articulated by Malcolm Knowles (1980) and Stephen Brookfield (1986, 1990).

world of knowledge construction and to test themselves and their ideas out in wider arenas.

Jewish Knowers and Their Teachers

The Belenky typology of knowers has proved useful for me in reflection on my own development as a Jewish knower, as well as in conversations with Jewish professionals about their work with Jewish adults. Exhibit 4-1 presents my adaptation of the Belenky model with respect to different types of Jewish adult knowers. In this configuration, Jewish silent knowers are adults who believe that their experience as Jews has rendered them Jewishly illiterate and thus has made them unwelcome in Jewish learning settings. Because they have never seen themselves as part of the "Jewish conversation," these adults cannot fathom that they can actually study Jewish texts or participate in meaningful discussion of Jewish ideas. They may be secular and immigrant Jews who as children did not receive any formal Jewish education, women who were not permitted to learn Hebrew or read Torah, adults whose formal Jewish education was simplistic and ended in adolescence, or adults whose Jewish educational experiences were marred by authoritarian teachers who scolded them for asking questions, and so on.

Jewish received knowers are found among the people who faithfully sit in a class or lecture and passively acquire information delivered by the teacher. They have a strong sense of themselves as "learners," but rather than engage ideas on their own, they will listen to the teacher and repeat back what is heard. Typically, such adults like to accumulate information but do not want to participate in discussion, probe the opinions of classmates, or pursue inquiry in a systematic or independent way. Typically they insist that they want to hear only what the teacher—"and not all the other people"—has to say.

Jewish subjective knowers are found among adults who view what they have learned through the lens of their own experience. Although these learners can engage in dialogue about what they have learned, they tend to overlook alternative perspectives or become so immersed in one view that they cannot imagine "stepping back" to consider other interpretations or explanations. They may be congregants who are wedded to a specific *siddur* and cannot imagine the benefits of changing to a new prayer book. Or they may be text learners who react impatiently to suggestions that their understanding of biblical stories would be enhanced by comparing different

EXHIBIT 4-1

Jewish Adult Learners as "Knowers"

RECEIVED KNOWERS
- See knowledge as coming from outside authorities
- Are dependent on others when forming opinions
- Prefer lecture and "facts"

Example: "I will go to the lecture about Pesach and I will do all the things the rabbi says so that I can do the seder the right way."

SILENT KNOWERS
- Don't know they have the right to know
- Don't know how to begin to acquire knowledge
- Silent observers

Example: "I'll attend the seder but I won't feel comfortable asking what it all means."

SUBJECTIVE KNOWERS
- Rely on personal experience as basis for knowledge
- Have strong convictions that their knowledge is correct
- Use intuition

Example: "The only meaningful way to do seder is to go to my parents' home and do what we've always done. My gut tells me that that's what will work best for everyone."

PROCEDURAL KNOWERS
- Recognize the value of multiple perspectives
- Develop tools to analyze data
- Able to conceptualize and debate opposing views

Example: "I'll learn Hebrew and compare different haggadot so that I can participate more fully at the seder."

CONSTRUCTED KNOWERS
- Develop own knowledge base after careful analysis
- Push back boundaries of own perspectives
- Create new ways of seeing old ideas
- Take risks in teaching others

Example: "I will lead the seder and will give my own interpretation of what each item on the seder plate symbolizes for Jews today."

Adapted from Mary Belenky, Blythe Clinchy, Nancy Goldberger, and Jill Tarule, *Women's Ways of Knowing* (New York: Basic Books, 1986).

translations of the *Tanach* instead of clinging to an old or familiar version. Or, too, they may be holiday celebrants who want to maintain certain family traditions without examining what underlies those traditions or members of a synagogue who insist that a new musical setting for a prayer decreases their ability to "relate" to the prayer.

Jewish procedural knowers are learners who enjoy the "procedures" involved in gathering and analyzing ideas and acquiring the skills for more sophisticated knowledge manipulation. These learners are found in text study groups that encourage debate; they are the people in adult Hebrew classes who enthusiastically explore the roots of words and the complex usages of syntax; they are library and Internet users who love to search out different interpretations of a text. Jewish procedural knowers appreciate being shown *how* to learn—how to find and use resources, how to construct an argument, how to understand the subtext of a story or the hidden meanings of a work. They also enjoy being given challenges of translation or of comparing several interpretations of a phrase or concept or piece of text.

Finally, Jewish constructed knowers are learners who have developed their critical thinking, analytic skills, and meaning-making abilities to the point that they are able to construct new meanings and assert their independent ideas with a sense of personal authority. These learners take intellectual risks and bring their insights and experiences to the creation of new knowledge; at the same time, they yearn to integrate Jewish ideas into their own lives and way of thinking. Jewish constructed knowers enjoy writing commentaries on what they are reading or creating new prayers or rituals to express their new insights about Judaism and themselves as Jews. They are excited to find new Jewish learning communities where they can diversify their knowledge base and build relationships with other learners who are committed to serious study. The more these learners engage in constructing Jewish knowledge for themselves, the more they are willing to share their learning and insights with others.

Like children at the seder table whose questions command different responses from the parent, these different types of Jewish knowers represent differing challenges for Jewish professionals who wish to be responsive to their learning needs. Exhibit 4-2 describes some of the challenges that teachers face with each of these types of knowers and presents a number of approaches Jewish professionals can use to be more "connected" in their teaching. Today, more and more Jewish adult learners seek teachers whose

EXHIBIT 4-2

Connected Teaching with Jewish Knowers

Characteristics of Jewish Knowers	The Jewish Professional's Connected Response
Jewish Silent Knower Lacks confidence in Jewish learning ability Doesn't feel he or she has the "right" to an opinion on a Jewish issue Hasn't "claimed" his or her Jewish story Hasn't had opportunity to be "heard" as a Jew	Offer safe spaces for Jewish conversation Invite reflection on the learner's Jewish story Provide opportunities for silent knowers to hear others' stories, including the teacher's Engage people in nurturant Jewish activities
Jewish Received Knower Likes to listen to speakers and not engage in dialogue or debate on Jewish issues Likes literal meanings and is often dualistic (right/wrong; us/them) in own assessment of situations involving Jews or Jewish ideas Is more comfortable articulating the views of authorities than asserting own opinion	Accept the received knower on his/her own terms but encourage critical thinking In group settings, invite the learner to summarize (compare/contrast) others' observations and to offer his or her own commentary Share your own learning stories and offer to help learner identify his or her own Jewish questions
Jewish Subjective Knower Has intuitive sense of own Jewish "truth" Pays close attention to own inner voice Recognizes that there may be many truths, but maintains highly personal attachment to own truth Is pragmatic and will refer back to own Jewish experience rather than gravitate toward consideration of alternative ideas or practices	Encourage the learner to document own and others' Jewish experiences and viewpoints Suggest that the learner explore unfamiliar Jewish ideas and experiences and then compare own findings with those of others Help the learner to experiment with new Jewish practices Affirm the learner's passion for Judaism
Jewish Procedural Knower Engages in conscious, deliberate, systematic analysis of Jewish texts and ideas Likes to acquire and apply procedures for obtaining and communicating Jewish knowledge Is interested in how others formulate their ideas Is able to take the perspective of others and debate alternative points of view Recognizes that Jewish learning involves continuing interpretation	Introduce the learner to sources and methods of textual analysis and research Help learners to find suitable study partners *(chevruta)* or study groups Lead study groups and ask participants to debate ideas and consider multiple perspectives Help learners to plan future Jewish learning projects that will involve a variety of learning strategies
Jewish Constructed Knower Seeks to integrate intuitive Jewish understanding with knowledge from outside sources Recognizes that all knowledge is constructed, that knower's experience is part of the known Seeks to examine, question, and develop processes for assessing own ideas Has a passion for learning Enjoys sharing own learning with others	Encourage the learner to synthesize learning and to claim own expertise Validate the learner's participation in the ongoing Jewish conversation Invite the learner to write and publicly share insights and ideas with other Jews Create opportunities for the learner to become a Jewish teacher and role model

pedagogical approach conforms to the model of the connected teacher. They want teachers who will help them to do more than just *stand* at Sinai—by helping them to acquire skills and knowledge that will enable them to make their own way "through the wilderness." They like rabbis and educators who pose questions that make them reflect critically about their Jewish identity and values. They are hungry for contact with Jewish professionals who can help them reflect on their Jewish knowledge and then challenge them to move beyond that knowledge. They appreciate teachers who are open about their own Jewish learning experiences and willing to disclose how they have dealt with questions and doubts; rather than insisting on teachers who have all the answers, these learners value individuals who have struggled with the questions.

Meeting a Constructed Knower: Allison's Story

When I began studying Jewish adult learners, one of my goals was to "follow" a number of adult Jewish learners through several years of their adult Jewish growth. Accordingly, I designed a small-scale longitudinal research project in which I would periodically interview individuals who were engaged in ongoing, systematic programs of Jewish study. One of my first interviewees was a young woman named Allison Benveniste-Henderson. I had heard about Allison from a colleague, Rabbi Sidney Shaberman, who told me that Allison was a "model adult Jewish learner." In describing Allison to me, Rabbi Shaberman commented: "This woman has an insatiable hunger for Jewish knowledge. For someone who hardly knew the *Sh'ma* five years ago, Allison has become a proficient Torah reader. And she insists on understanding what she's reading!" He mentioned that he had invited Allison to read and comment on the *parashah hashavua* the next week and suggested that I come to the service.

Listening to Allison chant Torah, I was immediately drawn to the energy of this thirty-eight-year-old woman. Her love of Torah radiated the minute she began to chant *Parashat Pinchas*, and her *d'var Torah* about the Rabbis' inclusive attitude toward Zelophehad's daughters seemed to come from deep within Allison's spirit. I later watched as a dozen women crowded around Allison, animatedly congratulating her and asking how she had become so proficient in Hebrew and confident about text interpretation. I learned from these conversations that although Allison had lived in the community for several years, few of the congregants had met her before. She explained that when she had decided to pursue Jewish learning, her highest priority had been to find a teacher who would help her one-on-one to "come in close to Torah." She said she had been inspired by her cousin Talia, a rabbi in the Midwest, who had encouraged her to "find her own voice" as a Jew. Allison was guided in her learning by Rabbi Judy Davis, the director of a nearby university Hillel, who had showed her "how to study Judaism in a serious way." Allison told the women that even though she had had an adult bat mitzvah under Rabbi Davis's direction, being asked by Rabbi Shaberman to give a *d'var Torah* at their congregation represented "an even more important rite of passage on my journey to Jewish adulthood."

When the crowd of admirers thinned, I approached Allison and asked her to tell me more about her story. That evening we began a conversation that continued over several years. In a series of interviews, encapsulated in Story 4, this dynamic young woman described her experiences of "more than just standing at Sinai." She recounted her own development as a learner and told me how Jewish professionals had helped her to become a knower and teacher to others.

◈◈ Story 4 ◈◈

ALLISON

Allison Benveniste-Henderson was born in a small East Coast city in 1956 to parents who "didn't know much about Judaism." Allison and her older sisters attended religious school at a Reform synagogue in a neighboring city, but their parents were not involved: "They sent us to Sunday school in a taxi."

Early on, Allison was troubled by what she regarded as her parents' hypocrisy about Judaism. She argued frequently with her father, resenting that he "expected us to date Jewish men, but there were none around." She felt alienated from the synagogue community and her Jewish peer group:

> I just didn't feel connected to anything. We were like one of three Jewish families in our town, and it was a temple that served many communities. By the time I was a teenager, I was dating non-Jewish guys, and I regarded the temple kids as cliquey and materialistic. In college, none of my close friends were Jewish.

After college, Allison became engaged to John Henderson, who had grown up in a large Methodist family in the Midwest. When she and John discussed their wedding plans with his parents, Allison stated that she wanted her Jewish heritage to be affirmed in the wedding ceremony. She was surprised by this assertion and by her desire to express her Jewish identity in this way. Subsequently, she sought advice from her second cousin, Talia, who had become a rabbi. Although Talia said she would not officiate at the wedding, she made herself available to Allison and John to talk about their interfaith relationship. She encouraged the couple to remain loyal to their individual religious identities and urged Allison to become Jewishly educated. She sent them a book about Jewish weddings, which prompted Allison and John to incorporate a number of Jewish prayers and practices into their ceremony. Allison was delighted that the wedding guests danced "both the hora and the beer barrel polka" (a Henderson family tradition), and she later recalled that her wedding preparations served as the first step on her adult Jewish learning journey.

After the birth of her second child, Allison quit her job as a technical consultant to stay at home with the children. Her cousin Talia sent her another book—this time one on Jewish family learning activities—and Allison was excited by the authors' creative ideas for making Judaism "accessible to our whole family." Although she liked what she had read, she did not feel ready to affiliate with a synagogue, where she imagined that interfaith couples would not be well received.

During her children's preschool years, Allison continued to read about Jewish holidays and traditions. She learned how to create Chanukah and Passover celebrations in her home. Allison gradually realized that although she had thought she was "doing it for the children," she actually wanted to learn about Judaism for herself. An eager reader, she initially assumed she could learn about Judaism by "reading, getting ideas, and following instructions." However, over time she began to reframe her understanding of the challenges of becoming Jewishly literate:

> I went through about two years of trying to read on my own, just some really basic Judaism books. . . . Heschel's book on the Sabbath, thinking I want to start out with Shabbat. Eventually I realized that I wanted to know—I wanted to learn more. Reading is great, but I

wanted to know what's *in* the Torah. Here I was reading how important Torah is, I was reading how Torah guides our lives, but I didn't
know Torah or how you "study Torah."

At the urging of her cousin, Allison decided to look for a teacher
who could to help her to figure out a personal Jewish learning agenda:

> First I called the educator at a local synagogue, but he said the only
> way to study there was to be in the adult bar mitzvah class that was
> held every other year. At that time the class was already midway
> through a cycle, so it wasn't open to me for many months. I knew
> that I didn't really want a group class anyway, so instead I called the
> Hillel at the university where I'd done my master's. I reached Rabbi
> Judy Davis, and she was very smart with how she dealt with me. She
> really welcomed me and challenged me. It was a process that had no
> beginning and no end—a process of, "Well, now let's start. Start by
> learning Hebrew. And then come see me: We need to *talk!*" So I got
> a Hebrew tutor and listened to tapes and then called Rabbi Davis for
> an appointment.

Allison recalled that, as early as their first conversation, Rabbi Davis
pushed her to assert her ideas and form opinions—to trust her own
thoughts. She said that the rabbi explained how it was customary for
Jews to come together to debate ideas and how important it was for
Allison to "enter into the conversation" of Jewish thought:

> We had amazing discussions. Rabbi Davis really opened my eyes to
> a lot of things I hadn't seen before—to think about, to write about.
> I did a lot of writing for her. She taught me about *d'var Torah*, about
> all the books, about commentary, about how my questions *and* my
> opinions count.

As Allison began to reflect critically on her Jewish identity and her
assumptions about Judaism, Rabbi Davis helped her to think in new
and intellectually "flexible" ways:

> It was really a different perspective, because when I went to her with
> my ideas or questions, she would say, "But of course—what you're
> saying makes sense," or "See, that's the next step, the next question
> for you." So it was like "Oof, I'm not crazy." And I said, "Is it all right

to do it this way?" And she said, "The wonderful thing about Judaism is that as you learn things, you can also bring in your own reality. Absolutely, that's what it's all about. And you don't have to be a rabbi to learn. You just have to have a desire to learn—and I would love to teach you."

With Rabbi Davis's support, Allison immersed herself in Jewish learning activities:

I joined a text study group, and I got tapes to learn Torah trope. I learned about Jewish mysticism and studied about Jewish women's prayers. I read about Jewish history, and I read people's stories. That was probably one of the best things I could have done—reading other people's stories—because it really made *my* story seem just as important.

After Allison had studied for about a year, Rabbi Davis encouraged her to take steps to publicly celebrate her learning journey. Allison became excited about the idea of an adult bat mitzvah when Rabbi Davis explained that she could exercise considerable choice about how and what the bat mitzvah service would include:

She suggested I begin by looking for "my" Torah portion and pointed out that there are choices one can make as an adult—that I didn't have to do a portion just because it happened to fall around my birthday. She said, "It's really up to you what you do. You should do what you *want* to do." So she suggested some portions to look at, and said "Go ahead and start thinking about how you would put together a service. I'll help you, but you will put it together."

For Allison, the service during which she became a bat mitzvah, held in the garden of her home, was a "blessed event." Surrounded by her family and close friends, she took her first steps to claiming her voice as a Jew:

I decided to learn *B'shalach* and wrote a whole service about times of celebration. I talked about how God makes it possible for all of us to "cross the sea" and grow. I taught everyone about the joyousness of the *Mi Chamochah*, and we sang it over and over. My cousin Talia participated in the service. So did my sisters. Everyone had a role, even my parents and my in-laws. My husband gave me a beautiful tambourine as a gift. It was a wonderful celebration for our whole family.

Shortly after Allison became a bat mitzvah, a local synagogue rabbi, Sidney Shaberman, heard about Allison's Jewish learning journey. He invited her to read Torah and present a *d'var Torah* at a Shabbat service. Although Allison had been leery of the synagogue—assuming it would feel as alienating as her childhood synagogue—she was thrilled by the invitation and startled by the enthusiastic response to her participation in the service. A number of congregants thanked her for coming and showing them that it was "possible for adults to have such a deeply personal connection with the Torah." Several women asked if she would be willing to tutor them in Hebrew. Allison recalled that evening as a "real coming of age—exactly what a bat mitzvah is supposed to be: you teach the community."

Despite this achievement, Allison felt like a novice Jewish learner. Thus she was very shocked a few months later when the rabbi asked her to join the synagogue staff and redesign the bar mitzvah preparation program:

> I was stunned when Rabbi Shaberman called and asked, "Will you be our *m'lamedet* [teacher]?" I said, "How can I do that? I don't know anything about doing this. I'm not competent to do this." He said, "Do the job and I'll work with you, I'll help you. Let me share my experience with you." What an opportunity: I grabbed it! Because he was willing to work with me, to teach me "from the inside," and even to cut me slack while I was learning.

Over the next few years, Allison worked with both children and adults as they prepared for becoming *b'nei mitzvah*. Her excitement about Jewish learning continued as she shared her growing knowledge with others. As her confidence grew, she began to write prayers and to read about her family's Sephardic background. She wrote and presented *divrei Torah* on a regular basis, sometimes comparing opinions she had found in on-line Torah commentaries. And, as she began to think of herself as a Jewish educator, she sought out other Jewish professionals, attending a Coalition for the Advancement of Jewish Education (CAJE) conference and meetings of a regional bureau of Jewish education.

When interviewed at age forty-six, Allison said that becoming literate in Torah and finding her voice as a Jewish adult represented the fulfillment of an adult dream:

> I wanted to be able to—if somebody said, "I want you to chant this portion next Saturday morning"—I wanted to be able to put on my *tallit* and be able to know what it says, be able to comment on it. Because, to me, to really do it consistently, to chant Torah, to read from it, you need to be able to comment on it. That's the gift of Torah: to take Torah and to relate it to what's going on around you today, to the world. That's what we do in Judaism. That's what sets us apart. That's what makes it so wonderful: your commentary counts, it's important, what *you* have to say matters.

Allison's Story: A Developmentalist's Perspective

Allison's experience as a Jewish adult learner illustrates two related themes found in the literature on adult development and learning:

- When adults move from "silence to voice," they increase their sense of efficacy and improve their self-esteem. Correspondingly, when Jewish adults acquire a "Jewish voice," they become more confident and positive about themselves as Jews.
- When adult learners acquire a sense of personal authority, they feel empowered to share what they have learned. By passing their knowledge along to others, Jewish adult learners can achieve a meaningful sense of *Jewish generativity.*

The Growth of Efficacy and Self-Esteem in Adulthood

In order to become a Jewish constructed knower, an adult must have positive Jewish self-esteem. According to adult learning expert Daniele Flannery (2000, p. 56), "self esteem has to do with how people feel about their identities." Writing about the connection between identity and self-esteem in adulthood, Flannery distinguishes between "core self esteem" (which forms in early childhood and is grounded in whether a person feels loved and valued unconditionally) and "situational self esteem" (which derives from a person's sense of what he or she can do well or from the responses of others). She argues that an adult's situational self-esteem can change as personal circumstances change. If, say, a woman does poorly in high school, she may for years believe herself to be intellectually wanting and suffer poor "school-related" self-esteem. However, if that woman later returns to school and does well academically, her damaged self-esteem—and self-image—can dramatically improve.

Flannery further notes that because most contemporary adults have "multiple identities" (such as a work identity plus a quite separate community identity, as well as distinctive family, student, leisure time, religious and/or ethnic identities), an individual's self-esteem will vary depending on the social context in which a particular identity comes into play. Thus, a person who feels competent and confident in work situations may simultaneously feel incompetent and insecure in avocational settings. Or a person who feels effective in secular activities in the community may feel awkward and ineffectual in religious milieus. Fortunately, because adults are able to learn new skills and develop a strong sense of *agency* (or mastery), a damaged self-esteem can be overcome through educational experiences. In this sense, just as identity is fluid in adulthood, so too is one's self-esteem.

The starting point of the psychological literature on Jewish self-esteem frequently focuses on *negative* Jewish identity and how internalized anti-Semitism causes contemporary Jews to distance themselves from being identified as Jewish or "too Jewish" (Klein, 1980). Jewish men and women both suffer from encounters with stereotypes that characterize Jews as having features outside the norm of what is desirable or lovable. For example, according to psychologist Rachel Josefowitz Siegel (1995), there are anti-Jewish stereotypes that offer Jewish women no attractive option:

> As Jewish American Princess, she is caricatured as too selfish, too demanding, too loud and pushy, either over-sexed or too frigid; as Jewish Mother, she is misportrayed as too self-less, too nurturing, too unassertive and desexualized. Either way she falls short of what she is expected to be. . . . (p. 50)

Siegel says that the consequence of such stereotyping is that the Jewish woman may respond with "self-doubts and lowered self esteem" and may struggle with "having to choose between hiding her feelings from herself, hiding her Jewishness, or retreating from painful situations" (1995, p. 50). Similarly, Rabbi Jeffrey Salkin (1999) describes the impact of centuries of anti-Semitic iconography that portrayed Jewish men as both evil/in league with the devil and hypermasculine/hypersexual. Salkin writes of his own struggle to feel pride in being an ethical "mensch" in a world that preferred him to "be a [macho] man." Several psychotherapists have called for ethnotherapy (Klein, 1980; Crohn, Markman, Blumberg, and Levine, 2000) or other Jewish psycho-educational programs (Hammer, 1995) that can help adults overcome the deep damage that has been inflicted on their self-image and identity as Jews.

Although little has been written about the role Jewish adult learning plays in helping people to increase their Jewish self-esteem, personal accounts from learners like Allison demonstrate how Jewish learning can lead to positive Jewish identity and "voice." In Allison's case, her childhood and adolescence were marked by a progressive alienation from Judaism and the Jewish community. Her parents did not create a nurturing Jewish environment, and her Jewish education failed to give her a sense of connection to the Jewish people. That she wanted some kind of Jewish connection at her wedding surprised even Allison herself. Nonetheless, when she later opened herself up to Jewish learning—first by taking note of her cousin's counsel, then by reading books on Jewish themes, and finally by studying with Rabbi Davis—Allison took her first steps toward developing a sense of Jewish efficacy and positive Jewish identity. Her studies with Rabbi Davis helped her to gain a clearer sense of her right to participate in a Jewish discourse and to assert what mattered to her as a Jew. She started in a position of silence (not even knowing that her opinions counted) to received knowing (reading books) to procedural knowing (learning Hebrew, analyzing other people's Jewish stories, participating in text study). As she became more familiar with the Torah and learned about commentary, she acquired the confidence to begin to *construct meanings* for herself. When she crafted *divrei Torah*, Allison drew on a variety of textual materials, studied the opinions of a range of scholars, organized insights provided by her teachers, and reflected on the relationship between her own experience and messages of Torah. She recognized that, like generations of Jews before her, she could "enter into the conversation" about Jewish texts. Rather than seeing "authority" as something vested only in others, she discovered that she too could speak with a measure of authority about Judaism and Jewish life. As she developed into a constructed knower, she became more confident in her ability to be a Jewish educator and cultivated relationships with other knowers, both in her role as a teacher and as a colleague to other professionals in the Jewish community.

More than Just Standing at Sinai: The Generative Jewish Adult

In earlier chapters I noted that, in the view of theorist Erik Erikson, human development is marked by "tasks" that become salient at different times during the life cycle. I also pointed out that some tasks—such as developing a sense of competence in childhood or forming an identity in adolescence—might even be reconceptualized as important "Jewish tasks" that adults must "work through" as part of successful Jewish growth. When I reflect on *generativity*—the task Erikson associated with adulthood—I am struck by how "Jewish" this concept is. In our daily prayers we pledge to continue our covenant with God *l'dor vador*, "from generation to generation." We are, like Joshua who handed the Torah to the elders, obligated to pass the Torah from one generation to the next. Jews have always cautioned that parents must teach their children and that continuity depends on how Judaism is conveyed to one's children and one's children's children. The explanation of "what generativity is about" by three of Erikson's disciples could readily be considered a restatement of Jewish philosophy:

- Generativity is about the next generation, about bearing, raising, caring for children—one's own and others.
- It is about assuming the role of responsible parent, mentor, shepherd, guardian, guide, and so on, vis-à-vis those whose development and well-being benefit from the care that role provides.
- It is even about assuming such a role vis-à-vis society writ large, about being a responsible citizen, a contributing member of a community, a leader, a mover, and a shaker.
- In addition, it is about *generating:* creating and producing things, people, and outcomes that are aimed at benefiting, in some sense, the next generation, and even the next. (McAdams, Hart, and Maruna, 1998, p. 7)

In their book on generativity, McAdams, Hart, and Maruna say that although generativity may stem from a person's inner desires, frequently it is determined by cultural expectations that are placed on people during their adult years:

One of the reasons that generativity emerges as a psychosocial issue in the *adult* years is that society comes to demand that adults take responsibility for the next generation, in their roles as parents, teachers, mentors, leaders, organizers, creative ritualizers and "keepers of the meaning." (p. 10)

From a Jewish perspective, the idea of generativity is at the center of our daily responsibilities—to teach children, to reaffirm the covenant between God and the Jewish people, to remember and pass along to others our heritage as a people who have weathered oppression and emerged as survivors. However, whereas most Jewish adults today are highly generative in their work, family, and community pursuits, many do not function in a generative way in Jewish domains. Lacking sufficient Jewish education or feeling disconnected from Judaism or the Jewish community, they cannot fill the teaching-mentoring-leading-ritualizing roles that would enable them to transmit the meaning of Judaism to others. They often grieve the "disconnect" and wish they could help their children or non-Jewish in-laws or Christian colleagues and neighbors to understand Judaism, but they have not done the learning that might equip them to teach with authority or credibility.

Allison's experience as a Jewish adult learner stimulated a desire to share her Jewish learning with others. Initially she was content to teach within her family; her bat mitzvah provided an important opportunity to create a Jewish learning community with those closest to her. But later, when invited to read Torah and present a *d'var Torah* at a local synagogue, Allison felt she had finally become a Jewish adult. Her sense of being able to be Jewishly generative mushroomed within several years. By taking on new responsibilities as a Jewish educator, she created many opportunities to "shape" the Jewish lives of people of all ages in her community. By writing prayers and continuing to give Torah commentaries, Allison influenced others through her insights and her role modeling. And by broadening her involvement in the world of Jewish education, Allison helped strengthen the community of professionals who do more than just "stand" at Sinai, by actively transmitting Jewish knowledge from generation to generation.

From Theory to Practice: Helping Learners
Do More than Just Stand at Sinai

Becoming connected to learners—and helping learners eventually to connect to other learners—is one of the most exciting dimensions of work in today's Jewish adult learning community. The current generation of learners represents an extraordinary resource for the future in Jewish adult education. Helping these learners become teachers to others—to transmit what they have learned to the next generation of learners—is part of how Jewish professionals can themselves do more than just "stand" at Sinai.

To connect more effectively with Jewish adult learners, Jewish professionals should:

1. Help learners to see what kind of "knowers" they are and assess what it might take for them to shift to more proactive learning modes. At the same time, be respectful of the learners' choices, and do not expect learners to leave their "comfort zone" until they are ready.

2. Encourage learners to plan for their own Jewish generativity. Ask them what they want to pass on to future generations of Jews, including the generation of people around them who do not have as much Jewish learning as they do. Foster opportunities for Jewish learners to tutor, teach, and mentor other learners and prospective learners.

3. Develop a consultation group for adult learners who wish to become teachers. Share your teaching experiences with them. Offer to co-teach with them. Help them to pair with one another to plan and evaluate their teaching experiences.

5

Wrestling with the Angel:
Grappling with Tough Questions

That same night he arose . . . he crossed the ford of the Jabbok . . .
Jacob was left alone. And a man wrestled with him until the break
of dawn. . . . So Jacob named the place Peniel, meaning, "I have
seen a divine being face to face, yet my life has been preserved."
—*Genesis 32:23, 25, 31*

Contemporary Jewish adult learning stories are replete with examples of how learners "wrestle to find meaning"—to engage in what Rabbi Daniel Gordis (1995) describes as "the enterprise of asking life's hardest questions, of searching for life's most elusive answers, and of building relationships with each other, with a Force Jews commonly call God, and with our tradition as we commonly go through that process" (pp. 45–46). In *God Was Not in the Fire*, Gordis talks about how prevalent "journey stories" are in Jewish tradition, noting that, for Jews, "the magic and the power of religious life is in the 'quest.' " A central feature of the quest, Rabbi Gordis points out, is *questioning*:

> The Jewish tradition recognizes that to be a human being is to perpetually ask questions, to wonder without fully satisfying our wondering. Frustrating though many of our deepest and most personal questions are, we cannot put them aside, no matter how hard we try. (p. 46)

Moreover, Gordis says, questioning—wrestling with whatever angels we meet on our respective journeys—means "resigning ourselves to the inevitability of not completely understanding the world in which we live, but at the same time committing ourselves to persisting in trying" (p. 46). When adults begin to struggle—with their lives, dreams, losses, legacy to the next generation, and the threat of the unknown—they customarily look to a religious tradition for help.

Indeed, experts in the field of adult religious education suggest that meaning-making is the central activity of their work with adults. Leon McKenzie (1986) explains:

> We come into the world with question marks in our heads. We strive for intelligibility and purpose. We seek a perspective or framework for our being-in-the-world. The first purpose of religious education is to make a particular meaning framework available. (p. 11)

According to McKenzie, acquiring a meaning framework provides adults with "order and stability" in their lives. Learning helps adults to clarify their identities and achieve greater personal coherence in their sense of self. McKenzie suggests three ways that religious professionals can help adults develop a meaning framework and a stronger religious identity:

1. Help learners to explore the richness of their religious heritage.
2. Help learners to explore and expand their initial meaning structures by relating the religious tradition to their life experiences.
3. Help learners to question the religious tradition critically.

The literature on adult religious education draws heavily on work in the fields of cognitive psychology and adult learning. To date, the insights from these disciplines have not been applied to the experiences of Jewish adult learners. The more Jewish professionals understand how Jewish adults wrestle with meaning-making, the more they will be prepared to help these adults find relevant answers about Judaism and Jewish life.

Meaning-Making: The View from Cognitive Psychology

According to Sharon Daloz Parks (2000), a leading adult development psychologist, meaning-making is "the activity of composing a sense of connections among things: a sense of pattern, order, form, and significance" (p. 19). To be human, Parks explains, is to "seek coherence and correspondence . . . to want to be oriented to one's surroundings . . . to desire relationship among the disparate elements of existence" (p. 19). Over the life cycle, each person is engaged in a continual process of "composing"—taking in information, adapting the input to our individual realities, and responding idiosyncratically. Meaning-making helps us to make sense of our experiences, find explanations for puzzling events, and understand other people's choices and ways of knowing. It also pushes us to ask fundamental questions about who we are as human beings and why we are here on earth.

More than fifty years ago, the Swiss psychologist Jean Piaget (1952) described how the meaning-making process begins in early childhood when infants begin to organize information about objects in their range of sight. First, children develop the ability to label and manipulate details about phenomena in their immediate experience ("Mama" to indicate mother; "the ball is blue" to categorize information; "c-a-t spells 'cat' " or "one-plus-one equals two" to manipulate symbolic elements). As children mature, they enlarge their capacities for meaning-making, begin to think in increasingly abstract terms, and develop the ability to use symbols and metaphors. Thus, the school-age child is able to "imagine" one-plus-one rather than counting the total on fingers; similarly, the young adolescent is able to conceptualize and act on abstract concepts (e.g., fairness or loyalty) rather than needing to test and prove a particular concept each time it is encountered. The move from "concrete" thought to more "abstract" thinking (also referred to as hypothetical thinking) is a sign of intellectual maturity.

One of the ways that people demonstrate that they are moving to abstract thought is seen in how they respond to complex life situations. As Robert Kegan, author of *In Over Our Heads: The Mental Demands of Modern Life* (1994) points out, the development of abstract thinking is crucial for successful functioning in the postmodern world. The more people can imagine options, consider alternatives, see things from others' perspectives, and consciously reflect on what they are thinking, the better prepared they are to cope with life's complexities and unexpected demands.

During adulthood, meaning-making becomes especially salient at midlife. This is when family structures change (children becoming independent and leaving home; parents becoming ill and dying) and when adults come to terms with their own physical decline and mortality. When confronted with changing realities and roles, most adults find themselves driven to understand life in deeper and more coherent ways than before. In this quest, they typically encounter internal paradoxes that prompt them to rethink their values and assess how they reconcile competing tensions in their lives. In *The Seasons of a Man's Life* (1978),

Daniel Levinson and his colleagues refer to these competing tensions as "polarities" and say that, over the years, adults struggle to integrate opposing "tendencies" such as being young versus getting older, yielding to destructive (and self-destructive) impulses versus cultivating creative urges, investing in self-promotion versus nurturing others, and becoming more separate versus becoming more connected and interdependent.

Faith development theorist James Fowler (1995) hypothesizes that midlife adults who are trying to reconcile conflicts and paradoxes may begin to see life situations in more nuanced ways. Having moved from the "conformist" thinking of adolescence to the more individualistic stance of early adulthood (a time of active choice making about work, family, politics, and lifestyle), these individuals begin to notice the "bigger picture," as well as the subtle distinctions of how different people "construct" reality. As they grow older, people who are developing cognitively become less dichotomous (either/or, black/white) in their thinking and more able to see "both (or the many) sides of an issue simultaneously" (Fowler, 1995, p. 185). Fowler calls this emergent consciousness "conjunctive faith," and says that the adults who move toward this kind of thinking see that "things are organically related to each other." They also accept that there are phenomena that don't "fit into" previously held assumptions. When moving toward conjunctive faith thinking, adults become more flexible in how they "organize" information and more fluid about the meanings they ascribe to experiences. They also become more "dialogic"—willing to engage in internal and interpersonal dialogues about the nature of life and the relationship between individual concerns and universal issues.

The cognitive process of sorting out the "big picture" can seem highly destabilizing to people who are unwilling to change their views or are intimidated when they find that old assumptions don't work any more. On the other hand, people who take intellectual risks and entertain new possibilities find that they develop a greater tolerance for the unknown and greater curiosity about puzzling ambiguities. The more that adults struggle with their questions, dualities, and doubts, the more they are able to face their conflicts and discover their personal truths. Ultimately, grappling with life's paradoxes and tough questions—"wrestling with the angel"—enables adults to make meaning of their experiences and the unknown and to move toward mature spiritual integration.

Meaning-Making: The View from Adult Learning Theory

Adults who struggle with questions of meaning frequently turn to "new learning" situations in order to understand their changes and sort out their ideas. Adult meaning-making is maximized in learning that is *transformative* rather than *informational* (Taylor, Marienau, and Fiddler, 2000). Informational learning focuses on how people acquire and store knowledge; the information they receive is from outside themselves and is obtained through memorizing or reproducing. While this kind of learning is crucial as a starting point, it tends to be fairly concrete and may not be long lasting; the learner doesn't have to "do" anything with the knowledge and thus may stay relatively detached from it. If people are detached from ideas, then they will not use those ideas in a personally meaningful way.

Alternatively, transformative learning "centers on the learner's abstraction of meaning; [it] is a *deep approach* to learning" that is interpretive and helps the learner to better understand reality and cope with change (Taylor, Marienau, and Fiddler, 2000, p. 14). Educators who encourage transformative learning assume that the learner will *change perspective* by virtue of going through a process of reflection, analysis, and interpretation (or reinterpretation) of information. According to theorist Jack Mezirow (2000), transformative learning involves a ten-step *personal transformation* sequence in which, cognitively, the learner moves from dissonance (what he refers to as "disorienting dilemmas") to evaluation of old assumptions to exploration of new ways of thinking to new ways of behaving or understanding. His sequence is delineated in Exhibit 5-1.

Mezirow has written extensively about what happens to adults when they have "disorienting dilemmas"—confounding life events that cannot be understood or resolved using old problem-solving strategies (e.g., the death of a loved one, a difficult job change, unanticipated illness, or value conflicts with one's family members). In his view, adult educators play important roles in helping learners to make new meaning of these events and to change their behavior in positive ways. Later in this chapter are some specific suggestions for how Jewish professionals can create learning environments that can promote perspective transformation in Jewish adults. First, though, let's consider some of the principles of adult cognitive development and meaning-making in light of a specific story. We turn now to meet Phil, an executive in the computer indus-

EXHIBIT 5-1

Jack Mezirow's Ten Phases of Perspective Transformation

Transformation involves changing a frame of reference about "habits of mind" and points of view that are no longer meaningful. A person transforms a frame of reference by becoming critically reflective of his or her assumptions and aware of how those beliefs were acquired. Through reflection and consideration of alternative beliefs, the individual comes to a new understanding and recognizes the potential for a change in behavior. The *process* of perspective transformation occurs when a person

1. Experiences a disorienting dilemma
2. Undergoes self-examination that may involve feelings of fear, anger, guilt, or shame
3. Conducts a critical assessment of previously held assumptions
4. Recognizes that one's discontent and the process of transformation are shared by others—that one's problems are not exclusively a private matter
5. Explores options for new roles, relationships, and actions
6. Plans a course of action
7. Acquires knowledge and skills for implementing one's plans
8. Tries out new roles on a provisional basis and assesses feedback
9. Builds competence and self-confidence in new roles and relationships
10. Reintegrates information into one's life on the basis of conditions dictated by the new perspective

Adapted from Patricia Cranton, *Understanding and Promoting Transformative Learning* (San Francisco: Jossey-Bass, 1994), and Jack Mezirow, "Learning to Think Like an Adult," in Jack Mezirow and Associates, *Learning as Transformation* (San Francisco: Jossey-Bass, 2000).

try who began his Jewish adult learning journey in his midforties. Following the story is my commentary on Phil's experience and a discussion of how people like Phil can be helped to grow.

Phil's Story

For a number of years, I attended a summer study retreat that attracts Jewish adults who are seeking intensive Jewish living-and-learning experiences. One year, I became friends with Phil Sapphire, a fifty-two-year-old information technology executive, who was my study partner in a class on prayer. Phil was a highly methodical learner who took time to reflect on ideas and assess his own relationship to them. He was particularly self-reflexive about the *Kaddish* (his father had recently died), and his comments prompted other members of the class to think critically about some of their assumptions about the role of prayer in their lives.

At the retreat, I also became friends with Phil's wife, Carla, who said that she had come to the program to try to understand what was pulling Phil into such intense involvement in Jewish learning. She mentioned that he spent many hours on-line with Jewish study partners. Before we left for home, I asked Phil to tell me about his Jewish learning journey. As we will see in Story 5, Phil Sapphire's adult Jewish growth reflected his long-standing desire to resolve unanswered questions in his life and to figure out how Judaism fit into his ways of "making meaning."

❧ Story 5 ☙

PHIL

Philip Sapphire grew up in Milwaukee. His parents owned a printing business and were active in their Conservative congregation. After his bar mitzvah, Phil joined AZA (Aleph Zadik Aleph, the high school boys division of the B'nai B'rith Youth Organization) and attended a regional Jewish camp. He found these groups appealing, especially compared to the youth group at home, which was "too social":

> I remember at camp things like putting on our own services. I remember a lot of funky, social action stuff, and also some feel-good readings from Kahlil Gibran and Anne Frank. . . . There was one

counselor who got some of us involved in intensive Torah study, which I loved. That was the first time in my life that I felt "authentic" as a Jew. I was shy, but at camp I really had a sense of being part of things—innately part of things. . . .

Although Phil enjoyed the camaraderie of camp, at home he never felt part of the Jewish "in crowd." He disliked his mother's "country club" relatives and avoided the family's annual Purim party: "Lots of liquor, lots of noise, no way to talk to anybody—which I probably wouldn't have been much interested in anyway." And while his mother was president of the synagogue Sisterhood, Phil perceived his parents' commitment to Judaism as superficial: "They did all the 'right things'—Shabbat dinners, attending services, giving *tzedakah*—but they never wanted to talk about why they did what they did."

When he got to college at the University of Wisconsin in 1969, Phil attended events at Hillel but was disconcerted to find that it was dominated by students who had grown up in a more traditional worship environment: "They davened fast and talked about the Mishnah. I simply didn't have the background." Although he had thought he would join a Jewish fraternity, once he arrived on campus he changed his mind: "The sixties happened, and the whole fraternity scene—and the idea of exclusive Jewish organizations—seemed increasingly irrelevant, even offensive."

During his last year of college, Phil became involved socially with a group that experimented with drugs and sought "higher consciousness." A friend suggested that he read Ram Dass's *Be Here Now,* and he was excited by the book's messages that all life is connected and contemplation can lead to joy. But in a Zen Buddhist meditation group, he realized that he wasn't feeling joyful and wasn't comfortable with Eastern philosophy:

> In meditating there, I got some glimpses of the connectedness of the whole world, but only the merest glimpses. When you meditate, just when you start recognizing what's happening, you lose it. As soon as you go "Oh God, this feels good," it's gone. That was hard for me to deal with. And, even more: I had a lot of trouble with the laissez-faire approach of Buddhist philosophy. I couldn't buy into the idea that "this is all an illusion." I feel it's the works in this world that are important. I feel very accountable, and I couldn't dismiss my history.

I believe in history—I have a Jewish belief in history. And that's different from the "nothingness" that's at the center of Buddhist thought.

In his twenties, Phil moved to Seattle, where he began a career in the emerging computer industry. He threw himself into work in data management and built a reputation as a troubleshooter who could find creative solutions to complex problems. He occasionally attended Jewish singles events, where he met other young adults who had questions and concerns similar to his own:

> I remember going to a group that met on Friday evenings. Most were people who were pretty disaffected from religious observance, but still committed to Judaism in various ways. We would have dinner and discussion—usually about the restrictiveness of a law-driven religion that considered itself "superior." There was something really intense about this for me. I liked being with people who thought critically, who asked what it means to "buy in" to a set of values when you've got some basic objections to the underlying framework. And I liked hanging out with other Jews. But I also was wary—always suspicious of anything that smacked of "cliquish" Jewish snobbery.

Through work, Phil met Carla, a human resources administrator who had grown up in a traditional Jewish household in Cleveland. Also a "child of the sixties," Carla had "run from" the Jewish community, which she found smothering and repressive. Although they were married in a Jewish ceremony, Phil and Carla agreed that they didn't want to live the "ghetto-ized" life of their parents. After a few years, they moved to the Silicon Valley in California and were delighted to blend into an ethnically mixed neighborhood in San Jose. After their daughter, Shira, was born, they occasionally participated in seders sponsored by a Reconstructionist *chavurah* in their community, but they did not enroll Shira in the *chavurah's* lay-led education program. Looking back on those years, Phil recalled:

> We pretty much picked and chose those elements of Jewish life that appealed to us. We attended lectures at the Jewish Community Center, contributed to the construction of the Holocaust Memorial

Museum in Washington, lobbied against Christmas trees in Shira's school, sometimes had a subscription to *Tikkun* magazine. When Shira was in high school, she got involved with a group of Jewish environmentalists, so we "went Green" for awhile.

In the spring of 1993, Phil turned forty-five. The previous fall, Shira had left for college, and as the year went along Phil felt increasingly depressed. He realized that much of his "sense of personal meaning" had been bound up in parenting; he missed Shira tremendously. At work, he had enjoyed mentoring several younger employees, but now one of his protégés was outdistancing him and stood ready to manage Phil's own division. The computer industry was changing rapidly, and Phil feared that his knowledge base might soon be regarded as obsolete. Meanwhile, Carla's widowed mother, still in Cleveland, moved to an assisted living facility, and Carla began to get calls from the facility's staff that her mother was having problems with mental disorientation. Carla arranged her work schedule so that she could fly to Cleveland once a month. Suddenly Phil had many weekends alone and found himself at a loss for activity. He joined a gym and also took some piano lessons, but the depression did not lift.

Phil decided to visit his parents. When he called to make arrangements, his mother asked him to come for the bar mitzvah of her cousin Stanley's grandson. Phil agreed to attend the bar mitzvah—his first family event in many years. When he arrived "home," his mother pointed out that Phil's *tallis* bag was still in the drawer in his old bedroom. Phil had mixed feelings when he took the *tallis* out of the bag: "I felt both sentimental and detached." At the bar mitzvah, however, he had an intense emotional response:

My mother had been telling me that the synagogue had changed a lot—that there were swings and slides where there used to be only fur coats. At the service it hit me full force that what Judaism does is to really *embrace the generations*. It was Saturday morning and they brought a little baby girl up to be named. And then there was the bar mitzvah where my great-uncle passed the Torah to his son, who passed it on to his son. And, of course, people said the *Kaddish*. There were old people and young people—and what hit me was the comprehensive way in which everyone was *held* by the community and that the prayers seemed more about love and compassion than about obeying a controlling, angry God.

When Phil returned to San Jose, he could not stop thinking about what he had observed at the service. He told Carla that, to his shock—even bewilderment—he had found it comforting to be with other Jews and appealing to "look at the old prayers with new eyes." He said he was hungry for the kind of close Jewish community that he had seen in Milwaukee and remembered from his days at camp. With Carla's support, he called a local rabbi, Marshall Young, and said he was wondering how to resume his Jewish education "after thirty years in the wilderness." After hearing about Phil's background and questions, Rabbi Young recommended Phil check out an early morning *parashat hashavua* group that met in a downtown accounting firm.

From his first visit to the text study group, Phil was struck by how comfortable he felt with the study experience and being part of the conversation: "It all felt so familiar to me. Even though I hadn't studied with other Jews for three decades, I seemed to know how to begin." He began to attend the study group on a regular basis and was energized by the learning experience:

I became a steady member of this group. And one of the things I learned early on was that in text study you have to dig under the obvious story. This is exactly what you do with computer software: you don't look for the obvious, you look for the silence rather than the norms, you look for the unspoken rather than the spoken. Doing so felt so natural to me that I fell right in with it as if I had been doing it my whole life. And, for the first time since the singles group in Seattle, I was with other Jews who were motivated to really probe Jewish ideas, to look at the complexities of Jewish thought.

As Phil became involved with text study, he began to rethink some of his assumptions about—even prejudices against—Jewish tradition. He realized that he had assumed that Judaism would be rigid and prescriptive, rather than open to challenge and interpretation. He was surprised by how much he identified with the conflicts of biblical figures and was intrigued by the complexity of the relationship between God and man. To deepen his understanding, he began to assemble a personal library of Jewish books: "I started doing a lot of reading—books on midrash, halachah, philosophy, prayer—and was just amazed at how rich Judaism is, on so many different levels."

Using his computer skills, Phil also began to explore Jewish Web sites and was startled to discover how many study and dialogue opportunities there were on-line. He subscribed to several listservs to receive Torah commentaries and began to follow discussions on Rabbi Judith Abrams's Maqom Web site (for adult Talmud study). He liked becoming part of a "virtual community" of learners and enjoyed telling people about the wonders of studying with "Jews in cyberspace."

Phil's increasing involvement with Jewish learning caused tensions between him and Carla, who, preoccupied with her mother's situation, felt that Phil was paying more attention to his on-line study partners than to her. Carla's resentment was fueled when Phil accepted an invitation from his father, Maurice, to join him on a trip to Israel. Phil was not interested in traveling with an organized tour but proposed instead that he and his father find a way to "do some Jewish learning" in Jerusalem. One of his Internet correspondents told him about a yeshivah for English speakers where they would be welcome to study on a short-term basis. Their three-week trip was, in Phil's view, an unqualified success. A "transcendent" moment occurred when he and Maurice entered the yeshivah's *beit midrash*:

> We walked in and it was as if I could "see" my great-grandfather studying at one of those wooden tables. I felt like I was in a familiar place—not physically, but in a sacred space created by the teacher, the students, the conversation, and the text. It was so familiar to me that I almost had to think to myself that in another life I had been there. That I had been a *cheder* boy or something. It was as if my father and I were meant for studying like that. We joined right in and became one another's *chevruta*.

For six months following the trip, Phil and Maurice engaged in steady dialogue about Judaism and Jewish values. They sent one another Torah commentaries and exchanged brief *divrei Torah* via e-mail. They spoke weekly on the phone about favorite books on Jewish subjects. When Phil developed some back problems that required him to stay off his feet, he wrote to his father that he found solace in reading about the end of Moses' life:

> I sent my dad an e-mail and said I'd been thinking about how Moses says, "There's the Promised Land. I'm ready to go," but

God says, "You can't go." I told him I figured that story is about as stark as you can get possibly get. It's saying: Just because you're a good guy and you work hard doesn't mean that you will get the reward. That just 'cause you do good things and you're powerful and you're wise and you're an agent of God doesn't mean that you're going to accomplish everything in your lifetime. It may be that you simply set things in motion that in some other person's lifetime will work. It was pretty amazing to write that kind of thing to my own father—to link that to my own life and, really, to his life as well.

Then, unexpectedly, Maurice suffered a fatal heart attack. For many months, Phil was grief stricken: there were so many things he wished he had said to his father; he missed their dialogue; he wanted his father to know that Shira had applied to be a counselor at the Jewish camp Phil had attended years before. Although he attended a daily minyan to say *Kaddish,* Phil felt spiritually unfulfilled. He would recite the prayers but didn't feel connected to them or better able to accept his profound sense of loss. He was "angry at God" but also felt disingenuous because he had "never really been 'on speaking terms' with God."

As the year of mourning ended, Phil found himself longing for relief from his gnawing anger and depression. He imagined quitting his job and moving to Jerusalem, but he knew that that would destroy his marriage and not really provide the spiritual answers he was seeking. He persuaded Carla to accompany him to a weeklong retreat for Jewish adult learners. The experience had a positive impact:

We took a class on Jewish prayer. Every day, we got into heavy discussions about prayer, arguing different views about what prayer is and how Jews use it in their lives. This came at a good time for Carla: her mother was deteriorating, and Carla was struggling with her own spiritual questions. The class clarified how each of us has to work out a relationship with a prayer ritual and discipline. I realized that for me, "prayer" is what happens when I *study.* It's when I'm learning with others that I feel the most connected, even where I find something "sacred." I'd never made that connection before. Just getting that language helped me begin to explain myself to my wife.

Phil's Story: A Developmentalist's Perspective

Phil's story highlights three themes in the cognitive development literature on meaning-making that are relevant to the experiences of contemporary Jewish adult learners:

- When Jewish adults have disruptive or "disorienting" experiences that challenge previously held worldviews (such as the death of their parents, the intermarriage of children, encounters with anti-Semitism, divorce, or relocation to a new community), they sometimes wonder if Judaism can help them to "understand" their situation in new ways. When these adults embark on new meaning-making, new learning can transform their view of themselves as Jews.
- As Jewish adults mature and grapple with pressing questions and ambiguities, they discover paradoxes in their thinking about Judaism and their lives as Jews. These paradoxical struggles may become especially salient when individuals attempt to "make meaning" during the adult years.
- When Jewish adults are grappling with questions of meaning, they find it beneficial to engage in learning and discourse with other learners. The opportunity to actively dialogue with other Jews contributes significantly to Jewish meaning-making and adult Jewish growth.

Transformative Learning and Jewish Meaning-Making

Adults who struggle with questions of meaning often seek new learning in order to understand what is occurring in their lives. Transformative learning begins when the learner has a disorienting dilemma and cannot rely on old strategies to understand current events. To change his or her perspective, the learner must go through a process of critically reflecting on past assumptions, exploring new options, discussing ideas with others, and engaging in new learning activities.

When Jewish adults become "disoriented" and begin a search for meaning, they often turn to Jewish tradition. Some people hope to learn from Jewish teachings new ways to look at their lives. Others feel a need to sort out what meaning Judaism (or being Jewish) has for them in their lives. Regardless of how these adults engage Jewish questions, they find that there are no simple answers. Indeed, to "make meaning" Jewishly, one must "wrestle" toward personal transformation. And, indeed, the Jewish learning tradition has long recognized that learners thrive when they are challenged to think critically, consider alternative viewpoints, and debate alternative meanings. For Jewish adults who have never before looked closely at their Jewish identity or the role of Judaism in their lives, transformative learning begins when learners and teachers come together purposefully to grapple with questions, doubts, and other concerns.

Over the course of Phil Sapphire's life, there were several instances of "disorientation" about his life as a Jew: his discovery at college that he didn't "fit in" with the dominant crowd at Hillel; the realization during Buddhist meditation that his Jewish sense of history and reality were at odds with basic Buddhist thought; his unexpected insights about the benefits of synagogue participation when he visited his parents; and his despair and anger when his father died unexpectedly. Although in his early adult years Phil searched for learning environments that might help him to assess the meaning of Judaism in his life at that time, he did not have teachers or peers to reinforce his questioning in a lasting way.

Phil's Jewish transformative education began at midlife when he approached Rabbi Young to talk about resuming his "interrupted" Jewish education. Rabbi Young helped Phil to choose a suitable venue in which to assess some of his assumptions and to think critically about Judaism and his relationship to Jewish tradition. In the Torah study group, Phil acquired knowledge that helped him to become a more active and informed Jewish adult learner. Later, when his father died and Phil became despondent and spiritually bereft, the weeklong Jewish study retreat offered him the opportunity to examine his feelings of loss and to analyze how prayer (and study) could help him to "reintegrate" his life in the face of deep grief.

Phil's responses were consistent with the steps to personal transformation described by Mezirow. His disorienting dilemmas led to self-examination and a critical assessment of his assumptions about Judaism, Jewish law, and Jewish community; participation in group discussions (in the Torah study group and at the study retreat) helped him to compare his views with others' and to explore alternative ways of thinking; and as he took deliberate steps to become more informed Jewishly, his self-confidence as a Jewish thinker increased and his dialogues about Judaism deepened (as evidenced by his discussions with his father and his participation in the on-line Talmud study program).

Coping with Multiple Meanings:
Paradox in the Lives of Jewish Adults

As we have learned from the insights of Daniel Levinson and associates (1978) and James Fowler (1995), adult life is fraught with encounters with paradoxical or competing ideas. When people move from "dualistic" (black-and-white) thinking to more complex ways of seeing the world, they find themselves debating what may seem like opposing answers to difficult questions. They learn about the challenges of dialectical thinking and gradually develop the ability to "hold differences in one hand." Some adults surprise themselves by becoming comfortable with ambiguity; others struggle with unresolved issues, realizing that there are consequences for any choice and no easy or perfect answers. In the best of circumstances, this more pluralistic and flexible thinking leads to a sense of personal integration in which the individual discerns connections among disparate ideas and feels a sense of "oneness" beyond the self.

For Jewish adults, internal (and sometimes interpersonal) dialectical debates about Jewish values and way of life tend to surface at times of personal change. Contemporary Jews typically live in "several worlds" and thus grapple with the challenges of having more than one cultural identity. Their lives are not parochial, and they value the "multiplistic" perspective that comes from living in a diverse society. At the same time, many long for the comforts of being part of "a tribe" and find themselves drawn to communal activities with their "own kind." Also, having received the benefits of higher education, these adults value modern, rational inquiry; their advanced learning has given them a healthy skepticism that they bring to "religious" or spiritual questions that don't fit into scientific frames. Yet they yearn for spiritual wholeness and a sense of connection with something larger than themselves; they are curious about how the wisdom of Judaism can contribute to their quest for well-being during the stressful adult years. Some of the paradoxes Jewish adults wrestle as they try to "make meaning" Jewishly are presented in Exhibit 5-2.

Phil's story offers several examples of the kinds of paradoxes suggested in Exhibit 5-2. As a college student, Phil wanted to find a Jewish peer group *and* he was both "put off" by students at Hillel and skeptical of fraternities that, by design, were exclusive to one group. Early in adulthood, when he attended Jewish singles events, he liked "hanging out with other Jews" *and* was wary of " 'cliquish' Jewish snobbery." Later, he was glad to find like-

EXHIBIT 5-2

Sample Paradoxes in Contemporary Jewish Lives

Paradox 1	I feel competent in my work and family roles; I feel adult in most aspects of my life	*and*	I feel insecure in Jewish roles; I don't feel fully adult/ authentic as a Jew
Paradox 2	I want to be part of the Jewish community, to share common values and goals with the group	*and*	I feel like a stranger with other Jews in diverse Jewish settings
Paradox 3	I want to feel a sense of home and intimacy within a homogeneous Jewish community	*and*	I want to feel "at home" in a pluralistic Jewish world; I resist "ghettoizing" or appearing different or separate from others
Paradox 4	I feel I should be part of something larger than myself	*and*	I want to maintain my personal boundaries; I don't want to get too enmeshed or feel a loss of my individual identity
Paradox 5	I feel pulled toward Jewish tradition and a sense of continuity	*and*	I am put off by Jewish traditions and dated, obsolete practices
Paradox 6	I feel responsible for the survival of the Jewish community	*and*	I am barely able to meet my personal obligations and survival needs
Paradox 7	I hunger for a Jewish spiritual connection and a sense of meaning in Jewish life	*and*	I lack a connection to Jewish spiritual tradition and prayer; I don't even know what I believe or if it's "Jewish"

minded Jews in his community and join them for activities *and* he wanted to selectively pick and choose only those elements of Jewish affiliation that "appealed." In each of these instances, Phil was pulled by both sides of issues and found no easy answers. As he struggled to "make meaning" of his life choices, he had to reflect on past choices, evaluate options, tolerate ambiguities, and accept that there might be no fixed answers to his questions. At the same time, because of his willingness to "wrestle" with conflicting feelings and ideas, he was able to find new pathways for meaning and growth.

Learning Communities and Meaning-Making: *Dialogue and Adult Jewish Growth*

The literature on adult learning in general, and transformative learning in particular, stresses the value of dialogue in adult meaning-making. According to Taylor, Marienau, and Fiddler (2000), in dialogue "two or more people exchange ideas and beliefs" and thus get exposed to "ideas and ways of thinking different from their own" (p. 34). This exposure to how others make meaning pushes each person to examine what underlies their differences and to surface potentially distorting assumptions. It is only when people examine their own and others' ways of making meaning that they can authentically sort out and differentiate their own meanings and sustain genuine communication. Dialogue involves moving below the surface of mere conversation:

> Dialogue is not to be confused with aimless discussion in which partic-
> ipants take turns saying what they think they already know. Rather,
> learners *inquire into and respond openly to others' ideas*, at the same time
> thinking about and being willing to *surface and question assumptions*
> *underlying their own and others' statements.* (p . 34)

The dialogic process helps people to discover their own truths and to share those truths with others. It helps participants to see their views in social context and to move beyond subjective perceptions. It also helps people to feel less alone when they struggle with complex questions. By wrestling with others' ideas, they come to know both themselves and their "angels" more completely.

Dialogue also fosters a sense of connection with others. Significant relationships help adults to think about the needs and views of people outside themselves; through relationships we develop compassion and understanding, as well as the capacity for mutual support. Dialogue and interpersonal connection also serve to enlarge how people think about their responsibility to the greater community:

> People who have moved toward connection with others are also likely to *experience themselves as part of something larger.* Though they may not necessarily follow an activist social agenda, they are likely to be more aware of the ways in which human society is mutually interdependent. Along with this realization comes the desire to *contribute one's voice to the collective endeavor.* (p. 42)

Phil's Jewish dialogue experiences—in the Torah study group, with his father, in on-line discussions, and at the study retreat—had a significant impact on his relationship to Judaism, Jewish tradition, and the Jewish community. In the Torah study group, he discovered how gratifying it was to have dialogue partners who were willing to probe Jewish tradition in a thoughtful way; by sharing personal interpretations, he began to understand alternative views and to see that different people make meaning in different ways. In his conversations with his father, he deepened his personal connection to Judaism and saw how his own life mirrored experiences of earlier generations of Jews. Participation in the on-line Talmud study program provided Phil with a variety of study partners and with the sense that he was "contributing his voice" to the larger "Jewish conversation." Also, through discussions with classmates at the study retreat, Phil finally began to differentiate what mattered to him about prayer and to understand how Jewish learning was helping him to achieve some of the personal integration he had long been seeking.

Although Phil's experience in learning communities helped him to grow Jewishly, his involvement with Jewish study contributed to stress between him and his wife. Indeed, as Phil increased his level of dialogue with fellow learners, he apparently did not include his wife in conversations about his search for new meaning or recognize that she too might engage in spiritual questions. In my interview with Phil, it sounded like the class on prayer might have given him and Carla some shared language with which to begin meaningful dialogue, but it was unclear how their individual Jewish journeys would intersect or how they could become mutually supportive as their lives evolved. Indeed, as Phil and Carla each wrestle with the "disorienting dilemmas" that are a by-product of change, it remains to be seen how their respective attempts to "make meaning" will impact their relationship and the future of their marriage.

From Theory to Practice: Helping Adults Wrestle with Meaning

The primary role of the Jewish professional in the meaning-making process is to create conditions for the kind of questioning and wondering that characterize healthy adult development and learning. Rather than providing answers, Jewish professionals best serve adult learners by encouraging them to grapple with the unresolved questions of their lives. They support the learner's quest for new information and, whenever possible, offer opportunities for dialogue. Laurent Daloz, who has written extensively about the teacher as mentor, urges educators to think of their job as "not to instruct but rather to understand [the] student's thought and . . . raise questions about it" (1999, p. 219). He further suggests that the teacher who helps learners to "live" inside their own and others' questions sends the message that meaning-making is at the center of learning—that "we all have the potential to evolve toward increasingly integrated and differentiated ways of making sense of the world" (p. 48).

To create the kind of meaning-making learning environments that help Jewish adults like Phil Sapphire to grow cognitively and find new ways to make meaning, Jewish professionals should:

1. Be on the lookout for Jewish adults who have had "disorienting dilemmas" and offer to help them chart a course of Jewish learning that can help them with their specific meaning-making needs. This means helping learners to assess what they want and need to know and showing them where to find support for their Jewish growth. It also means helping people to understand that (a) disorienting dilemmas are the first step on the journey of new understanding and (b) Judaism has resources that can help them deal with the ambiguities and paradoxes in their lives.

2. Validate the paradoxes that Jewish adults struggle with by offering opportunities for discussion about those conflicts. This includes incorporating dialogic activities into classes and programs that are "informational," helping people to find study partners, working with learn-

ers to help them develop critical thinking skills, and encouraging individuals to study collaboratively about controversial topics.

3. Build dialogue into all adult Jewish learning activities. Help learners to create dialogues with themselves (through journal writing and other reflective activities), with their teachers, and with one another. Encourage them, as well, to see "wrestling with angels" as a crucial and potentially valuable aspect of adult Jewish growth.

4. Introduce learners to resources that will help them to learn about a range of alternative points of view. Encourage them to consult books, periodicals, Internet resources,[4] and study programs, and then to discuss what they have learned with you and others.

5. Recognize that while Jewish adult learning can provide new frameworks that support Jewish adults in new meaning-making, it can also "destabilize" learners' lives and cause them to experience a sense of alienation with the people closest to them. Encourage learners to begin dialogues with family members whose lives may be affected by their growth and change. Serve as a supportive resource to these families, helping each person to see that there are multiple ways to find meaning in Judaism.

---

4. Two helpful Internet resources that link adult learners to a range of resources are www.myjewishlearning.com (co-produced by Hebrew College and Jewish Family & Life) and www.kolel.org (produced by Kolel: The Adult Centre for Liberal Jewish Learning).

6

Know Before Whom You Stand:
Preparing to Meet the Learners

*When you pray, know before whom you stand. And in this way you
will win the future world.*
                        —*Babylonian Talmud,* B'rachot *28b*

Da lifnei mi atah omeid. The words of Reb Eliezer are clear: "When you
pray, *know before whom you stand.*" When Jews enter a sanctuary or begin a
moment of personal prayer to God or even come "face-to-face" with other
humans, we are reminded by the Talmud to "be prepared," to pay attention
to what we are about to encounter. In the classroom, Jewish professionals
face a special challenge: not only do they stand before God, they stand
before their adult audience as well.

In the preceding chapters, I have described how important it is for
Jewish professionals to understand and respond to the *developmental* tasks
Jewish adults face in their lives and learning. We turn now to some of
the challenges involved in *teaching* adults—in meeting the range of needs
and expectations that these students bring to the classroom beyond the
developmental issues we have discussed. We will also explore some of
the strategies educators can use to motivate adults to "stretch and grow"
as learners and as Jews.

When I consult with rabbis and educators about working with Jewish
adults, I typically am asked questions about how professionals can effectively serve learners and their needs. The questions reveal how challenging Jewish professionals find it to respond appropriately to the daunting range of backgrounds, expectations, learning styles, and priorities
found in any group of Jewish adults. Indeed, when I recently gave a
workshop on adult learning at a meeting of Jewish professionals, I received
such questions as:

How do I deal with a class that includes people with traditional backgrounds *and* people who barely know how to bless the Shabbat candles (and everything in between!)?

What is the best way to accommodate a group when some people want lectures and others prefer study and conversation?

Some learners come for *torah lishmah,* but others come to "get the basics." And then there are the "schmoozers" who are just glad to get together—they aren't that interested in content per se. What's the best way to design a curriculum when there's such a mix of attitudes about what people are coming for?

How can I integrate newcomers into a study group that has been meeting for a long time?

How can I get younger people and more men to come to Jewish adult learning programs?

Rabbi Ariel Jordan's Story

To illustrate some of the challenges of working with a mix of learners, let's consider the experience of Rabbi Ariel Jordan, a rabbi at a small synagogue in the Southwest, who occasionally consults with me about her work with adult learners. Only two years into her career, Rabbi Jordan aspires to become successful as an adult educator and is beginning to appreciate the challenge of (1) designing programs that will attract adults to Jewish learning and (2) being responsive to the diversity of learners who come to the door. Story 6 illustrates the different kinds of learners often found in contemporary adult Jewish learning activities and highlights some of the strategies Jewish professionals might use to accommodate the mix of people before whom they stand.

◈ Story 6 ◈

RABBI ARIEL JORDAN

Rabbi Ariel Jordan was hired after her ordination in 1999 by Congregation Kulanu (CK), a synagogue of 180 families. During the first two years at CK, she developed a family education program in which she got her first taste of teaching Jewish adults. Having spent many years as a religious school teacher and camp counselor, Rabbi Jordan had been somewhat apprehensive about working with parents and other adult learners: her teaching style was more experiential than academic, and she feared that many of her adult members would be patronizing (after all, to some she was young enough to be their daughter!) or resistive to her "hands-on" approach to Jewish education.

Nonetheless, in her Rosh HaShanah sermon in 2001, Rabbi Jordan announced that she would teach a four-session course, "Making Meaning of *Tzedakah*," later that fall. In the sermon she explained that the idea for the course had been sparked by her cherished memories of Friday evenings of her childhood, when her grandmother, a life member of Hadassah, would put a contribution to Hadassah Hospital into a special *tzedakah* box. Rabbi Jordan said that she especially remembered her grandmother's annual "emptying of the box" that resulted in a check being sent off to the hospital in Jerusalem. Moreover, she commented:

> When I went to Hebrew University during my junior year of college, I volunteered on a children's ward at Hadassah Hospital. And every time I walked onto the hospital campus, I was moved by the realization that my grandmother had seen herself as personally obligated to get those buildings built and those labs equipped and both Jewish and non-Jewish patients treated. My grandma never questioned her responsibility to act justly—to do the mitzvah of *tzedakah* and think of the needs of others. To her that was what Jews just *do*.

Rabbi Jordan told the congregation that later, when she became a Jewish professional, her deepest hope was to help others understand the meaning of *tzedakah*. She said she wanted to raise this issue for study and group dialogue at CK and "to begin to create a community conversation about *tzedakah* as a core value of Judaism rather than as a knee-jerk reaction associated with reaching—or not reaching—for one's checkbook."

To Rabbi Jordan's delight, nine people showed up at the first session of the "Making Meaning of *Tzedakah*" class. When she asked why they had come, she was intrigued by the variety of responses.

Annette, age thirty-two, said that she had grown up in a "vaguely Christian" family but now was married to a Jewish man who "wants the children to grow up in a Jewish home and wants us to have a united front teaching our kids Jewish values." Annette said that she eventually might convert to Judaism but first wanted to take some general classes: "I need to learn basic Jewish ideas and practices. I want to know what people mean when they use certain words or phrases. I've heard the term *tzedakah,* but I don't know what it really means or how it translates into meaningful action."

Bob, age forty-five, explained that he grew up in a Conservative family and became a bar mitzvah. As a teenager he attended Young Judea camps and after college spent a year working on a kibbutz in Israel. "For many years, my Jewish identity was all about Israel. I've been active in Federation and B'nai B'rith—lots of fund-raising." However, after Bob's mother died three years ago, he found himself attracted to "the more spiritual side of Judaism." He and his sister attended a retreat about Jewish grief, and he was deeply moved by the experience of "finding people like myself to say *Kaddish* with." Now Bob has been diagnosed with hepatitis C, and as he faces months of treatment, he said he is seeking new learning experiences that will help him put his Judaism and Jewish values in perspective.

Cele, age seventy-eight, mentioned that her parents had been founding members of Congregation Kulanu in the 1930s and that she was a member of the temple's first religious school classes: "I guess I started Sunday school when I was about nine, and I've been going to classes here ever since!" Cele said that in recent years she has started to learn some Hebrew from an Israeli neighbor: "After all those years as a classical Reform Jew, I finally decided it was time to learn the *alef-bet.*" Cele mentioned that except when she travels to visit her grandchildren, she attends every adult learning Jewish event held in the community.

Dorit, age fifty-three, said that she was raised in a secular family in Israel but learned *Tanach* in school and later studied text with other adults in Jerusalem. Now married to an information sciences professor who is on leave from his university in Tel Aviv, Dorit has lived in the United States for four years and said she enjoys having the chance to immerse herself in study on a regular basis: "In Israel, I was always having to squeeze in text study after long days of working and commuting. Here I am more at leisure and am able to take classes or find out things on the Internet." She noted that although she knows a lot about *tzedakah*, she hopes the class will point her to interesting commentaries about the topic: "Once I begin thinking about something, I do a lot of reading on my own."

Earl, age fifty, introduced himself by saying that he's not a scholar and may not "fit into a class with all you serious people." Earl's parents were Jewish, but he received no formal Jewish education. His ex-wife insisted they join CK when their children were young, but the only time Earl came to the congregation was when the children were participating in a family service. In recent years, Earl and his wife have divorced, and the children live with their mother in a nearby community. Earl said he has been quite isolated and is now spending time at CK and the Jewish Community Center so that he can meet other Jewish adults.

Francine, age forty-two, said that although she was confirmed at a Reform synagogue, little of her Jewish education "stuck." Now, as a parent to children in a liberal Jewish day school, she is eager to become Jewishly informed: "It's been important to understand what my children are learning and to be able to talk to them about Judaism in a way that feels authentic." She said that soon her oldest child will have to do a *tzedakah* project as part of her bat mitzvah year, and Francine doesn't want to ask her to "do *tzedakah* without understanding what that really means."

Gina, age thity-eight, recounted a "very positive life as a Jewish learner," both in her family's Reconstructionist congregation and later when she studied comparative religion in college. She recalled getting a lot out of a class CK's former rabbi taught about *Pirkei Avot* and hopes that this class will get her back into some regular Jewish study. Gina recently received custody of her eight-year-old son and said she was looking for some new ways to think about the challenges she faces as she tries to balance her career as a systems analyst with the responsibilities of single parenting.

Helene, age sixty-six, a retired librarian, has recently moved to CK's community "to be near my children and grandchildren." Helene grew up in a Conservative home but raised her children Reform: "My husband had a minimal Jewish background and was always more comfortable in a Reform setting." Ten years ago Helene became an adult bat mitzvah and found that preparing for that event rekindled an old passion for Jewish learning. In her previous community, she participated in a two-year Jewish literacy program for adults and resolved always to have a Jewish study group with whom to exchange ideas. She said she now hopes to start a Jewish book group for her Hadassah chapter but wants more scholarly grounding before she brings people together to learn.

Irving, age fifty-one, attended an Orthodox *cheder* until age thirteen, but lost all interest in Judaism when his father died prematurely right before Irving's bar mitzvah. He mentioned how resentful he was that when his father died, the synagogue's treasurer had insensitively approached his mother about paying off a pledge to their *shul*'s building fund: "Here was my mother, wondering how we were going to meet our house payments, and this s.o.b. is hocking her for money." Irving said he distanced himself from the organized Jewish community for many years, but recently has found himself "wanting to revisit Judaism and get rid of the baggage after all these years of feeling like an outsider." He said he decided it would be easiest to find "a way in" in a Reform congregation where people are "committed to making informed choices about Judaism." Planning to take early retirement, Irving wants to learn about ways an affluent Jew like himself can "give back to the community."

As shown in Exhibit 6-1, the group before Rabbi Jordan found herself "standing" ranged in age (thirty-two to seventy-eight), Jewish background (secular to Orthodox, plus one non-Jew), level of Jewish education (none to *cheder*), familiarity with Hebrew (none to a native Hebrew speaker), and types of interest in the course topic (nine different agendas). In addition, women outnumbered men by two to one.

In planning for the class, Rabbi Jordan had known that she wanted to give the learners an opportunity to think about the meaning of *tzedakah* in their own lives. She planned to include some text study but sensed that in a congregation that did not have a core group of experienced text learners, an introductory adult learning course would not be the time to focus exclusively on traditional sources. She anticipated that there would be some diversity among class members in terms of age, gender, Jewish educational background, and learning preferences. Accordingly, she planned a course with the intent to employ a variety of teaching strategies to accommodate a range of

EXHIBIT 6-1

Background and Interests of Learners at Congregation Kulanu

Name	Age	Jewish Background	Jewish Education	Stated Interests
Annette	32	(Christian)	None	Wants to learn basic Jewish ideas and practices to help raise Jewish children "authentically"
Bob	45	Conservative	Bar mitzvah; Israel kibbutz experience; Jewish spiritual retreat	Wants to understand *tzedakah* so that he can find spiritual meaning in the face of life-threatening disease
Cele	78	Reform (classical)	Has attended classes at CK since childhood	Sees learning as the way to maintain ongoing connection in the CK community
Dorit	53	Secular; Israeli	Educated in Israel; ongoing text study	Is a lifelong learner who wants to understand all aspects of Judaism through text and commentaries
Earl	50	Secular	None	Recently divorced; looking for places to meet other Jews
Francine	42	Secular	Introduction to Judaism class; Hebrew and family education workshops	Wants to help her daughter do a *tzedakah* project for her bat mitzvah
Gina	38	Reconstructionist	Bat mitzvah; confirmation; comparative religion major in college	Is facing new parenting challenges and wonders if Jewish learning can provide a new perspective
Helene	66	Conservative	Religious school; adult bat mitzvah; graduate of a two-year Jewish literacy program for adults	Would like to start a Jewish book group, but wants to get more background about Judaism and Jewish values
Irving	51	Orthodox	*Cheder* until age 13	Wants to "revisit" Judaism after many years of alienation

learning needs and styles. Shortly before the first class, a colleague sent her information about a nationwide *tzedakah* program being envisioned by a coalition of Reform, Conservative, and Reconstructionist synagogue leaders; she decided to use the last part of the course to invite the learners to become involved in this program, the Corners of the Field project. Exhibit 6-2 presents Rabbi Jordan's course plan.

Rabbi Jordan's "Making Meaning of *Tzedakah*" class met for four consecutive weeks. Structurally, the class proceeded along the lines the rabbi had envisioned. However, the dynamics were not always what she expected. As she interacted with and observed the learners, Rabbi Jordan noted differences among the students in terms of their classroom behavior, level of comfort with text study, values about *tzedakah,* and priorities as learners.

Diverse Classroom Behaviors. From the first class onward, Rabbi Jordan was aware that Irving and Cele were ready to "jump in" to discussions, while Dorit and Francine were more interested in analyzing written materials. Earl tended to ask many "how-to" questions, and Bob used his laptop to record many notes. When, in the second class, Rabbi Jordan asked class members to write down personal lists of times they had been aware of *tzedakah* in their lives, both Irving and Cele enthusiastically started making an accounting and then engaged one another in a lively conversation about their experiences; at the same time, Francine and Gina made what appeared to be perfunctory lists and spent most of the pair-share time talking about their children's busy lives. Later in that session, when Rabbi Jordan proposed role playing to tap into the feelings people have when they are asked for contributions, Dorit was clearly impatient and went outside to use her cell phone during that activity. Other people—especially gregarious Earl—took to the role playing with gusto, prompting considerable levity in the class as people shared their reactions to solicitations by representatives of the Jewish Federation and other organizations. After the second class session, when Bob was undergoing treatment for hepatitis C and was too tired to come to class, he called and asked Rabbi Jordan to send him materials he could study on his own. And after the third class, when Rabbi Jordan asked people to find *tzedakah* commentaries on the Internet, Gina responded by e-mailing the group the addresses of several dozen Web sites she had found that, she said,

EXHIBIT 6-2

Course Plan for "Making Meaning of *Tzedakah*"

Session 1
1. Introductions
2. Small groups (triads): Discuss Maimonides' "Laws Concerning Gifts to the Poor."
3. Discussion: Is charitable giving as "an obligation to promote the common good" different from giving as "a way to make oneself feel good."
4. Lecture on the evolution of the concept of *tzedakah*.

Session 2
1. Read story from *Four Centuries of Jewish Women's Spirituality.**
2. Discussion: What is the difference between *tzedakah* and charity?
3. Personal reflection: List times when you were aware of *tzedakah* in your life or through the behavior of others. Pair-share lists.
4. Large group: Role-play telephone conversations with phone solicitors who call at dinnertime. Discuss how contemporary Jews view "obligation" versus "choice."

Session 3
1. Text study orientation: Show learners how to read a text, find commentaries, identify arguments, personalize material.
2. Review Miriam Steinberg's d'var Torah on *tzedakah* (2001).
3. Text study (hevruta-style) of portions of Leviticus, Amos, Maimonides' Mishneh Torah, and *Pirkei Avot*.
   Questions: How is *tzedakah* portrayed in traditional texts? What can we infer about the different meanings of the term *tzedakah?*
4. Homework: For Session 4, use the Internet or library to find a commentary or d'var Torah that extends your thinking about *tzedakah*. (See, for example: "Deepening our *Tzedakah*" article at www.Socialaction.com).

Session 4
1. Large group: Discuss commentaries on *tzedakah* that students bring to class.
2. Text study (hevruta-style) on verses about "the corners of the field."
3. Wrap up: Starting a "corners of the field" project at Congregation Kulanu.

---

*Story by Rabbi Sue Levi Elwell (1992) about a poor seamstress who transformed remnants from garments she sewed for the rich into Rosh HaShanah outfits for poor children in an orphanage; the seamstress's *tzedakah* took the form of notes the children found tucked into the pockets of these outfits. Many years later, a wealthy philanthropist explained that he came to do *tzedakah* because of the impact of receiving those notes—knowing that someone had felt it her responsibility to let him know he was "not alone in the world" during his lonely childhood.

"really opened my eyes—and my heart—to what *tzedakah* means in our lives today."

Diverse Levels of Comfort with Course Content. In the text study sessions, Dorit, Irving, and Helene enjoyed learning with one another; each had previous experience with text study, and they all appeared eager to get into meaningful conversations about the texts and commentaries. Conversely, Annette and Earl indicated early on that they were unfamiliar with text study and would need considerable guidance. Annette opted not to attend the session that was devoted to text study and later left Rabbi Jordan a message saying she felt she might be better off in a course for potential converts. Earl also decided to skip the text study session, telling Rabbi Jordan that the focus on texts wasn't going to help him with his immediate goal of getting to know people better.

Differing Values. Although everyone in the class was interested in *tzedakah*, there were marked differences in the group regarding priorities and concerns. The older learners, Cele and Helene, spoke affectionately of Israel and said that Rabbi Jordan's Rosh HaShanah remarks about Hadassah Hospital had kindled positive memories of fund-raising for Zionist causes. The younger class members, especially Gina and Francine, talked of their more immediate concerns—issues of hunger and unfair treatment of immigrants that they felt Jews should be addressing more conscientiously. Rabbi Jordan also noted that there was an interesting divide in terms of gender: as a group, the women had more recent and compelling experience with Jewish learning than did the men. Nonetheless, the men were eager to advance their views, and class discussions were not dominated by one gender or the other.

Differing Priorities as Learners. Even though the *content* of each class seemed to interest the learners, in the long run Rabbi Jordan sensed that what mattered most to these Jewish adults was the opportunity to come together in a warm and inclusive atmosphere that helped them to talk about something of relevance in their lives. By the fourth session, it was clear to her that many of these learners would be responsive to the idea of getting involved in the Corners of the Field project.

While initially she had been concerned that the course she designed wasn't "academic" enough, in the long run she found that providing a range of learning experiences and modalities seemed to work well for the majority of the students.

Rabbi Jordan's Story: Insights from the Adult Learning Experts

Rabbi Ariel Jordan's story provides the basis for discussing a number of issues that have been addressed in scholarship about what adults bring to learning situations and how educators can understand the learners before whom they stand:

- Groups of adult learners tend to be marked by the learners' differences from one another as much as their commonalities. The diversity of backgrounds, aspirations, educational needs, and learning styles among adults creates a particular challenge for educators who wish to set up welcoming learning environments.
- Diversity also extends to issues of age and gender, both of which influence what occurs in adult learning settings. Adults born in different eras, countries, and social contexts bring varying expectations to their learning. These additional aspects of diversity must be taken into account when educators plan adult learning programs.
- Adult learners are different from child learners because they bring to the learning situation a breadth of life experiences that influences their stance and expectations as learners. Educators need to be attentive to learners' needs for self-direction, reservoir of experience, social roles, and interest in immediate application.
- Although adults may be eager to learn, educators can increase their motivation by actively encouraging their participation in the learning process. Motivational strategies can help to make learners feel included and can offer them ways to find relevance, broaden perspective, and acquire feedback about how their learning interfaces with their lives.

Learning Orientations

Studies of adult learners reveal that they each bring different expectations to the learning experience, especially in terms of what they perceive as the value of the learning itself. By first assessing learners' orientations, an educator can design programs that meet people "where they are at" rather than assuming that a one-size-fits-all model will work.

Although little empirical research has been conducted about Jewish adult learners, the typology of learning orientations reported by researcher Cyril Houle provides a useful framework for assessing the learners in Rabbi Jordan's class. According to Houle (1961), most adult learners bring one of three orientations to their learning.

- Some are *goal-oriented* individuals who look to learning as a means to obtain a specific objective; typically these learners will use their new knowledge in order to gain a change in status in their personal or professional lives.
- Other learners are more *activity-oriented* and participate in learning primarily for the sake of the activity itself; rather than looking to develop a skill or learn content, these people like the social dimensions of education and enjoy having the opportunity to interact with other learners.
- Some learners are *learning-oriented* individuals who tend to pursue learning for its own sake; they possess a fundamental desire to know and to grow through new inquiry.

A fourth learning orientation that has yet to be established empirically but may be particularly relevant to adults in religious education settings pertains to learners who are *spiritually-oriented,* who use learning to deepen their self-understanding and to acquire a sense of meaning or coherence in their lives.[5]

As shown in Exhibit 6-3, the learners in the "Making Meaning of *Tzedakah*" class can be described in terms of these four different learning orientations. Annette, Francine, and Irving are goal-oriented: each wants to learn about *tzedakah* to function more effectively in their present life circumstances. Cele and Earl can be described as primarily activity-oriented learners: Cele attends Jewish education activities as a way to maintain active involvement with the synagogue community; Earl, who has recently divorced, seeks out synagogue events to meet new people and have activities

---

5. I am grateful to Dr. Jonathan Mirvis, International Director of the Florence Melton Adult Mini-School, for suggesting this fourth type of adult learner orientation to me.

EXHIBIT 6-3

Learning Orientations and Preferences

Rabbi Jordan's Students	Learning Orientation	Learning Preferences
Annette: Wants to learn Jewish approaches to effective parenting. **Francine:** Wants to understand *tzedakah* to help daughter with bat mitzvah project. **Irving:** Hopes to "reconnect" with Judaism and get a clearer understanding of how to practice *tzedakah*.	**Goal-oriented learners** use learning to gain specific objectives that help them to change their "status" in their personal or professional lives.	Demonstrations Hands-on activities Information sessions Action guidelines
Cele: Attends Jewish learning programs to maintain involvement in the synagogue and Jewish community. **Earl:** Looks for activities that may bring him into social contact with Jewish people.	**Activity-oriented learners** participate in learning primarily for the sake of the activity itself (including the social aspects) rather than to develop a skill or learn a subject.	Personal sharing Group discussions Cooperative learning projects Retreats Field trips Extracurricular activities
Dorit: Studies *lishmah*, for the sake of learning. Uses learning to spark further learning, often independently. **Helene:** Wants to acquire Jewish knowledge to teach others.	**Learning-oriented learners** pursue learning for its own sake and possess a fundamental desire to know and to grow through learning.	Text analysis Comparing commentaries Case studies Reflective writing exercises Debates Independent learning projects
Bob: Facing personal losses and medical problems; hopes that learning can help him clarify his Jewish values. **Gina:** Looks to Jewish tradition for spiritual guidance and support in parenting.	**Spiritually-oriented learners** use learning to acquire a sense of meaning or coherence in their lives.	Autobiographical exercises Reading spiritual stories Handmade midrash Bibliodrama Values clarification activities Reflective writing exercises

to attend. By contrast, Dorit and Helene bring to adult Jewish learning more of a *torah lishmah* (study "for its own sake" or learning-centered) orientation: Dorit, fluent in Hebrew, has studied Jewish texts for many years and learns "for the sake of learning"; as a learner, she wants to "go beyond" the text and study what various commentators have written. Helene, a retired librarian, hopes to develop a Jewish book group but first wants to immerse herself in ideas that will help her to think more globally about Judaism and Jewish values. Finally, Bob and Gina each wonder if Jewish learning might help them with the current changes in their lives: Bob has recently been diagnosed with hepatitis C and faces months of drug therapy. Gina has just received legal custody of her eight-year-old son and is finding herself overwhelmed emotionally with the changes implicit in her new roles and responsibilities. These individuals may be seen as *spiritually-oriented* learners who hope some of their needs may be met through Jewish learning experiences.

Exhibit 6-3 also demonstrates that adults who have different learning orientations tend to prefer different kinds of learning activities. Jewish professionals need to be attuned not only to the different expectations learners bring into the learning environment, but the kinds of activities that will engage them (or possibly turn them off). By mixing and matching activities, an educator can create an environment that serves the needs of different groups. At the same time, because learning orientations often shift as learners become involved in the learning process (e.g., goal-oriented learners become more spiritually-oriented; activity-oriented learners become more learning-oriented), participation in diverse activities will expose them to a range of approaches and alternative ways to think about Judaism and Jewish learning.

Learning Styles

Beyond distinct learning orientations, adults also have preferred learning styles. While there are many "typologies" that categorize learning styles, the work of Jerold Apps (1991), as presented in Exhibit 6-4, captures the essence of the different ways people process information or look to education for help. According to Apps, *sequential* learners prefer carefully planned and structured learning activities; *practical* learners prefer fast-paced instruction that leads to immediate application; and *intuitive* learners prefer learning that involves reflection and personal

EXHIBIT 6-4

Learning Styles

Rabbi Jordan's Students	Learning Style	Preferred Teaching Strategies
Bob: Likes written materials he can study on his own. **Francine:** Wants a curriculum about *tzedakah* that is organized and explicit.	**Sequential learners:** Appreciate carefully planned learning experiences where they know exactly what is to be learned and how they should learn it. Prefer to learn things in order and to have units of information build on one another.	Lecture Print materials Handouts Programmed instruction
Annette: Likes demonstrations and simulations that help her to practice Jewish rituals. **Dorit:** Wants to focus on text and avoid personal storytelling. **Earl:** Wants to learn from explicit examples. **Irving:** Looking for information that will help him make decisions about *tzedakah*.	**Practical learners:** Want fast-paced teaching that has immediate application. Have little patience for "getting acquainted" teaching tools and other activities that foster a sense of community. Prefer teaching approaches that use examples directly applicable to their situation. Have little time for what they perceive as theoretical material unless they can see immediate application to practice.	Debates Demonstrations Simulation games Case studies
Cele: Enjoys sharing her own ideas and learning from others. **Gina:** Wants to learn from others so as to better understand own life and parenting situation. **Helene:** Wants to learn by engaging in study with others.	**Intuitive learners:** Prefer learning when both feeling and thinking are combined. Want to find meaning for themselves. Resent having a teacher tell them what/how they should learn. Appreciate getting to know other learners as people and for the knowledge fellow learners have to share.	Discussions Breakout groups Role playing Dyads or triads Group projects Panels Field trips

meaning-making. These differing learning styles cause learners to respond to some teaching strategies more favorably than others. Although Jewish professionals can't please all the learners all the time, they can incorporate a range of teaching strategies into their adult learning programs, thus providing options for individuals who have different learning preferences.

The responses of Rabbi Jordan's students suggest that they may have different learning style preferences. Francine and Bob are *sequential learners* who prefer classes where there is a lecture and a clear outline of material. Francine likes learning that is structured and focused; she wants a curriculum about *tzedakah* that will help her to organize her thinking and guide her in supporting her daughter when she undertakes a bat mitzvah *tzedakah* project. Bob prefers receiving written materials that he can study on his own; he is interested in "building a case" about *tzedakah* and requests information that can help him organize his ideas.

Dorit, Earl, and Annette are *practical learners*: each comes at learning with a desire to gather information in an active, efficient manner. In order to assess the value of rabbinical texts on *tzedakah*, Dorit has little patience for group activities such as role playing; she wants to focus on the texts and avoid personal storytelling. Earl, a newcomer to Jewish learning, asks for practical guidelines that will make Judaism more immediate and relevant. As someone considering conversion, Annette is preoccupied with learning the basics of Judaism; she prefers learning that helps her to efficiently translate abstract concepts into her daily behavior.

Cele, Gina, Helene, and Irving are *intuitive* learners. They seek meaning in what they read and discuss, and they are comfortable with group dialogue that includes personal sharing. These learners are willing to let the learning agenda evolve as the class moves along, expanding their understanding of content as befits the current moment.

Exhibit 6-5 synthesizes details about Rabbi Jordan's learners and reveals some of the complexity that faces a Jewish professional who stands before a group of adults and aspires to meet their learning needs most effectively. Optimally, an adult educator will respond to the diversity of the learners by becoming flexible and creative with teaching strategies. However, because learners bring such a range of orientations and learning styles to the classroom, and because different teachers have different teaching strengths, not all learners' preferences can be addressed at once.

EXHIBIT 6-5

Adult Learners at Congregation Kulanu

Name	Learning Orientation	Learning Style
Annette	Goal-oriented	Practical
Bob	Spiritually-oriented	Sequential
Cele	Activity-oriented	Intuitive
Dorit	Learning-oriented	Practical
Earl	Activity-oriented	Practical
Francine	Goal-oriented	Sequential
Gina	Spiritually-oriented	Intuitive
Helene	Learning-oriented	Intuitive
Irving	Goal-oriented	Practical

Birth Cohort Factors

Adult learner diversity has many dimensions. Returning to Exhibit 6-1, we are reminded that not only do the learners on Rabbi Jordan's list have different learning orientations and learning styles, they bring to their Jewish learning a range of backgrounds and life experiences. Their ages range from Annette, a thirty-two-year-old non-Jew, to Cele, who is seventy-eight and remembers when her father was the first president of the congregation when it was founded in the 1930s. Overall, the class members represent several "birth cohorts"— groups of individuals who grew up in a particular era and thus share a common understanding based on the times in which they have lived. Learners like Helene (age sixty-six) and Cele (age seventy-eight) came of age shortly after World War II; it is likely that their understanding of Jewish community and *tzedakah*, as well as many other issues about Jewish life, were shaped directly by family immigration patterns, the Holocaust, the founding of the State of Israel, Jewish migration to the suburbs, and other events and issues. Many people of this cohort (though by no means all) expect learning to be teacher centered: they were raised to respect the Jewish scholar as the expert, and when they attend learning events they expect to "sit and listen."

By contrast, baby boomers like Bob (age forty-five), Earl (age fifty), and Irving (age fifty-one) grew up in an era of economic prosperity and social activism; their generation of Jewish teens lived in the suburbs, often received a "watered-down" Jewish education, and associated Jewish learning more with social activism than classroom study. Accordingly, many (though not all) adults of this cohort approach Jewish learning with a measure of skepticism: why talk about it instead of "doing something"? Ironically, a significant proportion of this cohort have looked to—and even studied—other religious traditions (especially Eastern religions) but do not appreciate the depth or breadth of Jewish knowledge that could give a new sense of purpose to their lives. Almost universally college-educated, these adults are accustomed to bringing critical thinking skills to their learning and do not want to be "talked at." Once they begin to study in a serious way, they tend to become devotees of Jewish learning and, as they look toward retirement, seek multiple Jewish adult education opportunities on a continuing basis.

An even younger cohort is represented by Gina (age thirty-eight) and Francine (age forty-two), who came of age in the 1970s and 1980s—a time of Jewish institutional expansion. Many of these adults were socialized by Jewish camps and group trips to Israel; some were drawn to thriving Hillels and budding Jewish studies courses on their college campuses. Although many of this cohort may have had limited formal experience with Jewish learning, as adults they are accustomed to speedily accessing new information and ideas when they feel impelled to overcome ignorance. Accustomed to the postmodern approach to learning that routinely challenges "absolutes," adults of this group expect to look at Judaism and Jewish texts through "multiple lenses." They like to compare the Jewish experience with that of other groups, and many (though not all) resist narrow definitions of Jewish practice or identity.

Jewish professionals must pay attention to the cohort factors that influence the experience and outlook of their learners. Different groups will respond to the Jewish study experience based on how they were socialized earlier in life. Jewish adults bring to the learning situation frames of reference heavily influenced by when they were born, what their families experienced, and how Judaism and Jewish life were expressed during their formative years. Jewish professionals must show sensitivity to cohort factors and to the differential attitudes of adults who grew up at different times, in different places, knowing different Judaisms or Jewish communities.

Gender

Rabbi Jordan's group included six women and three men. These statistics are representative of more universal patterns of gender participation in adult Jewish learning activities today. In a recent survey of adult Jewish learning in America, Steven M. Cohen and Aryeh Davidson (2001) report that women surpass men in their frequency of participation in Jewish learning activities. Cohen and Davidson note that "women are generally more religious and community oriented, and more invested in their roles as spouses and Jewish parents as compared to men" (p. 13). They observe that in the larger community, females are more likely than males to "join communal organizations, participate in volunteer work and attend religious services." Accordingly, these authors speculate, it may be that, compared to men, women see Jewish learning as "more firmly linked to . . . Jewish familial, religious, and communal participation." In other words, given women's greater attention to family, religion, and community, it should be no surprise that women seek out Jewish learning more often than do men.

Cohen and Davidson also speculate that Jewish women may also be seeking to "compensate for weaker experiences in Jewish education as children." This, they note, becomes especially significant as more women become leaders in Jewish organizations previously controlled by men. With their ascendancy to leadership roles in synagogues, Federations, and major Jewish organizations, Jewish women may feel particularly motivated to acquire the literacy they missed (or were excluded from) before.

As discussed in chapter 5, a number of adult education researchers have theorized that women learners may bring different "ways of knowing" to the adult education classroom. Sometimes women's adult learning goals are different from those of men because of their different socialization. Thus, more women than men may prefer Jewish learning situations in which group support and sharing are the norm. But some men (like Bob) seek Jewish learning because they are looking for spiritual guidance, and some women (like Dorit and Helene) seek opportunities for rigorous discourse and debate. To date, there is no research that compares women and men in Jewish educational settings. What *is* known is that, in all Jewish adult learning programs outside the Orthodox community, more women than men enroll, women are highly motivated adult Jewish learners, and there is wide variability in Jewish women's learning needs, styles, and orientations.

Consequently, when planning learning programs for Jewish adults, Jewish professionals should expect a plurality of women (but, correspondingly, should also think about ways to reach out and be responsive to men). In addition, they should consider whether women-only, men-only, or mixed classes will serve the learning needs of people in their community. They need to be sensitive to gender differences in the classroom. And they need to think about how their own gender (as well as age) may impact their perceptions of their learners, as well as the expectations and attitudes of the learners before whom they stand.[6]

Knowing the Adult Learner: Andragogy and Beyond

Beyond the issue of learner diversity lies a broader issue that has been at the center of a lengthy academic debate about adult learners: *is adult learning different from children's learning?* Malcolm Knowles, who began writing about adult learners in the 1970s, coined the term "andragogy" to differentiate the adult learning experience from more child-centered "pedagogy." In Knowles's view, adult learners bring to the learning experience a set of characteristics that distinguish their learning needs from the needs of children. Knowles's theory of andragogy (1980) is based on five assumptions about the adult learner:

1. As a person matures, his or her self-concept moves from that of a dependent personality toward one of a self-directing human being.
2. An adult accumulates a growing reservoir of experience, which is a rich resource for learning.
3. The readiness to learn is closely related to the developmental tasks of a learner's social role.
4. There is a change in time perspective as people mature—from future application of knowledge to immediacy of application. Thus, as a learner, an adult is more "problem centered" (often wondering, "How

---

6. In *Women as Learners: The Significance of Gender in Adult Learning* (San Francisco: Jossey-Bass, 2000), Elisabeth Hayes and Daniele Flannery provide an insightful overview of these issues.

will this material apply to my current life situation?") than "subject centered" ("What is the scope of this content?").

5. Adults are motivated to learn by internal factors rather than external ones.

These principles about the adult learner have shaped the thinking of many adult education scholars. Allen Tough (1979) has studied Knowles's first point—*the self-direction of adult learners*—and has concluded that adults initiate new "learning projects" all the time. When motivated to learn something new, Tough notes, most people take the initiative to find the resources to become newly informed and expand their understanding of unfamiliar ideas or tasks. The self-direction of adult learners certainly can be seen in the widespread use of the Internet, which most people learn through independent self-tutelage, or in the popular consumption of how-to guides. Self-direction is also seen among students who participate in structured learning programs but then use the content as a jumping-off place for pursuing personal interests.

In recent years, the self-direction of adult Jewish learners is evident in their active use of Web sites devoted to Jewish study topics. The popularity of on-line *parashat hashavua* commentaries, Talmud discussion groups, and Jewish distance learning programs reflects the high motivation of Jewish adults to select and personally coordinate their Jewish learning activities.

Knowles's second point—*the distinctive role of accumulated experience* that informs an adult's learning—has been at the heart of a broad literature on what educators should do to work most effectively with adult learners. Paul Westmeyer (1988) writes that the implications of this assumption are as follows:

- The teacher must be as aware as possible of the individual backgrounds of his or her students and seek to tailor learning to accommodate what the learners bring to the educational experience.
- Course content should build on students' previous experiences and incorporate that experience into course activities (via case studies, simulations, demonstrations, etc.).
- Students in a class can draw on their own resources and backgrounds to help one another; sometimes student-to-student "instruction" is even more meaningful than input from the teacher.

- When course content permits, students' interests and experience should be extended via the use of individualized study plans or learning contracts.

Westmeyer's distillation of Knowles draws particular attention to how important it is for Jewish adult educators to *start with the learner's experience* and *help the learner to become involved in the planning of the learning experience.* Because Jewish adults come to Jewish adult education with such a wide variety of backgrounds, interests, and needs, their teachers should not expect them to adapt well to "one-size-fits-all" teaching approaches. Jewish professionals need to honor the full scope of each learner's experience—respecting and drawing on what the learner knows from his or her secular life and Jewish background.

Knowles's third point—*the relationship between developmental tasks and the adult's learning readiness*—was mentioned in chapter 3. The more Jewish professionals become familiar with the kinds of developmental tasks adults typically go through, the better they will be prepared to respond with meaningful educational offerings. Some of the developmental experiences that predispose adults for Jewish learning are associated with parenting, caring for aging parents, parental death, chronic and terminal illness, divorce and family reconfiguration, intermarriage, geographic relocation, job shift, and retirement. Each of these "social role" events may lead to "teachable moments" that are meaningful to Jewish adults who are in transition or are trying to redirect some aspect of their lives.

In Jewish adult education, Knowles's fourth point—adults' *preference for immediacy of application* (often referred to as "less theory, more practice")—is sometimes interpreted by educators (or program planners) as a learner desire for abbreviated content or one-shot learning events. And, in some cases, very pragmatic workshops—on holiday observance or community action or how to read the *siddur*—will help adults to quickly acquire and act on useful information. However, this "quick-fix" approach may have negative consequences for people who need more time to process unfamiliar ideas and customs before being able to make thoughtful decisions about practice. And even though information can be dispensed in small doses, adult learners generally benefit from a series of learning events that help them to try on ideas or activities and then revisit those experiences in a systematic way. Short courses (such as a "four Tuesday evenings" class or a weekend of learning activities that build on one another) provide "immediacy" while simultaneously enabling the learner to process information in a more reflective and thoughtful way.

Regardless of the structure of the learning event, Knowles's fourth point underscores that most adults seek relevance in whatever they are learning: they want to know "how will this benefit me?" or "how can I apply this to my current situation?" Even individuals who study *lishmah*—for the sheer joy of learning—are pleased to find connections between what they are learning and their current life situations. Most Jewish adults are intrigued when they realize that traditional texts and insights have credibility and meaning today. Jewish professionals need to anticipate the desire Jewish adults have to see how what they are learning pertains to their lives and themselves as Jews.

Knowles's fifth point—that *adults' learning activities stem more from their own internal needs and values than from the demands or expectations of others*—is grounded in theories of *intrinsic motivation*. Raymond Wlodkowski (1999), the leading contemporary writer about adult learner motivation, explains:

> It is part of human nature to be curious, to be active, to initiate thought and behavior, to make meaning from experience, and to be effective at what we value. These primary sources of motivation reside in all of us, across all cultures. When adults can see that what they are learning makes sense and is important according to their values and perspective, their motivation emerges. Like a cork rising through water, intrinsic motivation is an evocation, an energy called forth by circumstances that connect with what is culturally significant to the person. (p. 7)

The presence—or absence—of intrinsic motivation among Jewish adult learners is an issue that concerns many Jewish professionals today. At what point, we wonder, do Jewish adults develop the curiosity and initiative for Jewish understanding that will motivate them to learn Jewishly? What sparks a desire to come in close to Judaism or Jewish tradition? Does the motivation have to come from within the individual or can it be *utzed* (Yiddish for "pushed forward") by rabbis or educators who inspire people to find meaning in Jewish texts or experiences? And, even if a Jewish adult is motivated toward Jewish learning, what sustains that energy, what evokes an ongoing Jewish connection?

Wlodkowski (1999) has written extensively on adult learner motivation and on what educators can do to create educational environments that attract and retain learners. In *Enhancing Adult Motivation to Learn,* he recommends that educators should be guided by four goals:

- To establish an inclusive and respectful learning environment
- To help people see learning as a relevant, personal choice
- To enlarge learners' appreciation of alternative perspectives
- To help learners to feel that what they have learned is valuable and authentic in their lives

Strategies for achieving these goals are presented in Appendix 1, which synthesizes Wlodkowski's suggestions and presents strategies Jewish professionals can use to motivate and engage adult learners. Appendix 2 contains an assessment guide that Jewish educators and program administrators can use to evaluate the ways that adult learner motivation is being supported and reinforced.

In the "Making Meaning of *Tzedakah*" class, Rabbi Jordan adhered quite well to the principles advocated by Knowles and Wlodkowski. Rather than fostering learner dependency, Rabbi Jordan consistently encouraged class members to think for themselves and not look to her as the only authority. She tapped into the learners' previous experiences with learning and was respectful of what they brought to their understanding of *tzedakah* from the past. She recognized and acknowledged how their changing social roles were impacting their lives and learning. Because she believed that these learners wanted to find immediate relevance in what they were learning, she created learning activities that would help them find connections between traditional Jewish values and their current practices. She also created a supportive and inclusive learning environment that provided variety and stimulation to a diverse constituency of learners. Ultimately, Rabbi Jordan endeavored to motivate her students—to pique their curiosity and to excite them about how learning about Jewish concepts could enrich their lives. However, she also recognized that, regardless of her input, her learners would address the issue of *tzedakah* on their own terms when they were personally ready.

From Theory to Practice: Knowing Before Whom You Stand

In *Developing Teaching Style in Adult Education,* Joe Heimlich and Emmalou Norland (1994) compare the role of the educator to that of a "mad scientist": "We have a cauldron bubbling with some potent elixir. We add just a touch of some other highly potent chemical. What we hope to produce is some sort of life." Ultimately, Heimlich and Norland point out, beyond "methods, techniques, the arrangement of the room, [or] the selection and organization of the information," all educators must come to terms with the reality that they "work with that most nebulous and ethereal of factors— *other human beings*" (1994, pp. 139–140 [emphasis added]). It is those other human beings before whom Jewish professionals stand in their work as adult educators. To more fully grasp the nature and needs of their learners, Jewish professionals should:

1. Take time to find out about Jewish adult learners' orientations to learning, as well as their learning styles; create learning activities that will accommodate a range of learners, thereby acknowledging that there is more than one way to learn.

2. Pay attention to gender and cohort issues in adult Jewish learning settings. Help learners to see how they may have been socialized in terms of Jewish learning, and show them that learning is affected by past experiences. Help them to reframe their understanding of Jewish education, conceptualizing it as a lifelong process rather than something that ends in childhood.

3. Recognize that, despite what they may initially claim, Jewish adults strive to become self-directing in their learning. Accordingly, design learning programs that encourage Jewish adults to learn with peers and to share what they have learned with others. Reward learners for their "independent" learning, explaining that *every* Jewish adult can "come to the study table."

4. Accept that not all adult Jewish learners will respond positively to every Jewish professional's approach to teaching. Accommodate different learners' preferences and needs when possible, but also be prepared not to please all the people all the time. As appropriate, help learners to find alternative learning situations that better fit their needs or expectations. Sometimes this will mean steering the learner to a different teacher (or venue) that can meet his or her needs more effectively. Or it may mean helping the person to find a study partner with whom to pursue the kind of learning they prefer.

5. Encourage Jewish adults to think of Jewish professionals as *resources* for Jewish learning rather than as judgmental authority figures. Sometimes this means inviting the learner to read a book on a subject of interest and then meeting one-on-one to discuss the implications or unresolved issues. Or it might mean helping the learner to collaboratively forge an individualized study plan, with the Jewish professional serving as a mentor or coach as the learner works his or her way through thorny material. Or it may mean simply going for a walk or a cup of coffee with potential learners and exploring how their lives and their learning might be enriched by study and dialogue with other Jews.

6. Remember that not all learners can be pleased with all approaches all the time! Nor can an educator be expected to accommodate all learners' needs or expectations—especially in "one-shot" classes where there is little time to assess preferences or adapt teaching strategies. When possible, do offer a variety of classes that will reach out to different kinds of learners. And, as appropriate, work with "niche" groups of learners, tailoring the content and/or the teaching-learning process to the learners' needs and priorities.

7

Tzimtzum in Practice:
Rethinking the Teaching-Learning Partnership

The doctrine of tzimtzum, *of God's self-limitation, states that the primeval act of creation by God was not one in which the Infinite left its mysterious depths, an act of emanation from within to without, as in early Kabbalah, but that this primal step was in fact "the contraction of the Infinite from Himself to Himself," an act of self-gathering and contraction within Himself in order to create the possibility of the processes of the world. . . . Only after this act of contraction does the Infinite turn outwards, sending a thread of the light of His essence into the primeval void created by* tzimtzum, *from which there emanate the* sefirot.
—Gershom Scholem, 1997, p. 151

For decades, Jewish professionals have been intrigued with Isaac Luria's interpretation of the mystical concept of *tzimtzum* (contraction). It was through the deliberate act of *tzimtzum* at the time of Creation that God pulled back and made space for the universe and humans. As God contracted, the theory goes, divine light was dispersed, but the light was so strong that it shattered the vessels into which it was to have been contained. The shattering of the vessels sent sparks of light out into the world, and ever since, humans have been obligated to reunite the sparks and bring healing to the world.

In a widely cited essay, *"Tzimtzum:* A Mystic Model for Contemporary Leadership," Rabbi Eugene Borowitz (1974) suggests that the appeal of Luria's interpretation of the Creation story is that it provides a dynamic role for humans as co-creators with God: when God pulls back, then we can take on the mitzvah of "repairing the world." Contemporary Jews resonate to the notion that there are things people can do—can take responsibility for—to help fix the order of things and restore God's light. And, in Borowitz's view, even though there are cosmic risks when God or a parent or a leader surrenders control to subordinates, God's "withdrawal of power" ultimately assures that "His creatures . . . have full dignity" and discover their own creative potential.

In his essay, Borowitz urges Jewish professionals to contract and make space for the people they serve; by practicing *tzimtzum*, he opines, others will be energized to speak, take risks, and find their own way of improving themselves and the world. Speaking on behalf of laypeople, Borowitz admonishes Jewish leaders to beware their tendencies for excessive control:

> Normally both [teachers and clergy] are so busy doing things for us that they leave us little opportunity to do things on our own and thus find some personal independence. Both talk too much—so much so, that when they stop talking for a moment and ask for questions or honest comments, we don't believe them. We know if we stay quiet for a moment, they will start talking again. We realize that their professional roles have been built around creation by extension of the self, so they will have to prove to us by a rigorous practice of *tzimtzum* that they really want us to be persons in our own right. (1974, p. 338)

Borowitz's call to Jewish professionals to deliberately pull back and thus support the growth of their constituents corresponds with a perspective advanced by many leading adult education experts. Following on the work of Malcolm Knowles (described in chapter 6), Stephen Brookfield differentiates between the pedagogic stance of the "teacher-as-expert" and the "teacher-as-facilitator." By no means diminishing the value of the expertise the teacher brings to the learning situation, Brookfield focuses more on how an adult educator can create a learning environment that fosters the growth of the learner. He says that facilitative teachers recognize the voluntary nature of adult learner participation and respectfully acknowledge who the students are and what they bring to the learning experience. They help learners to work cooperatively and collaboratively, so that they can learn with and from one another. Additionally, facilitative teachers encourage their students to engage in a cyclical process of exploration, action, and reflection (called praxis) that helps them to see how they have arrived at certain ideas and how they might apply what they are learning. Ultimately, facilitators encourage learners to become self-directing, not dependent on the teacher when they take new steps in learning or living. Brookfield's principles of effective practice are summarized in Exhibit 7-1.

EXHIBIT 7-1

Principles of Effective Practice in Facilitating Learning

1. Participation in learning is voluntary; adults engage in learning as a result of their own volition.
2. Effective practice is characterized by a respect among participants for each other's self-worth. Foreign to facilitation are behaviors, practices, or statements that belittle others or that involve emotional or physical abuse.
3. Facilitation is collaborative. Facilitators and learners are engaged in a cooperative enterprise in which, at different times and for different purposes, leadership and facilitation roles will be assumed by different group members. This collaboration is seen in the diagnosis of needs, in the setting of objectives, in curriculum development . . . and in generating evaluative criteria.
4. Praxis is placed at the heart of effective facilitation. Learners and facilitators are involved in a continual process of activity, reflection upon activity, collaborative analysis of activity, new activity, further reflection and collaborative analysis, and so on.
5. Facilitation aims to foster in adults a spirit of critical reflection.
6. The aim of facilitation is the nurturing of self-directed, empowered adults who see themselves as proactive, initiating individuals.

Adapted from Stephen Brookfield, *Understanding and Facilitating Adult Learning* (San Francisco: Jossey-Bass, 1986).

Effective Jewish Adult Educators

Although much has been written about the characteristics and practices of adult educators in the secular community, to date there has been no systematic scholarship about teachers who work with Jewish adults. While our community is blessed with gifted individuals who do a wonderful job of helping Jewish adults to learn, we don't know much about what these teachers do in the classroom or lecture, how they see their learners, or what they believe "makes a difference" in the Jewish adult learning enterprise. To address this gap, in recent years I have asked outstanding Jewish adult educators to tell me about their teaching experiences, strategies, and philosophy, as well as their perceptions of Jewish adults as learners. In my research,

I have been fortunate to gather insights from several dozen talented rabbis and educators whose approaches shed light on *tzimtzum* and other elements of learner-centered education in the Jewish community. Jewish professionals will find their comments instructive as they reflect on how they, too, can "contract" and facilitate Jewish adult learning in meaningful ways.

Tzimtzum: *Insights from Rabbi David Nelson*

Rabbi David Nelson is an educator whose work for CLAL, the Center for Leadership and Learning (a national Jewish leadership development program), earned him a reputation as one of the finest Jewish adult teachers in America. In 2000, Rabbi Nelson served on the faculty of Kallah, a Jewish adult learning retreat sponsored by the Union of American Hebrew Congregations. Over five days, he taught a six-hour *limud* (study seminar) using rabbinic texts to illuminate the "invention" of prayer in post-biblical Judaism. Having heard from learners about how exciting they found Rabbi Nelson's *limud*, I asked David if I could interview him about his approach to Jewish adult education in general and his strategies for teaching text in particular. Initially, he asserted that while he loved to teach adults about Jewish texts, he rarely "reflected" on his practice. However, his responses to my questions were so thoughtful that I realized I was listening to someone who not only *facilitates* adult Jewish growth, but also routinely thinks about *what makes a difference* in his work as a Jewish educator.

Rabbi David Nelson's "story," as captured by his responses to my interview questions, provides compelling insight to some of the ways that *tzimtzum* can be practiced by Jewish adult education professionals. Let's begin with Rabbi Nelson's reflections and then consider a number of themes that he and other outstanding Jewish educators deem central to their work with Jewish adult learners.

ॐ Story 7 ॐ

AN INTERVIEW WITH RABBI DAVID NELSON

Diane: I've heard from many people—both your students and other teachers—that you are a "magical" text teacher. How do you teach text? Where do you begin?

David: When teaching text, I don't go, initially, into the text. Usually, first, I have people share some sort of personal story. I often do it with a physical prop, what my friend Vanessa Ochs calls "the value of playing with toys." One example of this is the Grab Bag Game, where you put a bunch of Jewish objects in a bag, and you put people in groups of five or six and tell them: "Reach into the bag, pull out an object, and tell a story or a memory."

Another example is: When I do a *shabbaton* on spirituality, I say, "Before we look at the texts—we're gonna do a lot of that this weekend—let's just get a sense, let's take the pulse of the group. Tell us about an event, a moment, an experience which you would define as spiritual, and then we'll analyze them afterwards." This does a couple of things. It allows each person, every single person in the room, to *speak,* to have their voice heard, which I think is *extremely* important. (The "new" Reform tradition of having people say the names for the *MiShebeirach* for the sick or *Kaddish* out loud has the same effect: it's very important for people just to hear their own voices.) That's the first thing.

And the second thing is that the first thing they're invited to say is something about which they are the ultimate expert: their own lives, their own experiences, their own memories, their own stories. Once you've done that, then you can move into "Well, there really are a lot of incredible stories from the group about your lives. Now we're going to expand a little bit and talk about our people's stories. . . . "

We have to get beyond the notion that either of these activities is "only an icebreaker." Because icebreakers are what get people to talk. And the first thing I want to do is, right when I get with a new group, I want to get them in a position where they can talk. And that's crucial—as opposed to: "Before we do anything else, before you say anything, before the question and answer period, I'm first gonna lecture to you." It should be: "You're the first ones that get to talk."

Diane: And after you get them talking . . . what do you do to involve people in the study process?

David: I start out with a text that I care about and I trust and I think has enough levels of meaning—it could be a biblical text or a rabbinic text, it could be anything. Once I have that text, I don't have an agenda. There isn't a set of five points that I need to make in the class. There's no great denouement where I say, "Aha! Now you've got it."

So, I sit down with the class with a text, and I have them read out loud, first of all. Because a major part of what I try to do is have them *own* the entire process. Have them own the text, have them own the process of thinking about it and analyzing it and interpreting it. They read a piece out loud, and then I'll ask a completely open-ended question, like: "What's going on here?" Or, "So what's this all about?"

My goal is severalfold. One, when they say something, I take it seriously and I repeat it back to them. "So, what you mean is that you think this text is doing such and such." I do this almost every single time someone says anything, for a few reasons. First, it's so that *I* can understand what *they* said. Second, it's so that *they* can hear what they've said. And third, it's so that if they've said something in a way that isn't really articulate enough for the other members of the class to understand, I can restate it in a way that is a little more articulate.

So that's the first methodological piece: really listening to them and validating what they are saying. I never say, "Well that's interesting, but does anyone have other ideas?" It's clear that a teacher who says that is fishing for a particular answer that he or she has in mind. I don't have an answer in mind! So wherever they go with the text, as long as they go somewhere, is interesting. I have enough confidence in my own ability to make connections that I'm willing to let them raise whatever they raise. And I'm pretty certain that I'll be able to make a connection for them to something else: "Oh that's interesting; there's a story in the Talmud that says a similar thing. Let me tell you. . . . " And I'll tell the story.

Diane: What do you do, once people are thinking about a text or a set of ideas, to move the discussion along?

David: I'll give you an example. This afternoon, in the third session of my *limud,* I said to the group, "OK. We've had two sessions already. Now what we're going to do for the first ten minutes is break into *chevruta.*"

(By the way, I write the word *chevruta* on the board. I never, never, never use a word that is unfamiliar without defining it—especially not a Hebrew word. If I forget, I apologize and ask them to stop me for any explanation.)

Then I split them into pairs: "Ten minutes. Your goal in these ten minutes is to come up with at least four questions, and then take two of these questions and come up with at least two answers for each question." They did it, and then I said, "Before we talk about your content, tell me: what was that like?"

"Well," said one person, "it was really interesting. I had to really listen." "Oh," I replied, "when you're in a big group you don't really have to listen." Then someone else said, "I could say whatever I wanted." "Very interesting," I said. "So when you're in a group of twenty, and there are five people who have their hands raised, and I say, 'OK, you're 1-2-3-4-5,' the person who's number 5 stops listening because all he or she is aware of is 'I have to remember what I want to say, I've got to think about how I say it.' Unfortunately, by the time it gets to be your turn, it's no longer relevant. Here, it's only you and your partner. He or she says something, and there are only two of you, so you've got to respond."

And then I said, "You know, as I walked around and listened to you, it sounded so wonderful. It sounded like a *beit midrash*." And that gives them a sense that they are not dumb, illiterate, ignorant fools, but that they're really part of the tradition. It validates them. It's after that—that validation—that we can begin to talk about their *chevruta* questions and answers.

Diane: I'm wondering if you have a "philosophy" of education—notions that guide how you think of your role as a teacher. What do you think you should be doing as a Jewish adult educator?

David: That's a big question. Let me talk about a number of different things.

1. *Making connections for people.* My role is to make connections. Someone says something, and I respond: "Think of how that point is emphasized in the *V'ahavta* prayer. Interesting point. Um, you know the very big movie last year, we all saw it. . . ." Then we all talk about the movie and how the idea under discussion was played out in the story, or whatever. That's the point that you can't teach to somebody. You have to have the kind of mind that can make those weird connections. And be confident enough. I've seen people who are very, very smart and know a lot, but if they have a string of points to make and someone asks a question that isn't in their string of points, they freeze.

2. *Personalizing from experience and decreasing the distance between the teacher and learner.* I knew a woman, a very fine scholar . . .

whose field was early, early twentieth-century American Jewish history. . . . But the first few years she worked with adults, she couldn't teach. Why? Because it was like an academic lecture. I bring in a lot of personal stuff, a lot of personal revelation. When I teach, I talk about my kids. I talk about my wife. I talk about my dog. I talk about my commuting into New York, by bus every day. . . . Why do I do this? For one thing, it seems to me that it takes what I'm doing, the activity we're engaged in, out of the realm of information acquisition and into the realm of human relationship. It makes it an interaction. One of the innovations of Jewish tradition is making Torah study a sacred activity. Because it's about being in relationship with the text and with your partner.

Being in relationship with the learner takes it out of the realm of "Wow, that's a really smart person up in front who's gonna tell me stuff I don't know and I'll write it down and then I'll know it." It takes it out of that realm and puts it into, "Good. Here's a person who integrates what I'm saying, and what the person across the room is saying, and what this other person is saying, into *life.*"

One of the tremendous sources of alienation for contemporary Jews is the nonpersonalization. We're back to the old joke that rabbis don't wear underwear, don't use the bathroom—that they're not really human. So when I say, "You know, my nine-year-old said such and such the other day, and I had a conversation with him," they say, "Oh, he has a nine-year-old kid, and they have conversations." And they think, "He's like me."

Most of the teaching I do is not designed to transmit bodies of information to people, but rather to change their sense of their relationship to Jewishness and Jewish tradition: "He's like me, he's involved with this. This means I can be involved with this." And I think probably my self-disclosure, self-revelation, makes me in their eyes a little more vulnerable, a little less distant. It brings down the distance. The same distance that is so deadly when a *bimah* is raised seven steps off the floor of the sanctuary: it's the same kind of distance. It's not something on my level—physically, emotionally, spiritually, intellectually.

3. *Lecturing (minimally) to provide a context.* Occasionally, when I think people are feeling overwhelmed and lost in the strangeness of the topic, I *will* lecture. When I do so, I make it very clear that this is *not* my usual—or my preferred—way of teaching and that the necessity of providing a framework overrides my normal tendency to facilitate discussion. So in a six- or seven-session class, I may lecture once, and always with apologies.

For example, in the first session of my *limud* here at Kallah, I said, "I need to give you a historical framework." And I talked for a half hour straight. I did a nutshell history of the Jewish people from the conquest of Canaan through the destruction of the Second Temple, through the Mishnah. So, I said to them, "I'm gonna do this; I do this very rarely. For the next half hour I'm gonna *talk,* give you dates and places and times. And that's gonna set the context for all the other discussions we're gonna have." *That* they find useful, but in very, very small doses, very few and far between. Especially now, in the era of CNN and sound bites, people want things packaged: "Don't give me four hours. Give me what's useful. Boil it down to the very bare minimum of what I need to understand what we're gonna do after this."

4. *Encouraging questioning and nonjudgmentalism.* I try to give people a lot of methodological hints at the beginning. If I'm going to be with a group for a weekend, I'll say to them at the beginning: "We're gonna start with the ground rules. The ground rules are: there are no ground rules. Any question is allowed. There's no such thing as a digression that we can't take." That's the first thing.

I also tell them: "Please. Don't start out by saying, 'This is probably a stupid question, but. . . .' Let's just stipulate that no question is stupid." That gives everyone permission to ask questions. I think that people find it very hard, very embarrassing, to ask questions. Because when they ask questions, what's going on in their heads? I know: I've been in their situation. They're thinking, "I am probably the only idiot in this room who doesn't know this. And if I open my mouth and ask, everyone's gonna know that I'm really stupid. . . . " So I say to people, "Not only are you not the only one who doesn't know, but you're probably the only one with the guts to ask the question. So you're doing everyone a big favor. So ask the question!"

And I also say: "The worst thing that will happen is that you'll ask me a question and I'll say, 'Let's hold that. Remind me of it later, if I forget. But hold that for later, 'cause it doesn't fit in here, but it will fit in later.'" But usually I just take the question.

5. *Attending to the vulnerability of the learner.* I had a conversation with one of the women in my *limud* this afternoon. She has a graduate degree in family counseling. She was talking about the fact that in her professional life, she feels really competent. She feels like an adult, if you will. Even if she doesn't know everything, she knows exactly where to look *anything* up. There's no problem in her professional life that she can't handle, even if she doesn't know it off the top of her head. When it comes to Jewish life, she feels like an incompetent imbecile.

And so part of my goal in my teaching is to get people to feel a little more in control. Because especially in today's world, most of us are in such positions of power and expertise. Take a lawyer who's pulling down $300,000 a year, billing $400 an hour, partner in a law firm, and walks into a room and everyone says, "Ooh, look who's here." Then he walks into *shul* and feels like a jerk, like a six-year-old. It's no surprise that he talks about religion as if he's a six-year-old. Asks theological questions that you would expect from a six-year-old. That disparity between my general sense of myself and my sense of my Jewish self, that's intolerable!

6. *Assessing the Hebrew abilities of the group.* I always gauge the Hebrew level of the learners. Last night in my *limud*, I said, "Here's a scale. One is you have no idea what Hebrew is, you've never seen it. Ten is you're absolutely fluent, you're a Hebrew Ph.D. Give yourself a number. Just go around and give me the numbers." And I got a sense that it was mostly 3's and 4's, with one 6 and a couple of 1½'s. I said, "OK, that gives me a sense of how much Hebrew I can use and what I have to translate."

7. *Helping people to experience Judaism.* I'm in the business to make people feel more comfortable exploring as many parts of their Jewishness as they can. I'm in the business of getting people to feel that, in principle, nothing Jewish, no part of Jewish tradi-

tion or text or history or literature, is foreign to them. Ideally, my students should get to the point where they can say, "I'm willing to look at anything. I'm willing to try any ritual. I've never done *mikveh* before (or put on *t'fillin* before, or whatever), but I'm willing to try it. It's probably not for me, but I'm willing to try it and see before I decide." As a teacher, I want to open people's access routes to Jewish stuff.

I do *shabbatonim* three to six times a year, with CLAL groups. Shabbat morning, I'll unroll the Torah and call people up for *aliyot.* I always make one *aliyah* for people who've never had an *aliyah* before. It never fails. "People, come on. We'll help you. Here's a *tallis.* Kiss this. Say these words." Then we sing *Siman tov u-mazal tov* or *Shehecheyanu.* We throw candy. And people come up to me afterwards—regularly—with tears in their eyes: "This was the most incredible thing. I've never done this before!"

Now the weird thing to me is that you don't have to be a rocket scientist to figure out that this affects people deeply. I can't figure out why most rabbis and most educators in most settings *don't* get it. I don't understand!

8. *Empowering the learner.* My philosophy, my approach to teaching probably correlates highly with a philosophy of an approach to parenting. It is a philosophy that says: My goal is to empower my kids, to make my kids be as independent and as fulfilled and realized in their own potential as they can be—and not direct them too much, but to facilitate. In my experience, the most important feature of parenting is the extent to which parents see their children as people and respect their views and their opinions and their personhood.

That carries over to my teaching. I try—and sometimes it's awfully difficult—to really respect the ideas, the opinions, the personhood of the students. In some groups it's easy; in others, it's very hard. I've had some wonderful teachers who were deeply disrespectful of their students. Completely disrespectful! Contemptuous. I said they were wonderful because they happened to teach me a lot of "stuff" or content, but if you look not only at the message, but also at the messenger and the medium, you're horrified.

I think that a lot of academics and a lot of rabbis do things—and I don't think they're conscious, I don't think they're malicious. I think they're unconscious. They do things to create a power differential. They'll use language, and not realize that language—the use of jargon or technical terminology—is a way of saying, "I know more than you. I'm superior to you." I try not to do that.

Other Voices, Similar Messages

Rabbi David Nelson's reflections on his practice point to three elements of *tzimtzum* that Jewish professionals should keep in mind in their work with Jewish adult learners. These elements were also mentioned in interviews with a number of other outstanding Jewish teachers who talked about how they (1) "come in close" with learners, (2) acknowledge the learners' needs for validation and respect, and (3) reflect on their teaching and learn from feedback from their students. The insights of these seasoned professionals bear further consideration.

Coming in Close

Articulated throughout David Nelson's remarks is his view that a crucial element of his success as an adult educator is his ability to "come in close" with learners. Ron Wolfson, Vice President of the University of Judaism and co-founder of Synagogue 2000, a national synagogue transformation initiative, explains how he decreases distance with the many adult audiences he addresses:

When I'm a guest scholar somewhere and I've got a group of people I don't know, I don't have the luxury of spending fifteen of my thirty minutes with them doing that [coming in close]. But I've developed some strategies for still sending a more personal message. First is: Greeting people before the lecture. I may not see everybody, but at least I meet some of them. That sets a tone and an environment. Secondly, I always start a lecture with a story about myself. That also creates an environment and a connection. Sometimes in the lecture, I'll ask people to turn to each other and discuss a topic, an issue—the whole thing is two minutes. These are little strategies that help to create an ambience without giving away all the time and without alienating the people who don't want to hear everybody else's story.

Dr. Wolfson's strategy to "connect" with learners via a story about himself is echoed in educator Judy Elkin's reflections on her work at Boston's Hebrew College with novice Jewish adult learners:

> I've found, as the educator, it's really important to say, "I'm there now." It's not "I've been there and now, look: I've come out on the other end and it's really great. Get in the pool, you'll love it." It's also, "I'm still there. We're all still there." It's important to acknowledge that I've also experienced periods of being "on the outside." I tell them, "I know how uncomfortable that feels, and I can only imagine how much more uncomfortable that must be for you." So I ask people to please take steps slowly, that this is not something they need to dive into 100 percent, that they're on a path, moving along on a path. And, I tell them, "We're all on a path, and sometimes we meet along the way."

As Ms. Elkin sees it, educators need to share with learners that they are learners themselves:

> I make sure to model my own learning: It's important for my adult students to know that I take a Talmud study class, that I go to Torah study, that there's a lot of stuff I still have to brush up on or learn for the first time. When Jewish adults first come to you with so little, they think of you as quite a maven. It's important to say to them, "There's so much I don't know. There's so much that's out there." And to say, "That's what actually attracts me to all of this Jewish study: It's a bottomless pit that can be daunting. But mostly it's a feeling of awe: Look how rich it is! Look at how amazingly deep it is!"

Sharing personal experience as a way to come in close is part of Rabbi Norman Cohen's approach as well. The provost of Hebrew Union College–Jewish Institute of Religion, Rabbi Cohen has taught in hundreds of adult learning settings. He described his views about "personalizing."

> I know that when people hear me personalize the text, which I do all the time, they are not passive agents. They're not passive; they are active learners. My story gives them the license, in fact pushes them, to personalize the stories in their own hearts and in their own heads. I recently gave a session on Moses as a leadership model, and I talked about Moses' loss of Miriam, his sister. I pointed out that just when Moses is at his own low, the people start to cry out: there's no water! Now how does Moses respond to the people of Israel

when he just lost his sister? I told them: "Those are the most difficult moments in one's profession, when you have to keep a balance
professionally and personally." And then I told them what it was like
for me, going to teach an adult education class out on Long Island
when I was going through a painful divorce. How hard it was to
find a sense of balance. Then I asked them: "How do *you* handle
times like that? How do *you* get the balance?"

According to Kathleen Taylor, Catherine Marienau, and Morris Fiddler
(2000), personalizing and self-disclosure accomplish many things in adult
learning settings:

> One of the most effective ways of abandoning our pedestal is to
> admit to being human, flawed, and still engaged in our own process
> of development and growth. . . . When an exercise calls for learners
> to describe aspects of their personal experience, we often begin by
> revealing the comparable and less than picture-perfect aspects of our
> own experiences. We talk openly about mistakes we have made in
> the past and current frustrations we have not resolved. This is not
> idle confessional chatter—it helps establish us as peers of adults
> whose experiences we share. Acknowledging to ourselves—and to
> our learners—that we, too, are adults engaged in a life-long process
> of growth reduces the temptation to accept implicit designations of
> our superiority. (p. 305)

Self-disclosure helps adult educators achieve "authenticity" in the view of
their learners. Stephen Brookfield (1990) writes that, for many years, he
"steadfastly refused to refer to anything to do with my life outside the classroom." However, over time he realized that his sharing his personal experience enriches the learner's learning:

> To me, personal disclosure smacked of amateur psychotherapy and
> indicated only that the teacher was using the learning group as a dump-
> ing ground for unresolved personal issues. There is no doubt that this
> can sometimes happen, but the authentic disclosure that students
> appreciate is very far from this. It is seen in teachers using incidents
> from their own daily lives to illustrate general principles, in their talk-
> ing about their passions that led them to develop an interest in their
> fields, and in referring to the enthusiasms that currently sustain and
> renew these interests. (p. 169)

Beginning with the Learners' Needs

Other people I interviewed revealed that a key element of their success as Jewish educators is their ability to "read" their learners' needs. Rabbi Sally Finestone of Wayland, Massachusetts, notes that potential learners are often "looking for justification" and want to be assured that their quest for knowledge is seen as worthwhile by a professional in the Jewish community:

> They wonder: Is it okay what I'm doing? Will it really make a difference in my life? Can you support me in what I'm doing? Will I be ostracized or rejected by the Jews who are more knowledgeable, more skilled than I am?

Similarly, Rabbi Judith Halevy of Malibu, California, says that Jewish adults are often looking for validation from Jewish professionals, who they hope will affirm them on their learning journeys:

> The learners—especially the women—are saying, "I want to feel whole, to feel I am a vessel that can hold all the pieces of my life. But I also want to feel validated and heard." This goes back to our story of the angel saying, "Tell me your name," and Jacob saying, "Bless me." The learners are saying, "I want to be blessed in where I am in my point in the struggle. Even though day may break and I may not have all the answers, I want to be blessed for the struggle I'm going through." Moreover, they want to be "seen," especially by Judy, that "gray-haired woman who went to Camp Tel Yehuda [a Zionist camp in Pennsylvania] and is now the spiritual leader of a Reconstructionist synagogue and a long-time teacher in the Jewish Renewal movement."

Rabbi Halevy's remarks call to mind a point made by adult educator Jane Vella, whose work in cross-cultural education has sensitized her to how important *respect* is to adult learners. Vella (1994) writes that educators can create respect through open-ended questioning and thoughtful listening—pedagogic approaches certainly modeled by David Nelson in his interactions with his learners:

> *Re-spectare* is the root of the word *respect*. It means: to see again. I suggest that it also implies hearing again. Listening without interrupting is a simple structure for assuring respect. We can do that even in large groups. Open dialogue can readily be structured in any event: teaching

a complex concept, practicing a skill, or learning an attitude. Concepts can be presented as open systems—as the hypotheses they are—and the adult learner can be invited to examine them, edit and add to them from their experience, do something with them. Such a dialogue builds a relationship that inevitably leads to learning and development. (p. 70)

Dr. Bernard Steinberg, director of Harvard-Radcliffe Hillel and a teacher in the Wexner Heritage leadership development program, says that one of the ways he meets learners' needs is by helping people to become aware of themselves as thinkers—and as Jewish thinkers:

My first job as a teacher is dissolving baggage so that people can be in touch with where they are in the here and now. So they will begin to think: "I am an adult person living in the universe, and whether I know it or not, I'm making life decisions on the basis of a bunch of assumptions that I haven't really looked at. But the assumptions are there. And I may make different decisions if I'm aware of the assumptions, because maybe I'm just reacting against what I assume."

Steinberg says that before learners can really grow as Jews, they have to see themselves as meaning-makers who will be faced with challenging questions and decisions:

One of the first things people have to come to terms with is that they are creatures of meaning and purpose. The deeper they are in touch with that process within themselves, the more satisfaction they have. Meaning creates meaning creates meaning. I see all Jewish learning as basically a deepening of the process of self-awareness. So the first step is obviously: "My self is a thinking, questioning human being." And a lot of people are not aware of that, they aren't aware that they are thinking, questioning human beings.

Dr. Steinberg's approach is to push learners to enter into dialogue with Judaism's "extraordinary legacy of three to four thousand years." He finds that most Jewish adults have insufficient awareness of how their "individual identities link with the collective identity of the Jewish people." So when he teaches text, he urges learners to discover the "voice of the text" and to talk back to that voice, to find meaning through dialogue and personal identification. By focusing on the learner's interaction with Jewish texts and tradition, Bernie Steinberg successfully avoids making himself the central mediator of the learner's meaning-making experience.

Tzimtzum and Reflection

Practicing *tzimtzum*—becoming a teacher who contracts and makes room for the learner to grow—does not occur by happenstance. Just as learners need to become aware of themselves as meaning-makers capable of new thought, educators, too, must reflect on their assumptions and why they do what they do. Parker Palmer (1998) tells us:

> Teaching, like any truly human activity, emerges from one's own inwardness. . . . Viewed from this angle, teaching holds a mirror to the soul. If I am willing to look in that mirror and not run from what I see, I have a chance to gain self-knowledge—and knowing myself is as crucial to good teaching as knowing my students and my subject. (p. 2)

Each of the Jewish adult educators I talked with revealed that, over time, they had spent time thinking about their teaching and about how to increase their effectiveness with adult learners. They acknowledged that although some of their classes or speeches had been enthusiastically received, others were less successful. They confessed that there were times when they had underestimated their students' needs or overestimated their own ability to convey ideas. They admitted how sometimes they were tempted to "repackage" old material or skimp on preparation. And they admitted that sometimes their egos had taken over, causing them to pay less attention to their students' needs and even discredit learners' ideas. At the same time, these highly effective teachers were able to comment on how they "got better"—what they routinely did to enliven their presentations, engage their students, and revitalize themselves as both teachers and learners.

Rabbi Donald Goor of Tarzana, California, participated in a professional consultation group about working with Jewish adult learners. He told me what he was learning from teaching an adult education class at his synagogue:

> I am in the middle of teaching a six-week class on prayer. Last fall, on my sabbatical, I wrote an article on prayer, so I saw this as a chance to "teach" about it. But now, after teaching two sessions, I realize that my questions aren't quite the students' questions. My questions are kind of rabbinic, in terms of liturgy and the Jewish context. And theirs are much more personal. It's not that my question isn't personal—the

underlying question is the same: "Why is prayer not working?" I think that's generally my question and theirs. But I now see that I'm much further along in the questioning than they are. And this is a crucial point, because I've done all this reading and already written what I thought was going to be the "right" answer.

But my students are going to change my thinking. Because I was wrong. Part of what I have to do is to accept that they come from a whole different place. The people who don't read Hebrew had a hard time with my opening questions. For them, prayer works just fine because they generally don't have a problem with the *siddur* and its translations. They assume they won't know the Hebrew, so they find something meaningful in the English. But there was a whole group of people who stayed afterwards the second evening to tell me how much they dislike services because of the *siddur*. They had all sorts of issues about the translations and what prayer is or should be. And those weren't the issues I had brought up. But, to them, those were the *real* prayer issues. So for tonight's class, given the texts I had in mind, I'm going to do it differently. I am going to have them read the prayers in Hebrew and in English and then ask them how they respond.

I've realized that before, in the past, I would walk into classes with a technique, knowing where I would "lead" people. But now the leading will be very different, because I had to step back and hear what they said and how they responded. Which, by the way, is the importance of *chevruta*—hearing things from another person. Until I got to the class, I'd done all my research and reading by myself. Once I got into the classroom I realized: I *had* to listen.

Rabbi Goor's reflections about his teaching conform to several key principles of *critically reflective practice,* a teacher self-assessment approach advocated by adult education scholars. First, to become more learner-centered and also to renew one's vitality as a teacher, the adult educator needs to be committed to dealing with problems that arise in the teaching situation; this includes problems that the teacher discerns and problems students may have with the teaching-learning process. As part of reflective practice, a teacher must be willing to ask for feedback and use input from others. Second, because reflection often leads to changes—in the teacher's behavior, in the interactions with students, in what is expected in the learning situation—the reflective practitioner must be willing to examine how those changes will impact all the parties involved. Third, reflective practice involves taking action, even if that action is deliberately choosing not to change.

In his account, Rabbi Donald Goor showed that he was attuned to the problems caused by the "curriculum" he had designed for his class on prayer; early on, he realized that his agenda differed greatly from that of his learners. His students also let him know that their questions led to a different type of discussion than Rabbi Goor had anticipated. Rather than taking a defensive position, Rabbi Goor used this critique as the basis for future action. As he planned the third class meeting, he decided to start with the learners' experience by asking them to read and comment on certain texts. He realized that he needed to listen more closely to the learners' views—to learn from the learners. And he saw that he needed to "step back"—to practice *tzimtzum*—in order to create a learning environment that drew not only on his expertise on prayer but on the learners' questions as well.

From Theory to Practice: Learner-Centered Teaching

The insights of successful Jewish adult educators about their understanding of their learners' needs and their own practice provide a useful framework for Jewish professionals who work with adults. Many elements of "best practices" that are contained in the comments and vignettes presented in this chapter may also be found in the burgeoning literature on "learner-centered teaching" in adult education. Exhibit 7-2 summarizes the recommendations of some of the best writers in the adult learning field. Additional perspective on these approaches is offered in chapter 8.

Ultimately, when working with adult Jewish learners, professionals need to ask themselves such questions as: What is my goal for my learners? What will help my learners to learn—and to want to continue to learn? How will I know what has been learned and whether it is of benefit to the people I serve? What do *I* need to learn in order to feel alive in my teaching? In what ways might I modify my practice or my material to more effectively impact the growth of my students?

In addition, Jewish professionals should:

1. Diversify your approaches to teaching and consider ways you might function as a "facilitator of learning." This does not mean overhauling your practice but, rather, involves careful assessment of your effectiveness and ways for helping adult learners to grow.

2. Decrease "distance" from the learners by sharing as much of your own experience as you feel comfortable doing. This does not require

EXHIBIT 7-2

The Learner-Centered Adult Educator

Sees learning as something that begins with the needs of the learner

Involves learners in diagnosing learning needs, formulating learning objectives, designing learning plans, and evaluating the learning experience

Provides an "organizing vision" and "maps" of content and context

Helps learners learn "how to learn"

Encourages learners to recognize and challenge their old assumptions

Shows learners how to engage in processes of inquiry and discovery

Encourages and models collaborative learning and dialogue

Fosters learners' self-esteem

Gives learners critical feedback in a constructive manner

Is efficient

Sets limits on class discussion

Functions more as a "guide on the side" than a "sage on the stage"

Is authentic and credible

Does not separate head from heart

Does not separate teaching from learning

Reflects critically on his or her teaching and invites learners' reflections on the learning experience

---

Sources: Apps, 1991; Brookfield, 1986, 1987, 1990; Daloz, 1999; Draves, 1984; Knowles, 1980; Knox, 1986; Palmer, 1998; Vella, 1994.

"spilling" your personal life but rather means drawing from "real" experiences that show that you are a real person. Learners appreciate understanding how the teacher's own Jewish journey has shaped current thinking or values; the more you disclose how you have arrived at your current position of Jewish understanding, the more you help the learners to reflect on their own growth and change.

3. Organize information in ways that help the learners to get a clear perspective on the context and the content of what you are teaching (see the description of roadmaps in chapter 8). Remember that adult

learners like to situate themselves and their knowledge base in relation to what you are teaching. Help the learners to see how much they already know, and then build on (and even challenge) their previous ideas and assumptions.

4. Reflect on your practice as a teacher—and as a learner. If possible, find other professionals with whom to share thoughts about adult Jewish learning, effective teaching, and the challenges of meeting the needs of contemporary Jewish adults. Seek feedback from your students, and when there is criticism, use it for personal assessment of how you are doing. When confronted by problematic teaching situations, consider whether you need to practice *tzimtzum*—to pull back and make space for the learner and the learner's needs rather than forge ahead and prove how much you know. On the other hand, do not sacrifice your role as an authority; in the long run, your learners value you for the expertise you bring, so long as you transmit your knowledge in a thoughtful and accessible way.

8

Tachlis: Practical Strategies
in the *Beit Midrash*

> Tachlis. *Pronounced TOKH-liss, to rhyme with "Bach Liss." From the Hebrew for "purpose," "end." The point, heart, nub, or substance of the matter. "Let's talk* tachlis*" means "Let's get down to brass tacks." "What's the* tachlis*?" means "What are the real effects, the practical aspect?"*
>
> *—Leo Rosten, 2001, p. 381*

In the opening pages of this book, I described several of my own Jewish adult learning experiences: an adult *b'nei mitzvah* class that I found alienating and that rekindled in me feelings of inadequacy and distance from Jewish observance; a one-on-one study experience in which I was able to make connections between Torah study and my own skills as a learner; and a class on midrash in which I discovered the joy of engaging in text analysis with other people who could offer insights different from my own. Over the past decade, I have been on my own Jewish learning journey, and along the way—in class after class, with teacher after teacher—I have asked: What makes this class work? What's going on in this learning situation that positively impacts the learner? What's the bottom line in effective Jewish adult education? What strategies might be considered the nuts and bolts of a *quality* Jewish adult learning experience?

According to one of the leading scholars of adult education, Jerold Apps, quality is what matters most to adult learners. As individuals who value personal enrichment but also are protective of their time and "investments," many adult learners bring a "consumerist" mentality to new pursuits. They tend to approach educational activities with the kinds of questions outlined in Exhibit 8-1. These questions reflect a genuine desire to gain something from the learning experience and to find vehicles for continued growth, as well as high standards for personal satisfaction.

EXHIBIT 8-1

Adult Learning Program "Quality" Questions

Is the teacher up-to-date?
Does the teacher keep up with ideas and new information through his or her own study, reading, travel, dialogue with colleagues, etc.?

Does the teacher use stimulating and varied teaching approaches?
Does the teacher recognize that participants bring a variety of preferred learning styles and that different subject matter lends itself better to certain teaching approaches?

Is the teacher able to relate theory to practice?
Can the teacher present the abstract, general, and theoretical side of the material as well as the concrete, practical, and applied side?

Is the teacher concerned about learners as human beings?
Is the teacher a caring, sharing person—not a machine that wants to treat learners as so many other machines into which information is poured and out of which learning performance is measured in carefully delineated numerical units?

Will I have something to say about what is taught?
For those topics where I have considerable experience and knowledge, will I have the opportunity to ask teachers to cover particular questions or subjects based on my interests and what I need?

Will I be challenged to move beyond where I am now?
Even if I think I know what I want to learn, will I nonetheless, upon completion of the course or workshop, discover some new territory I had not been aware of before?

Will I discover guideposts for continuing my learning in this area?
Will my teacher point me toward additional learning that I can do on my own, so I do not become dependent on formal course or workshop offerings as a sole means of meeting my learning needs and interests?

Will this course or workshop contribute to independent learning?
Will I gain not only new knowledge and skills, but also acquire skills that I can use on my own when I want to learn something else? These skills may include how to find information and how to sort out and make sense of information, as well as how to develop critical thinking skills.

Is the course convenient and accessible?
Are courses and workshops offered at times that are convenient for me, with parking and child care? Will I have access to supplementary materials such as library resources? If I miss a class or session, will I be able to get a tape or notes from the teacher?

Will I get my money's worth?
Compared to others offering similar courses or workshops, will I learn what I want and need to learn with this one? Will I have spent my educational dollar well?

Adapted from Jerold Apps, *Mastering the Teaching of Adults* (Malabar, Fla.: Krieger, 1991)

In my experience, Jewish adults also approach Jewish learning with the desire to grow as Jews and to have meaningful learning opportunities that enhance their sense of Jewish identity. As I have discussed throughout this book, contemporary Jewish adult learners wonder:

- Will I feel comfortable learning with other Jews?
- Will I be accepted by Jewish "authority figures" despite the limitations of my Jewish knowledge?
- Will I get help in acquiring skills for Jewish learning?
- Will my view of Judaism and religion be respected by teachers and fellow learners?
- Will I find relevance in Jewish learning?
- How will my learning affect my identity as a Jew?

In *Mastering the Teaching of Adults* (1991), Apps urges adult educators to anticipate their learners' questions and concerns and to actively create learning environments that respond in purposeful ways. In this chapter, I draw heavily on Apps's practical suggestions for effective adult education. His insights, as well as those of a number of other adult education scholars whose work is cited, have contributed to my thinking about the "brass tacks"—the *tachlis*—that are at the heart of planning top-quality Jewish adult learning programs.

But before we get to the *tachlis,* as with earlier chapters, let's begin with a story. This story, unlike earlier ones in this book, has been drawn solely from observations rather than from interviews; it has been crafted to highlight the complexities involved in *planning* and *delivering* quality adult Jewish learning events. This fictional story—of synagogue scholar-in-residence Professor August Fonferberg—reveals how a well-prepared Jewish adult educator can unintentionally "miss the mark" with learners. Invited by the Social Action Committee of an imaginary congregation, Temple Kehillah, to address the topic of "increasing intergenerational awareness and involvement in social action activities," Professor Fonferberg violates many of the principles of effective adult education practice. Following the story, I suggest some fundamental strategies and sensibilities that Jewish professionals should incorporate into their planning and implementation of adult Jewish learning endeavors.

❧ Story 8 ❧

PAVED WITH GOOD INTENTIONS: PROFESSOR FONFERBERG'S SCHOLAR-IN-RESIDENCE WEEKEND

Barbara and Reva, longstanding members of Temple Kehillah's Social Action Committee, willingly agreed to co-chair the synagogue's annual scholar-in-residence program. The program topic, "Social Responsibility: Reaching across Generations," derived from the committee's ongoing desire to create dialogue among congregants of all ages about the social justice values that distinguish Judaism. In planning the weekend, Barbara and Reva coordinated with several constituencies to organize a program that would appeal to a variety of age groups: the rabbi gave some sermons on social activism; the synagogue's Adult Education Committee e-mailed brief readings about social justice to the whole congregation; the educator developed a special eighth grade curriculum to correspond with the weekend theme and invited the eighth grade class to participate in the weekend sessions; and several members of the synagogue's senior citizens group actively recruited other seniors to sponsor (and presumably to attend) the series of learning events.

The weekend planners were especially excited that Dr. August Fonferberg, an economics professor with an interest in liberal Jewish causes, had agreed to be their visiting scholar. According to the professor's curriculum vitae, he had published articles about the ethics of social responsibility and had spearheaded a program in which Jewish faculty members served as consultants to businesses in the Hispanic immigrant community. When Barbara called to invite Professor Fonferberg, she was impressed by his questions about the congregation and by his willingness to engage a variety of groups during the weekend.

On the scheduled Friday evening, committee members handed out a handsome brochure detailing the weekend's events. The brochure established that Professor Fonferberg would speak briefly after services on Friday night (no more than twenty minutes) to set the tone; that he would make linkages between texts and Jewish activism at the Saturday text study group; that, as part of the Saturday evening dinner program, he would involve the participants in a dialogue about what they could learn from one another about social justice concerns; and that he would meet with religious school parents on Sunday morning to talk about how families could become involved in social justice issues.

After the evening *t'filah*, the rabbi kicked off the weekend of study by saying how pleased he was that his old friend "Augie" had agreed to serve as scholar. Barbara then introduced the speaker by reading the professor's lengthy biography, which described his scholarly achievements and teaching awards. When Dr. Fonferberg came to the *bimah*, he thanked everyone for the invitation and proceeded to read a paper he had written that, he believed, best framed the issues he hoped the congregation would discuss during the weekend. The reading went on for seventeen minutes—the paper was a well-sourced reflection about Judah as a model of social responsibility. When he finished, he said that he looked forward to hearing how members of Temple Kehillah could apply his "model of social justice" to their contemporary lives. He invited the audience to give examples of how their own communal behaviors compared with Judah's actions.

After a moment of silence, Reva stood up and said, "Well, I'm not prepared to compare my experience with Judah's, but the Social Action Committee meets on the second Tuesday of the month and we can get only a few people to come to the meetings. What would you recommend we do to get people involved?" Dr. Fonferberg looked a bit startled, and replied, "Yes, that's a problem. And let's talk about what the committee's doing when we meet with parents on Sunday. But tell me: What is *your* model of social responsibility?" Caught unprepared, Reva stumbled through an unformed response and sat down embarrassed. A couple of other people took a stab at the speaker's question and one older congregant defensively listed all the community programs he had helped to organize in the 1960s. From Dr. Fonferberg's reactions, however, it seemed that he was waiting for an answer that would get at some point he had been trying to make. When it became evident that no one in the audience intended to comment further, the rabbi came forward and said that he was sure Dr. Fonferberg would be glad to continue the conversation informally at the *Oneg Shabbat*. During coffee and cake, only a handful of people made their way over to introduce themselves to the scholar.

At the Torah group study session on Saturday morning, Dr. Fonferberg found that he had to take quite a bit of time reviewing the concepts he had presented the evening before. On the table was a handout that contained selections from Genesis 44, the Babylonian Talmud (*Kiddushin* 40a–40b), and *Pirkei Avot*. Whenever latecomers arrived, the professor waved toward the stack of handouts but never stopped to ask their names or to brief them about what he was discussing. When Dr. Fonferberg finished summarizing his points about Judah, he suggested that the group look at the handout and ask themselves such questions as "How am I like Judah in approach to social responsibility?", "Could I do what he did?", "How did his behavior set up a model for future generations of Jews?", and "What alternative models are now in evidence in our community?"

After the group looked at the handout, Dr. Fonferberg restated his questions. Valerie, a member of the congregation's ongoing *parashat hashavua* group, said that she wondered if he could help them to link the material about Judah to the current Torah portion *(Parashat Vayikra)*, so that the "regulars" would not lose momentum in their study routine. She said perhaps the group could talk about the meaning of sacrifices. Her usual study partner, Ethel, began distributing copies of the *Tanach*, and several people said they needed time to review what *Vayikra* was about. In passing, Ethel asked Professor Fonferberg whether he found it instructive to study the Torah every week. Before he could answer, Valerie commented that she'd never realized how "bloody" *Vayikra* was, which led several other people to comment on how offensive they found it to read details of slaughter in the Torah. After about fifteen minutes of conversation about ways to understand the message of the *parashah*, Professor Fonferberg looked at his watch and announced:

> Well, I was hoping we would do some *chevruta* study today to get at the intergenerational issues, but we're nearly out of time. It's too bad none of the teenagers came this morning, because I want to get them involved in this conversation. But, before we go, would anyone like to comment on the topic of social responsibility across generations?

In response, several individuals described the ways their children and grandchildren volunteered at the synagogue's Mitzvah Day and other community service activities. Dr. Fonferberg complimented these individuals for being so committed to transmitting the values of social justice and said he hoped the group would come back Saturday evening to contribute to the discussion of the weekend's theme.

That evening, dinner was served in the synagogue's "meeting room" (a classroom during the day that was turned into a meeting space in the evening). Because only twenty-six congregants had made dinner reservations, the weekend planners had decided this space was more "intimate" than the synagogue's cavernous social hall. Unfortunately, the tables were crowded, and the noise level made it hard for people to hear one another across their tables. The room was hot, so people occasionally left to stand in the hallway to get some fresh air. During the meal, the teens were clustered at the end of one long table. Dr. Fonferberg sat at the end of another table, talking mostly with the rabbi and his wife.

Following dinner, the tables were cleared, and Dr. Fonferberg asked people to rearrange themselves into two groups, which he dubbed the Alefs and the Bets; he singled out two of the eighth graders in the Alef group, asking them to separate from their friends and join the Bets. The professor then distributed statements by Leonard Fein about the decline in Jewish social activism, and several pages from *The Jew Within* about the self-involvement of the baby boomer generation. He asked the groups to discuss whether involvement in social justice activities was a reasonable expectation in the contemporary Jewish community. He suggested that the group members read and discuss the authors' points of view and "if you want, talk about your own experiences with social justice." He asked them to reconvene in twenty minutes so that "the Alef-Bet [ha-ha] can come together for a juicy debate."

The Alef group spent the next five minutes silently reading the statements. When the group finished reading, they briefly acknowledged each author's position and then one by one reminisced about their experiences as community volunteers. In the conversation, they did not explicitly connect those experiences to the points made in the materials Dr. Fonferberg had distributed.

In the Bet group, the members decided to pair off to read and summarize how the authors agreed or disagreed. Barbara was in this group and suggested that each eighth grader partner with an adult for this activity; she noticed that in these pairs, the adults were very solicitous when asking the girls about their volunteer work in the synagogue and larger community. One of the adult pairs sought out Dr. Fonferberg to get his opinion on current events in Israel, so the scholar did not circulate to the discussion groups. When he suddenly realized that the twenty minutes had passed and "checked in" with each group, he discovered that neither group had fully understood what was expected in preparation for the "debate."

Dr. Fonferberg reconvened the large group and began to suggest what might serve as good "rules of discourse." However, before he could articulate some guidelines, a man named Herman launched into a lengthy statement praising the professor for selecting "interesting commentaries on the self-absorption of the younger generation." In response, a woman named Myrna declared that she didn't see how the quotes applied to life at Temple Kehillah: "There are lots of people here doing lots of wonderful things: collecting food for the hungry, visiting the sick, building homes for the poor, tutoring illiterate migrant workers, donating stuffed animals for kids at the children's hospital. I can't see how you can say anybody here is that self-absorbed." Herman and Myrna's exchange escalated to a rather contentious argument, with Herman dismissing the acts of *tzedakah* as "Band-Aids that people use to appease their guilt" rather than "conscious decisions to create a community of cooperation and mutual support." When Myrna shot back that Herman was an idealist who didn't really know the people he was criticizing, Reva spoke up and suggested that Dr. Fonferberg explain to the group the points he had hoped to cover before the evening ended.

Turning to the teenagers, Dr. Fonferberg said, "Well, what are the intergenerational issues at stake here? What does the younger generation have to say? What do you young ladies want to tell us old folks about how we get today's kids to be more socially responsible?" The eighth grade girls looked at one another self-consciously; one finally said she didn't know. The rabbi jumped in at that point, describing the synagogue educator's new social justice curriculum and commending the school principal for her efforts to raise student awareness about social responsibility. Dr. Fonferberg said he had received a copy of the curriculum but hadn't yet had time to review it. Barbara suggested that perhaps everyone could look at the educator's notebook of materials during the parents' meeting on Sunday morning.

Over bagels the next day, Dr. Fonferberg gave a "high-tech" presentation about social justice projects and their impact on volunteers of all ages. He told several jokes and poked fun at himself as someone who had to rely on his twelve-year-old daughter for computer tutoring. Twenty religious school parents attended and appeared intrigued by the professor's list of "Eighteen Great Jewish Social Justice Web Sites." Indeed, several people said they didn't know there was so much information about Jewish things on the Internet, and Dr. Fonferberg regaled them with amusing stories of how world Jewry had been transformed by the evolution of "the Jewish diaspora in cyberspace." One parent asked how to determine which Web sites were "legitimate," and that led to a dynamic discussion of how parents should monitor their children's use of computers. The discussion lasted for most of the allotted time but did not refer to the social justice curriculum or address how these parents might convey ideas to their children about taking social responsibility. The gathering ended when the parents left to pick up their children at the end of religious school and Dr. Fonferberg rushed off to catch a flight back to his home community.

Dr. Fonferberg's Story: An Adult Educator's Perspective

How do I, as an adult educator, reflect on Dr. Fonferberg and his rather bumbling performance as a teacher? What can we learn from this "cautionary tale" about the kinds of problems that can override even the most carefully planned adult learning programs? What did the key players in this story—the scholar, the planning committee, and the learners—do that impacted the quality or the learning outcomes of the weekend? In analyzing what occurred, we can assume that Dr. Fonferberg came to this scholar-in-residence experience with outstanding intentions: he prepared his remarks, he tried to envision effective discussion activities, he assembled materials he thought would be valuable to his audience, and he continually indicated that he hoped to create an interactive and personally meaningful program for synagogue members. We even can assume that this professor is a well-versed expert who has much to teach Jewish adults and has sought in his own life to practice the values he "preaches."

Yet, after the weekend, when Barbara asked a number of participants what they thought of the program, most said they hadn't "learned much" from the presentations or discussions. Several people commented that while they respected Dr. Fonferberg and appreciated his efforts, they had come to the weekend hoping to learn how to teach their children about social action. Instead, they demurred, they wound up feeling disconnected from the professor's "abstract" content, that the program didn't adequately address the topic advertised, and that Dr. Fonferberg had failed to provide practical suggestions about intergenerational involvement in social justice.

Barbara's co-chair, Reva, was particularly critical of the visiting scholar. She felt Professor Fonferberg had not "read" or managed his audiences well. She was especially discouraged by the teenagers' reactions: "Maybe I shouldn't have even asked them for their feedback," she sighed to Barbara, "I forget how teenagers say it all with one 'look.'" She elaborated: "One girl actually rolled her eyes and said, 'The pasta was good.' And another one shrugged and said, 'Well, at least it made my grandma happy that I was there.'" Reva went on to say that she felt especially bad for the synagogue's educator:

> Lisa worked so hard to make the curriculum relevant and to get the kids involved. But after Friday night, the word got out that Dr. Fonferberg was b-o-r-i-n-g. I'm amazed that as many as five kids showed up after that. I think it will be awhile before we will be able to talk "intergenerational" programming with our teenagers!

At the same time, the religious school parents enjoyed the professor's presentation and were intrigued by the possibilities of using the Internet to increase their awareness of Jewish issues. Nonetheless, the discussion on Sunday morning did not contribute directly to the overriding goals of the weekend: to increase social action consciousness and to foster intergenerational dialogue among congregants.

What made this well-planned weekend "miss the mark" for so many people? What can we learn by analyzing what occurred and what may have contributed to the generally lukewarm response to the speaker and the weekend's events? To get down to the *tachlis*, I have identified ten factors that contribute to the success of quality adult learning programs. Let us analyze this weekend in relation to them. The issues are as follows:

1. Attunement between the teacher's and learners' goals and expectations
2. The teacher's credibility and authenticity
3. The setting of the learning "climate"

4. Attention to the physical conditions
5. The scope of content and materials
6. Lectures
7. Discussions
8. Questions
9. The use of diverse teaching strategies
10. Evaluation

Attunement Between the Teacher's and Learners' Goals and Expectations

As I discussed in chapter 7, quality adult education is learner-centered. It begins with the needs and goals of the learners. To achieve "attunement" with those needs, a teacher must assess who the audience is from "day one"—when a course is envisioned or a speaking invitation is extended or a class meets for the first time. The teacher has the responsibility to adapt his or her expectations to the reality of the group. This does not mean discarding one's expertise but, rather, may require figuring out how one's knowledge and resources can be most useful to the learners. Adult learners expect their teachers to pay close attention to them—to meet them where they are "at" and to be committed to helping them find meaningful "ways in" to new learning. Part of being an effective educator is "reading" each group of learners and responding appropriately.

In *Models of Adult Religious Education Practice* (1991), R. E. Y. Wickett explains that the reason teachers like Dr. Fonferberg often fail to "reach" adult learners is that they set goals without thinking adequately about the audience's needs or the best way to meet those needs. "Learning can be based upon goals and objectives toward which the learner strives. We must organize our learning in relation to the end product . . . by formulating the objectives in a manner which is appropriate to aid the teaching and learning process" (pp. 53–54).

In the present situation, the teacher's attunement skills were not strong. Although initially Dr. Fonferberg thought to inquire about the makeup of the congregation, ultimately he failed to pay heed to what his hosts had said about the weekend or the likely audience. His first "mistake" was not honoring a request his hosts had made: to keep Friday evening brief and engaging, with a view toward inspiring people to "come back for more" the next day. Instead, he read a dense text and proposed an abstract theoretical framework that was hard for most audience members to follow. He then asked people to apply concepts before they had time to process the input. While his goal may have been to honor the congregation by not "speaking down" to them on Friday night, most people in the congregation were not looking for a talk at the level of an academic conference presentation. Dr. Fonferberg overlooked the needs of his audience and thus "turned off" people who might have come back Saturday and Sunday.

A second mistake Dr. Fonferberg made on Friday night was announcing his expectation that people would, the next morning, be able to "apply" what he had taught them the evening before. However, few of the people who had signed up for the weekend activities were prepared to make this quick "transfer of knowledge" the next day; thus the professor had to go back to basic concepts (about Judah as a model of social responsibility) before the learners were able to make connections between the text and their own lives. Although Dr. Fonferberg had reproduced texts for the Saturday morning study session, it would have been helpful had he provided a "roadmap" that included key concepts, terminology, and questions to consider. The intended goal for the text study session—to have a lively conversation that built on a conceptual framework—could not be met because the learners did not yet have the vocabulary required for such discourse. And, of course, he should have anticipated the need for quality handouts with type that was easy for congregants of all ages to read.

On Saturday evening, Dr. Fonferberg also failed to attune his goals with the learners' needs. His goal was to engage people in debate about what "the experts" had to say, but the learners' focus was more on their own immediate experiences with social justice. He also "missed the mark" with the teenagers by assuming they would readily join into an open discussion with the adults. He did not try to get to know the girls during the Saturday night dinner and thus could not assess their readiness for the discussion or whether they would need extra encouragement to openly share their views.

Dr. Fonferberg's computerized presentation on Sunday morning did attune quite well with parents who came to learn about the general idea of social justice but, aside from its "entertainment value," the presentation was not designed to get the audience either to think critically about social justice issues or to expand their involvement in social action activities. Consequently, the Sunday session was not attuned to the plans of the weekend organizers and likely did not help increase congregants' activism or bring members to the synagogue's Social Action Committee.

In the long run, Dr. Fonferberg's objectives proved incompatible with those of most of the learners at the scholar-in-residence weekend. Even though the professor had spoken with the weekend's organizers prior to the event, both he and the synagogue representatives had refrained from discussing the details of the weekend in depth. The organizers didn't want to pressure him to spell out his plans, and based on his years of college teaching, he was confident that he could create a meaningful set of learning experiences. As often happens with invited guest speakers, the professor made decisions about the weekend program without adequate input from his hosts and made faulty presumptions about how most program participants would respond to the activities he had in mind.

We can conclude from Dr. Fonferberg's experience that to set and strive toward appropriate, learner-centered goals, adult educators should systematically devise curricular plans that clearly answer four questions:

1. What are the learners' goals?
2. What activities (e.g., text study, large-group discussion, lecture, demonstration) can I provide that will lead the learner to achieve those goals?
3. By what processes (e.g., reflective writing exercises, pair-share conversations, feedback questionnaires) will the learner be helped to integrate ideas sparked by those activities?
4. How can the learners indicate that their goals have been effectively met?

Masterful curriculum and program planning require the teacher to think about the learner, the content, and the learning process. While the teacher's goal—to disseminate the information he or she is best equipped to share—cannot be discounted, the issue of attunement between that goal and the expectations of the learners must not be overlooked.

The Teacher's Credibility and Authenticity

In his insightful book, *The Skillful Teacher* (1990), Stephen Brookfield points out that adult learners seek a blend of credibility and authenticity in their teachers. He explains that credibility stems from the students' perception that the teacher has something genuine to offer:

> Teacher credibility refers to teachers' ability to present themselves as people with something to offer students. When teachers have this credibility, students see them as possessing a breadth of knowledge, depth of insight, and length of experience that far exceeds the students' own. (pp. 163–164)

Brookfield writes that students want to learn from people who, because of their "knowledge, skill, and expertise," can guide them through the "contradictions, complexities, and dilemmas" that are part of adult life. Even though adults seek teachers who have well-honed interpersonal skills, they consider those skills "empty" if they are not accompanied with content mastery.

At the same time, to gain student respect, a teacher must be "authentic." Brookfield explains:

> Authentic teachers are, essentially, those that students feel they can trust. They are also those whom students see as real flesh-and-blood human beings with passions, frailties, and emotions. They are remembered as whole persons, not as people who hide behind a collection of learned role behaviors. . . . (p. 164)

Phoniness, arrogance, and other forms of self-importance are not tolerated for long by most adult learners. They expect their teachers to (a) use words and actions that are congruent; (b) admit to errors and acknowledge fallibility; (c) allow aspects of their personhood outside their role as teachers to be revealed to students; and (d) show respect for learners by listening carefully to students' expression of concern, by taking care to create opportunities for students' voices to be heard, and by being open to changing their practice as a result of students' suggestions. Teachers who abuse their authority will be challenged by adult learners because they are not impressed or intimidated by mere credentials. If a teacher fails to be a real person or fails to demonstrate suitable empathy, adults will "vote with their feet" and discontinue participation in the learning endeavor.

Brookfield writes, however, that finding the right balance between credibility and authenticity is far from easy. These are elusive concepts that "cannot be easily standardized." Teachers often feel they are erring too much on one side or the other. But, says Brookfield, part of being a skillful teacher is making a continual effort to build credibility or act authentically:

> If you neglect entirely the need to build credibility in students' eyes, then they will have little confidence in the value of what you ask them to do. And if you behave inauthentically, they will regard your asking them to do it as a self-serving confidence trick. (p. 176)

In the present case, it is likely that Dr. Fonferberg was seen as credible: he brought to the scholar-in-residence not only impressive academic credentials (almost always highly valued in the Jewish community), and he brought content about social justice that had immediate relevance to the lives of the synagogue members. At the same time, he came off as pompous and inaccessible, failing to reach out and genuinely connect with the learners in a personable or respectful way. This lack of "authenticity" may have impacted the decreasing enrollments over the course of the weekend. It certainly was implicit in the evaluative remarks made about the weekend to Barbara and Reva.

Setting the Learning Climate

The way in which a speaker or teacher establishes a climate for learning is an especially important element in successful adult education programs. As we saw with Dr. Fonferberg's weekend, it is hard to change a learning climate once a pattern gets set. In the professor's story, even though he meant to give a message of inclusiveness and warmth, his initial behaviors—reading a dry paper that went on for too long (seventeen minutes of a twenty-minute time slot), putting the first questioner on the defensive, shortchanging the available time for questions—created an atmosphere (and a learning culture) that was hard to overcome during subsequent sessions. On Saturday morning, he created a top-down learning structure in which he situated himself as "the expert." His body language (waving newcomers toward the handouts), his failure to learn the participants' names, and his failure to create opportunities for meaningful group dialogue suggested that the *content* was more important than the *process.* On Saturday evening, his social stance compounded the problem: at dinner he sat with the rabbi (rather than making it a point to be fully available to the learners), and during the group activity he stayed off to the side. These choices "sent a message" that Dr.

Fonferberg wasn't disposed to reaching out to all the learners who came to the event. A particularly unfortunate aspect of his behavior was that he didn't use the dinner hour to interact with the eighth graders in attendance. That oversight meant that when he sought to draw the girls out later in the evening, he hadn't established an authentic relationship with them.

The learning climate changed dramatically on Sunday morning when Dr. Fonferberg met with the religious school parents. In this more informal setting, the professor seemed more relaxed; and when the parents were responsive to his "message," he loosened up and shared entertaining stories with his audience. Unfortunately, this group represented only a small fraction of the congregation he was visiting.

When teaching adults, educators need to think about how they can create a mood that puts *everyone* at ease. In *Mastering the Teaching of Adults* (1991), Jerold Apps suggests a range of "atmosphere creators" that teachers can use to set a climate that is positive, supportive, and "human" (see Exhibit 8-2). Apps's "tools" place a great emphasis on the immediate creation of dialogues—between teacher and learner, and learner and learner. By first engaging the learners in some kind of discussion about who they are, what they know, or what they would like to know, the teacher starts a process that affirms the learner and also models a learning style that is open and inclusive.

During most of the scholar-in-residence weekend, Dr. Fonferberg did not devote any time to the kinds of "class climate" activities that Apps recommends. Perhaps he did not understand why such activities would be useful, or maybe he felt they would consume too much time. Adult educators often assume that learners will not want them to take the time to do what might be considered "feel good" activities. However, as Apps and other adult education experts have found, quality adult learning is enriched by social interaction and community building. Taking just a few minutes to have participants "come in close" to one another is never a waste of time. Nor is providing an opportunity for the learners to share something about what they bring to the learning situation—their skills, background, or relevant experience—that will contribute to the development of an atmosphere of collaboration and collegiality.

Finally, according to Jerold Apps (1991), a crucially important dimension of climate setting in adult education involves the teacher's use of *humor*. Apps offers several reasons that educators should use humor to set the tone and create a positive learning atmosphere:

EXHIBIT 8-2

Tools for Setting the Climate

Atmosphere creators

Greet participants at the door when they come to the first session. Introduce yourself. Give each participant a handout that briefly describes something about you and your interests or preparation.

Give participants, as they enter the room, a copy of the course or workshop syllabus or agenda that includes objectives for the course or workshop, schedule, suggested topics for each session, suggested readings, information about how to reach you.

If appropriate, invite participants to articulate topics they particularly want to have covered. Write these topics on the board. Indicate whether you will or will not be able to cover the additional topic requests—so participants know what's in store for them.

Provide something eminently practical during the first time the course or workshop meets. This can be a new skill or a new piece of usable information. If possible, provide a handout that reinforces what has been learned and offers resources for further information.

If the group has 25 or fewer members, arrange the chairs in a circle so everyone can see everyone else. If more than 25 participants, arrange small groups around tables.

Introductions

Beyond having students introduce themselves by name and other background information, frame a question that elicits a past experience, a desired outcome, or a question they hope will be answered in the course.

Introduce yourself using the same criteria that you have set for the learners.

Have pairs interview one another; have partners introduce each other to the group.

Have students make name tags to wear (or display as stand-up cards) at the first session. Ask them to provide a logo or symbol that indicates something about themselves or their interest. Have each person explain the chosen symbol.

Information exchanges

Have students fill out confidential information cards that provide you with details about how to reach them. Ask for background information relevant to their current learning, including any concerns about learning now. Ask if there is anything that might get in the way of their learning (e.g., learning disabilities, health or family problems, performance anxiety, etc.) or may require special assistance.

Create a class roster by asking students to contribute their phone numbers and e-mail addresses. Xerox the students' list and encourage people to call one another about the class.

Adapted from Jerold Apps, *Mastering the Teaching of Adults* (Malabar, Fla: Krieger, 1991).

Humor in [adult education] can serve several functions. It can liberate creative capacity by offering novelty and helping learners break out of their ruts. Humor can also help learners see that mistakes are a normal part of the learning process and are something at which we can all laugh.

Likewise, you can become more human by laughing at those times when you commit an "oops." Humor can help you build relationships with learners, and relationships between and among learners result in building community. A humorous story or event that occurred in a class often provides a "hook" for remembering some important content. Humor can help reduce tension in a [learning situation], especially when the subject matter is difficult or controversial and learners are feeling tense or overwrought. Humor helps calm emotions and relax learners so they can concentrate more fully. And lastly, humor often opens the lines to you and your learners by showing you are human. (p. 77)

Dr. Fonferberg's sense of humor was uneven during the scholar-in-residence weekend. After dry remarks on Friday night and little animation on Saturday morning, he did attempt to be funny with his "joke" about combining the Alef and Bet groups on Saturday night. He also poked fun at himself as a computer novice on Sunday morning and then revealed his lighter side by telling stories about Jews in cyberspace. Nonetheless, humor was not readily evident in Dr. Fonferberg's approach to teaching. For the most part, in his effort to bring rich content, he conveyed a seriousness (and seriousness of purpose) that muted the potential dynamism of each of his sessions.

Attention to the Physical Setting

In addition to the climate of the classroom and other learning situations, the physical setting also contributes significantly to successful adult learning. In many adult learning programs, teachers have little control over the physical setting and are frustrated when they cannot create a learning environment suited to the needs of adults. As we saw in the account of the Saturday evening events with Dr. Fonferberg, physical factors such as noise level, dim lighting, and poor air circulation can cause learners to feel "disconnected" from the learning process. More than twenty years ago, Malcolm Knowles (1980) wrote about the importance of the physical atmosphere in adult education:

> The self-concept of being an adult has several consequences regarding
> the requirements of an environment that will be conducive to adult
> learning. It suggests that the physical environment should be one in
> which adults feel at ease. Furnishings and equipment should be adult-
> sized and comfortable; meeting rooms should be arranged informally
> and should be decorated according to adult tastes; and acoustics and
> lighting should take into account declining audiovisual acuity. (p. 46)

Creating learning environments that meet adult requirements is not
always an easy task, especially in facilities that have limited classroom or
meeting spaces or are designed primarily to serve the needs of children.
Adult educators need to evaluate the rooms they will use and determine
how to make adult learners feel comfortable in such settings. In the scholar-
in-residence story, neither the professor nor the weekend planners adequately anticipated the physical needs of the learners in the Saturday
evening program: the table arrangement precluded good conversation; the
seating isolated various participants from one another; the fan caused noise
and did not adequately cool the room. While none of these "inconvenienc-
es" make or break the success of an adult education program, adult learners
should not be subjected to such physical discomforts. To the contrary, in
quality adult learning programs, the physical needs of the learner are considered a top priority.

As shown in Exhibit 8-3, the "physical" dimensions of successful adult
education extend to more than just the size and location of rooms and fur-
niture. Adult learners need easy access to classrooms, restrooms, parking
spaces, working phones, and beverages. They need readable materials, good
sound systems, and adjustable temperature/ventilation mechanisms. And
they need physical "breaks" in which to stretch, snack, and attend to personal concerns.

In Jewish adult learning enterprises, the *location* of programs is a further
matter for consideration. For some learners, meeting on-site at a synagogue
or other Jewish organization is crucial to feeling "connected" with the
Jewish learning experience. For others, being able to enjoy Jewish learning
in their place of work or the larger community may enable them to achieve
a sense of integration between their personal and public lives. Still others
may find that gathering intimately to study in a teacher's home provides a
sense of Jewish authenticity they don't experience in more "institutional"
environments. And some people may look to places in nature in order to tap
into their spiritual connection with Jewish learning. Jewish adult educators

EXHIBIT 8-3

The Physical Setting in Jewish Adult Learning Programs

Convenience of location
Where and at what time(s) will the greatest number of adults be the most likely to assemble?

Room set-up
What will make classrooms (or meeting rooms) appealing and comfortable for adults?

What will enhance learner interaction and facilitate easy attention between learners and teacher?

Are the tables, chairs, lighting, and acoustics commensurate with adult needs?

Are visual aids (e.g., white boards) available?

What will make the room feel "Jewish"?

What Jewish learning resources are evident and accessible?

Access to parking, restrooms, and other facilities
What will make all learners feel safe—that their access needs have been anticipated?

How easily will learners be able to move from location to location?

Room temperature and ventilation
Is there enough climate control to adjust to adults' physical comfort needs?

Refreshments

What kinds of beverages and snacks will be valued by the learners at different times of the day or evening?

Who will supply refreshments?

Who will set up and clean up?

What backup food supplies may be necessary?

Adapted from Malcolm Knowles, *The Modern Practice of Adult Education* (Chicago: Follett, 1980).

need to create learning opportunities in a variety of physical settings and help Jewish adults find their preferred learning milieu. They need to understand how important physical spaces are to the adult learner and talk with program planners and learners themselves about how to provide settings that meet their needs.

The Scope of Content and Materials

Once a learning program is established and learners are welcomed, it is incumbent on the adult educator to decide the scope of material that can be accommodated in the time allotted. In *How to Teach Adults* (1984), William Draves pithily concludes that gauging how much material will be covered can be resolved by dividing material into three categories: "material *essential* for the students to know; material *important* for the students to know; and material that is *nice* for the students to know" (p. 26). Obviously, "essential" means different things to different people, and it is up to each teacher to decide what material can be covered and what they most want their learners to learn. That caveat notwithstanding, Draves reminds educators that, to effectively manage content, one must prepare:

> Every course needs preparation. Without it, your thoughts will be disjointed, the course structure fragmented, and the students will feel as though—well, you hadn't prepared. The dangers of underpreparation are many. You can forget points. You can give details out of sequence and confuse the students. You can talk too long and not leave time for other important topics. You can forget a visual aid or handout which would have helped in your presentation. Teaching is not just talking. (p. 23)

Deciding how to organize and deliver material to adult learners is one of the biggest challenges faced by adult educators. There are no formulas to be followed when one imposes one's own structure on a body of information and then proceeds to teach the delimited content. Most adult educators find that, in a given session or program, they cover far less than they expected, because as soon as audience members understand key concepts, they look for openings to ask the speaker how to apply the points to their own lives or worldviews. In some instances, speakers realize early on that some or all of the audience don't have the background for understanding the topic at hand; in such situations, the educator must adjust goals and use the time to present a framework that will be useful to the learners.

Regardless of the scope of the content, however, when planning for presentations, adult educators are well advised to organize their material around a limited number of points—three or four, and certainly no more than five—in a session. Moreover, they should plan to reiterate these points throughout the presentation, thus reminding the audience of key themes and giving them a way to organize (and reflect on) the concepts themselves. Speakers who use visual materials (such as handouts, slides, or Powerpoint presentations) to reinforce those organizing points help learners both to "see" the ideas and to have labels for arranging information in their heads.

As seen in Exhibit 8-4, Rosemary Caffarella (2002) suggests some use-

EXHIBIT 8-4

Guidelines for Organizing Content

1. Start by acknowledging and reviewing what participants know about the content.
2. Give participants a framework to use in organizing what they are to learn (an "advanced organizer") and understand how this learning could be transferred to their own settings.
3. Introduce key concepts, ideas, and terms early and revisit them throughout the instructional unit.
4. Explore materials familiar to the participants and then proceed to the less familiar.
5. Ensure prerequisite knowledge and skills are taught prior to moving to content that builds on these materials.
6. Proceed from the most important to the least important.
7. Teach from the less difficult to the most difficult.
8. Do not overload any activity with ideas and/or skills that are difficult to learn.
9. Provide for instructional activities that allow for learning transfer throughout the instructional segment.

Source: Rosemary Caffarella, *Planning Programs for Adult Learners* (San Francisco: Jossey-Bass, 2002).

ful guidelines for organizing content. Dr. Fonferberg's presentation would have benefited from many/most of Caffarella's recommendations. Certainly, his audience would have been more receptive if Dr. Fonferberg had begun by assessing what their previous knowledge was and tailoring his remarks to their level of understanding and learning needs. The people who attended the Friday night service would have appreciated being given a brief, easy-to-remember framework about "Judah as a model of social responsibility"—some basic concepts that they could revisit and more fully explore as the weekend progressed.

Dr. Fonferberg's biggest "mistake" may have been his failure to provide the learners with some kind of outline or guide that could help them to understand the progression of ideas the professor planned to cover during the weekend. Aside from the list of social action Web sites he prepared for the Sunday morning meeting with the parents, he did not give the learners tools for becoming more authoritative about what they were learning and needed to learn. Most adult educators can benefit from the counsel of Rabbi Michael Balinsky, Director of Faculty Development for the Florence Melton Adult Mini-School, who helps Jewish educators design course "roadmaps" (instructional handouts) that help learners understand the scope of what is being taught and how specific information fits into "the bigger picture." Roadmaps typically include key terms and concepts, questions on readings, questions for *chevruta* discussion and personal reflection, and bibliographic suggestions. More than a syllabus, a roadmap is a visual guide that both the learners and teachers can refer to as they navigate the complex journey of Jewish adult learning.

Dr. Fonferberg's study session on Saturday morning would have been enhanced by the use of a roadmap that summarized key points about Judah and taking social responsibility and that "situated" the texts included in the handout. Such a roadmap might also have offered some explicit "framing questions" about ideas to be discussed. The roadmap questions could have been coordinated with related (but not the same) questions the Alef and Bet groups would address on Saturday night.

Rabbi Balinsky's description of the value of roadmaps in the Mini-School's text-based courses is displayed in Exhibit 8-5. Two sample roadmaps by Mini-School teachers, Professor Sam Fleischacker and Rabbi Maralee Gordon, are found in Exhibits 8-6 and 8-7.

EXHIBIT 8-5

Constructing Roadmaps

1. Roadmaps shape the class and give the students a sense of completeness and of having covered the material in the lesson. They show students that the teacher is prepared.

2. Roadmaps can provide the key vocabulary, definitions and context of the texts to be studied. While this material will be covered in class, this simple visual aid will allow more time for the exciting give and take when studying the texts.

3. Roadmaps are excellent summary sheets and good for review by the student. Students appreciate their use as a "highlighter" of the key points of the class. They will come back to these [summaries] when they want to review a topic.

4. Roadmaps let students know where the class is headed and its intended goal. As new ideas are encountered, these may prompt important questions that can shift the intended direction of the class. While flexibility must be maintained, the use of roadmaps legitimate the focus and direction of the class and can help limit unnecessary digressions.

5. Roadmaps allow for chevruta and small group study by providing guided and open-ended questions on the texts. This allows for more interactive methodologies to be introduced and the increased engagement of the students with the texts and each other.

6. Roadmaps link students to . . . questions . . . that will not be covered in class.

7. Roadmaps can add questions of personal relevancy that emerge from the topic for which there may not be time in class. The roadmap can act as the bridge from literacy to relevancy.

Source: Michael Balinsky, *Preparing to Teach: Florence Melton Adult Mini-School Faculty Handbook* (Chicago: Florence Melton Adult Mini-School, 2001).

EXHIBIT 8-6

Sample Roadmap: Moral Awareness in Judaism

Vocabulary

Mishpat and *Tzedakah* are both words that mean something like "justice," although *tzedakah* is usually translated "righteousness" and has come to mean "charity."

Note how many times these words appear in the opening passage. The word shofet—"judge"—has the same root as *mishpat*: note Abraham's use of that fact in the question he asks God.

Lifnim mishurat ha'din: a phrase literally meaning "within the lines of the law" but idiomatically understood to mean "beyond the letter of the law."

Text Study

I. Genesis 18:17–26
What kind of attitude towards God does this text recommend? To what extent is Avraham an example for us? Where does Avraham get his notion of justice from? The last question leads to the central issue in today's class: *Is morality built into us, or commanded from without, in Judaism?*

Additional Texts

A. Deuteronomy 6:17–18. "(17) Carefully keep the commands of the Lord your God, and His testimonies and the statutes He has commanded you. (18) You shall do the right and the good in the eyes of the Lord . . . "

About verse 18 Rashi says, drawing on a Midrash: "This refers to going *lifnim mishurat ha'din*," and Nachmanides (the Ramban), building on Rashi, says that the verse demands that a person show decency to their fellow human beings beyond the letter of the Torah in every respect, "until he is worthy of being called 'good and upright.'"

At B. Talmud *Baba Mezia* 30b, Rabbi Yochanan says that Jerusalem was destroyed because people insisted on the letter of the Torah and refused to go *lifnim mishurat ha'din*.

B. Micah 6:8: "[God] has told you, human, what is good; and what does the Lord ask of you but to do justice (*mishpat*), and to love mercy, and to walk humbly with your God?"

C. Isaiah 5:16 (used throughout "the holy God is made holy in righteousness *[tzedakah]*)."

II. Deuteronomy 24:10–18 We will not cover this text in class. When looking at it on your own, note its interweaving of our relationship to God with our relationship to other people, the way in which it translates broad ethical themes into concrete laws, and the use it makes at the end of Jewish history to enrich an ethical ideal.

III. Confession *(Al-Het)* for Yom Kippur Why is the confession in an alphabetical acrostic? Why do we confess sins we have not committed?

Source: Professor Sam Fleischacker, Florence Melton Adult Mini-School, Chicago, 2001.

EXHIBIT 8-7

Sample Roadmap: Miracles

Prayer Inserted into the Amidah on Chanukah

We thank you for the miracles, for the redemption, for the mighty deeds and triumphs, and for the battles which You did perform for our ancestors, in those days at this season.

In the days of Mattathias son of Yohanan, the Hasmonean kohen gadol [high priest], and in the days of his sons, a cruel power rose against Israel, demanding that they abandon Your Torah and violate Your mitzvot. You, in great mercy, stood by Your people in time of trouble. You defended them, vindicated them and avenged their wrongs. You delivered the strong into the hands of the pure in heart, the guilty into the hands of the innocent. You delivered the arrogant into the hands of those who were faithful to Your Torah. You have wrought great victories and miraculous deliverance for Your people Israel to this day, revealing Your glory and Your holiness to all the world. Then Your children came into Your shrine, cleansed Your Temple, purified Your sanctuary, and kindled lights in Your sacred courts. They set aside these eight days as a season for giving thanks and reciting praises to You.

[Siddur Sim Shalom, p. 117]

Vocabulary

Nes	miracle, sign
Nes Galui	an overt, visible miracle, suspending the laws of nature
Nes Nistar Nissim Nistarim (pl.)	a hidden miracle, an event that can be explained through the laws of nature, in which God's hand is not readily apparent to all
Al Kiddush Hashem	Literally "For the sanctification of God's name." It most often refers to martyrdom but also connotes behavior in the life that engenders a sense of admiration for God and Judaism.

Hevruta questions for reading texts 4 & 5

On Text 4, BT Berachot 20a:
Why no more miracles?
Do you buy this argument? Why or why not?

On Text 5, Ba'al Shem Tov:
What are these miracles we miss?
What do we use to cover our eyes?

Key Names

Ramb_n (acronym for Rabbi Moshe ben Nachman)—**Moshe Nachmanides** (1194–1270). Spanish biblical exegete, kabbalist, talmudist, poet and physician. His works include a commentary on the Chumash, Chiddushim (new insights) on the Talmud and *Torat haAdam*.

Samson (Shimshon) Raphael Hirsch (1808–1888). German rabbi and writer, leading exponent of Neo-Orthodoxy which attempted to combine European culture with loyalty to traditional Judaism. His writings include an annotated Chumash, *Horeb*, and *Nineteen Letters on Judaism*.

Baal Shem Tov (Besht). "Master of the Good Name," the title given to Israel ben Eliezer (1698–1760), founder of the Chasidic movement.

Source: Rabbi Maralee Gordon, Florence Melton Adult Mini-School instructor, Forest River, Illinois, 2001.

Lectures

The tradition of lecturing in adult education is well established, and the popularity of the lecture series is ubiquitous in Jewish adult education programs. On the other hand, in his book on teaching adults, Jerold Apps (1991) begins a section about "lectures" by making the point that "some teachers of adults argue that the lecture should never be used." However, he goes on to explain:

> There is a place for lectures, particularly short, succinct presentations used in conjunction with other teaching tools. Lecturing continues to be one of the most efficient and effective tools for presenting information. In order to be effective, lectures must be done well. (p. 46)

The debate about lectures revolves around whether they sufficiently engage the active participation of the learner and impel the learner to think critically about the information presented. In the present story, the lecturer, Dr. Fonferberg, failed to engage his audience in a positive way (first, because he talked "at" them on Friday night and then put a member of the audience on the spot about her views). Although he hoped the lecture would provide a framework for the Torah study discussion, Dr. Fonferberg didn't provide an easily recognizable framework for people to pick up on the next morning.

Overall, Dr. Fonferberg's lecture did not serve as a vehicle for effective learning. However, his mistakes should not serve as an indictment of lecturing overall. In *The Courage to Teach*, Parker Palmer (1998) endorses the lecture process, especially if lecturing is the means by which a particular teacher can most dynamically get ideas across and even create community in a classroom. Palmer enthusiastically recalls the lectures of his mentor:

> In [my mentor's] courses on the history of social thought, he lectured nonstop while we sat in rows and took notes. But those classes were not teacher-centered: his lectures put the subject, not himself, at the center of our attention, and we somehow gathered around that subject and interacted with it, though we hardly said a word.
>
> How did my mentor manage to simulate the community of truth and draw his students into it? His lectures did not merely present the data on social theory; they staged the drama of social thought. He did this in part by telling stories from the lives of great thinkers as well as explaining their ideas. We could almost see Karl Marx, sitting alone in

the British Museum Library writing *Das Kapital*. Through active imagination we were brought into relationship with the thinker himself and with the personal and social conditions that stimulated his thought.

But the drama of my mentor's lectures went further still. He would make a strong Marxist statement, and we would transcribe it in our notebooks as if it were holy writ. Then a puzzled look would pass over his face. He would pause, step to one side, turn and look back at the space he had just exited, and argue with his own statement from a Hegelian point of view! This was not an artificial device but a genuine expression of the intellectual drama that continually occupied this teacher's mind and heart.

Drama does not mean histrionics, of course, and remembering that fact can help us name a form of community that is palpable and powerful without being overtly interactive or even face to face. When I see a good play, I sometimes feel strongly connected to the drama, as if my own life were being portrayed on the stage. But I have no desire to respond aloud to the line just spoken, no urge to run up the aisle, jump onto the stage, and join in the action. Sitting in the audience, I am already on stage "in person," connected in an inward and invisible way that we rarely credit as the powerful form of community that it is. (pp. 136–137)

Jerold Apps (1991) offers some concrete tips for preparing and delivering lectures. His suggestions, as outlined in Exhibit 8-8, provide a good starting point for Jewish professionals who wish (or need) to use the lecture mode to convey information, but aspire to do so in a stimulating and learner-friendly way. A good lecture not only makes the material vivid, it also provokes the listener to think and engage in the material—to be "in dialogue" with ideas, concepts, and a range of alternative perspectives.

Discussion

The benefits of group discussion in adult learning programs are widely recognized. According to Stephen Brookfield and Stephen Preskill (1999), good discussions "develop" student thinking by helping learners to (a) explore a diversity of perspectives, (b) recognize and investigate assumptions, (c) increase intellectual agility, (d) develop the capacity for clear communication of ideas, (e) strengthen skills of synthesis and integration, and (f) become co-creators of knowledge. Just as delivering effective lectures takes preparation and practice, facilitating good discussion also requires thought-

EXHIBIT 8-8

Tips for Preparing and Delivering Lectures

Do's

Lecture no longer than thirty minutes at a time.

Include no more than four or five major points, and be clear about which particular point you are discussing. Summarize main points at the end of your presentation.

Make sure you can be heard.

Enhance the impact of lectures with visuals such as chalkboard, newsprint, overhead projection visuals, slides, and videotape clips.

Use stories (not jokes, although stories may be humorous) to keep interest and help amplify major points.

Keep language as simple and concrete as subject matter allows. The more abstract the ideas, the more stories you need.

Keep eye contact with the group.

Allow learners time to take notes.

Make sure all learners can see visual material you use. Don't stand in front of the chalkboard or screen.

Allow time for audience questions at the end of the lecture.

Provide learners a written handout of major points covered in the lecture, and where they can find additional information on this topic.

Start on time, end on time.

Be enthusiastic; believe what you are saying.

Don'ts

Reading from a manuscript. You may put yourself to sleep.

Talking too fast, too slowly, too softly, or in a monotone.

Tugging your ear, shuffling your notes, clearing your throat, saying "and ah" or "you know." Watch yourself on videotape or have a friend or spouse sit in and honestly report your performance quirks.

Believing that lecturing is the one and only way to teach, now and forever.

Believing that lecturing is the ultimate in poor teaching and never should be used when teaching adults.

Adapted from Jerold Apps, *Mastering the Teaching of Adults* (Malabar, Fla.: Krieger, 1991).

ful planning by adult educators. Exhibit 8-9 synthesizes suggestions for "discussion management" made by Williams Draves (1984) and Barbara Gross Davis (2002).

From this detailed list, we can see a number of things that Dr. Fonferberg might have tried during the discussions that occurred during the scholar-in-residence weekend. As noted in Exhibit 8-9, when learners meet in groups to study texts on a particular question, they find it helpful if the teacher can put "a clearly defined question before the group." Lacking a clear question, group members are likely to set their own learning agenda (as did Valerie on Saturday morning) or may spend more time talking about personal experiences than getting to task (as did the Alef group on Saturday evening). Without specified guidelines, a group member may "hijack" the discussion (as Herman and Myrna did with their argument about what matters in practicing *tzedakah*) and prevent discourse from occurring in a way that can include a plurality of voices and ideas.

Dr. Fonferberg was not effective in containing the input of group members who wanted to discuss their own interests, nor did he recognize the cost of "singling out spokespersons" when he asked the eighth graders to speak for their whole generation at the end of Saturday evening. Overall, Dr. Fonferberg would have been more effective as a discussion facilitator if he realized the need for "shape or contour" that would have helped the discussion participants to "contain" the discourse and help the group to see the issues they had raised that could set a positive social justice agenda for the future.

To his credit, Dr. Fonferberg *did* plan programs that included some interactive learning strategies, but his discussion activities needed more shaping and management. Exhibit 8-10 describes a range of large- and small-group discussion techniques that Jewish adult educators can incorporate into learning programs.

Asking Good Questions

Learner-centered instruction is enhanced by a teacher's thoughtful questions. Posing good questions is the "gold key" to helping learners begin to learn. In *Tools for Teaching* (2002), Barbara Gross Davis devotes a full chapter to "question strategies" and ways to handle learners' responses. She urges educators to plan their questions and to listen carefully to what students

EXHIBIT 8-9

Tips for Facilitating Discussions

Setting the Tone

Arrange the group so that people can face one another and make eye contact.

Have everyone, including yourself, seated.

Allow fifteen minutes for the discussion to get under way.

Set a clearly defined question before the group. Sometimes it helps if the initial question is set in personal terms. For example, don't ask what a text is about. Ask, "How do you understand this text? What does is say to you?"

Managing the Discussion Process

Keep the discussion on track. Try to limit your participation to areas that are important or overlooked, but assume responsibility for the direction of the discussion.

Prompt learners to provide a fuller comment or explanation than initially offered.

Give learners time to complete their thoughts before moving on.

Maintaining a Positive Leadership Role

Make it clear that you value all comments.

Try not to allow your own difference of opinion to prevent communication or debate.

Monitor your own behavior in responding to students. Be evenhanded in inviting comments from women *and* men, more *and* less sophisticated learners, talkative *and* quiet members of the group.

Avoid singling out individuals as spokespersons. Do not ask anyone to speak for his or her whole group (e.g., "So, Phyllis, what would Jewish women have to say about that?").

Take time every once in a while to draw loose ends together.

Credit learners' comments during your summary (e.g., "As Sally said. . .").

Give a sense of progress or satisfaction with the discussion, add a shape or contour to it so participants can see what they have achieved, and end on a positive note.

EXHIBIT 8-9 (continued)

Managing disruptive or distracting group members

Step in if some students seem to be dominating or ignoring the viewpoints of others (e.g., "Suzanne, we've appreciated your comments. Now let's hear what the others have to say." or "Mark, why don't we give Rita and some of the others a chance to say something?").

Take aside students who are oblivious to their impact on others (e.g., "Evelyn, I know you learn best by contributing, and I appreciate the eagerness with which you are willing to pitch in to get discussions going, but I'm worried that with your confidence and your speed of articulation you may be unwittingly stifling the contributions of others . . .").

Intervene to prevent learners from interrupting one another.

Speak up promptly if a learner makes a disparaging or distasteful remark.

Break the group into smaller groups; pair yourself with the disruptive group member.

Engaging Reticent or Passive Group Members

Try to involve the quiet person at first in a "starter" question, like a response, yes-or-no answer, or personal opinion (e.g., "Anne, what do you think of what Miriam just said?" or "Jason, would you agree or disagree with that?").

Don't single out an individual as the quiet one or make a point of turning the group's attention to the individual. Instead, ask a number of people for their opinion, including the person you are trying to bring out.

Give a light, quick compliment to the person you are trying to bring out after a response. "Thank you," "Good," "Interesting point," are all nonelaborate yet encouraging words.

Adapted from Barbara Gross Davis, *Tools for Teaching* (San Francisco: Jossey-Bass, 2002), and William A. Draves, *How to Teach Adults* (Manhattan, Kans.: Learning Resources Network, 1984).

EXHIBIT 8-10

Large- and Small-Group Discussion Techniques

Large-Group Prompts

Ask for learners' questions and select one for the group to address.

Formulate questions that probe something the students already know about but do not have a single correct answer (e.g., instead of asking "Why are there two versions of the Creation story?" ask "What about the two versions of the Creation story stands out in your mind?").

Pose an opening question, and give learners a few minutes to write down an answer. After students have finished writing, solicit comments.

Ask learners to recall an event in their own lives that pertains to the topic under discussion. When several people have related incidents, explore their commonalities and differences, and connect the discussion to the readings or other course material.

Ask learners to recall specific images from a reading assignment (or film or exhibit or speaker). List the images on the board, and explore the themes that emerge.

Have the learners make a list of key points. Use these as a starting point for discussion by asking learners which points are or are not important.

Use brainstorming activities that encourage learners to consider a range of possible causes, consequences, solutions, reasons, or contributing factors to some phenomenon. After all ideas are written on the board, have the group critically evaluate all the ideas.

Small-Group Activities

Subgroup Discussions. Give pairs, trios, or small groups of students an explicit task: "Identify the two most obvious differences between today's and last week's material" or "Make a list of as many examples of today's topic as you can in five minutes." Give the groups a time limit, and ask them to select a spokesperson who will report back to the entire class.

Storyboard Technique. Divide a particular problem into three to five subtopics or questions, post each subtopic or question in large type on a flipchart, and place the flipcharts around the classroom. Divide the class into as many subgroups as there are charts. Students are to read the question on their flipchart, write solutions on slips of paper or Post-its—one idea per note—and attach the slips to the chart. After ten minutes, the groups move on to the next flipchart and post notes there. Continue until all groups have visited all flipcharts.

EXHIBIT 8-10 (continued)

Jigsaw Technique. Assign different aspects of a topic to different small groups (e.g., different portions of a text or different questions about the topic). Give each group questions to answer or material to master. Have groups inform one another about their conclusions by reporting out or by mixing and matching with other group members.

Cooperative Learning Technique. Provide small groups of learners with resources and a specific task or problem to solve. Encourage these groups to produce "products" to share with one another.

Adapted from Barbara Gross Davis, *Tools for Teaching* (San Francisco: Jossey-Bass, 2002), and William. A. Draves, *How to Teach Adults* (Manhattan, Kans.: Learning Resources Network, 1984).

answer: "When students respond to questions, you also gain insight into how well they are learning the material. Like other aspects of teaching, the ability to develop good questioning skills can be learned" (p. 82). Exhibit 8-11 summarizes Davis's suggestions.

In *Understanding by Design,* Grant Wiggins and Jay McTighe (1998) provide a list of questions that educators can use to "check for understanding"—to assess how learners are processing information and thinking about ideas *throughout* an instructional event. These questions and prompts encourage dialogue and help learners to consider perspectives other than their own. Examples of good questions and probes are shown in Exhibit 8-12.

At the scholar-in-residence weekend, Dr. Fonferberg asked many questions, but he was not successful in helping the participants move from question to reflection or dialogue. Like many educators, he asked more than one question at a time and didn't encourage the learners to "go deeper" with their responses. He also tended to "fill the silence" by restating questions and sometimes rephrasing what learners were striving to articulate before they could get their ideas out. By not using questions to "change the tempo and direction" of discussions, Dr. Fonferberg may have enabled a small number of weekend participants to dominate the discourse and inhibit other learners from active engagement.

EXHIBIT 8-11

Tactics for Effective Questioning

Ask one question at a time. Sometimes, in an effort to generate a response, teachers attempt to clarify a question by rephrasing it. But often the rephrasing constitutes an entirely new question. Keep your questions brief and clear.

Avoid yes/no questions. Ask "why" or "how" questions that lead students to try to figure out things for themselves.

Pose questions that lack a single right answer.

After you ask a question, wait silently for an answer. Do not be afraid of silence. Be patient. Waiting is a signal that you want thoughtful participation.

Search for consensus on correct responses. If one student immediately gives a correct response, follow up by asking others what they think. "Do you agree, Ari?" is a good way to get students involved in the discussion.

Structure your questions to encourage student-to-student interaction. "Lewis, could you relate to what Jill said earlier?" Be prepared to help Lewis recall what Jill said. Students become more attentive when you ask questions that require them to respond to each other.

Use questions to change the tempo and direction of the discussion:

- To lay out perspectives: "If you had to pick just one factor . . ." or "In a few words, what would you say is the most important reason. . . . "

- To move from abstract to concrete, or general to specific: "If you were to generalize . . ." or "Can you give some specific examples?"

- To acknowledge good points made previously: "Aaron, would you tend to agree with Julie Ann on this point?"

- To elicit a summary or give closure: "Josh, if you had to pick two themes that recurred most often today, what would they be?"

Use probing strategies. Probes are follow-up questions that focus students' attention on ideas or assumptions implicit to their first answer. Probes can ask for specifics, clarifications, consequences, elaborations, parallel examples, relationship to other issues, or explanations.

Listen to the student. Do not interrupt a student's answer, even if you think the student is heading toward an incorrect conclusion. Interrupting signals your impatience and hinders participation. Wait a second or two when the student stops talking before moving on.

Praise correct answers. Students look to their teachers for guidance and support. Teachers who are indifferent to students' responses or who chastise students soon find that participation drops off. Be enthusiastic, replying with "Excellent answer" or "Absolutely correct" rather than a bland "OK," "Yes," or "All right."

Tactfully correct wrong answers. Correct the answer, not the student: "I don't believe that answer is correct" instead of "Drew, you are wrong." Look beyond the thought process: "This is a hard concept to grasp; let's take this one step at a time."

Adapted from Barbara Gross Davis, *Tools for Teaching* (San Francisco: Jossey-Bass, 2002).

EXHIBIT 8-12

Useful Questions and Probes to Check for Understanding

Questions

How is _____ similar to/different from _____?

In what other ways might we show/illustrate _____?

What is the big idea, key concept, message in _____?

What ideas/details can you add to _____?

What might you infer from _____?

What question are we trying to answer?

What are you assuming about _____?

How did you arrive at your conclusion?

What evidence supports _____?

How might this be viewed from the perspective of _____?

What does _____ reveal about _____?

Probes

Why?

How do you know?

What do you mean by _____?

Could you give an example?

Let's unpack that.

Talk it through.

Tell us more.

I'm almost with you, but help me, give me some more explanation.

Can you find that in the text?

Do you agree

But what about _____?

Adapted from Grant Wiggins and Jay McTighe, *Understanding by Design* (Alexandria, Va.: Association for Supervision and Curriculum Development, 1998).

The Use of Diverse Teaching Strategies

In chapter 6, I discussed the different learning orientations and learning styles that adults bring to the learning situation. In the field of Jewish adult learning, the diversity of learners is especially great due to the huge range of educational backgrounds and experiences that characterizes contemporary Jewish adult learners. In a typical Jewish adult education program, one can expect to find people who have no formal Jewish education and people with college-level (or higher) backgrounds in Jewish studies; individuals who have no familiarity with Hebrew to native-born Hebrew speakers; a spread of ages, observance patterns, and views about Jewish life; and a range of expectations about what constitutes Jewish study. The Jewish professional must be prepared to respond to such heterogeneity and must develop a diverse set of teaching strategies to reach out to the different learners who walk through the door. The teacher who uses a variety of teaching approaches will keep learners engaged and will help them to develop alternative ways of thinking about material.

At the scholar-in-residence weekend, Dr. Fonferberg certainly encountered a variety of learners, and he also endeavored to offer a range of ways to help them think about social responsibility. His plans to foster *chevruta* study on Saturday morning and to stage a debate on Saturday night were well-intentioned. He recognized the importance of facilitating an exchange of views among learners and of including both younger and older participants. Unfortunately, his activities did not successfully capture the attention of many people who attended the weekend. In *Planning Programs for Adult Learners* (2002), Rosemary Caffarella advises adult educators to mix and match activities and to coordinate them with specific learning objectives. Exhibit 8-13 lists five such objectives and some of the teaching techniques that Caffarella suggests for achieving them.

In principle, even though most adult educators *likely* would agree that mixing and matching teaching approaches *likely* will benefit the learner and might even make teaching more interesting, most practitioners are reluctant to move out of their own "comfort zone" and embrace the unfamiliar. Ironically, many seasoned Jewish professionals who enjoyed *chevruta* study in their own learning resist introducing their learners to that experience. Or they put people into small groups for discussion, but then fail to debrief these groups' insights by asking what they had determined in their conversations. Or they urge people to attend midrash-writing or bibliodrama

EXHIBIT 8-13

Examples of Techniques by Learning Objectives

Learning Objective	Technique
To help the learner acquire specific knowledge	Lecture Panel presentation Group discussions Web-searching E-mail and listservs Audio- and videoconferencing
To enhance the learner's cognitive skills	Case study Debate Critical incident exercises Drawing Observation Game Computer-based simulations
To develop the learner's psychomotor skills	Demonstration Trial-and-error practice activity Fieldwork Simulation Game
To strengthen the learner's problem-solving and problem-finding capabilities	Problem-based learning Socratic dialogue Reflective practice Simulation
To help the learner change attitudes, beliefs, values, and/or feelings	Role playing Simulation Group discussion Storytelling Metaphor analysis Reflective practice On-line forums and chatrooms

Adapted from Rosemary Caffarella, *Planning Programs for Adult Learners* (San Francisco: Jossey-Bass, 2002).

workshops led by other teachers but never bring these practices into their own teaching.

Jerold Apps warns, "Teachers often prefer the tools they use well. Good speakers like to lecture. Some enjoy using audiovisual equipment. Teachers who like working out elaborate management schemes will probably choose complicated learner involvement tools" (1991, p. 92). To be truly effective, Apps says, adult educators must take risks to become versatile in their classroom approaches:

> Master teachers constantly push beyond their present limits of performance. This means taking risks, trying new ideas, examining what worked right and what didn't, and then trying it again. In this way, your bag of teaching tools will ever increase. You will feel that you are constantly growing as a teacher, not having to rely forever on old teaching tools that become a little stale in the doing. (1991, p. 93)

Experimenting with new teaching strategies most often occurs when a teacher has had the opportunity to observe another teacher utilize a different approach. Like their students, teachers learn from good role models. Jewish professionals need good peer learning experiences in which they can reflect on their teaching and explore options for effective practice. Collaborative teaching experiences can also help teachers to consider alternative methodologies and support one another in experimenting with new approaches. Dr. Fonferberg might have found it valuable to consult with the synagogue educator and a member of the Torah study group when planning activities for the weekend. He certainly might have tried out some of his programmatic ideas on the weekend co-chairs, Barbara and Reva. His consultation with his daughter about how to utilize the latest electronic resources apparently served him well as he prepared his Sunday morning presentation.

Evaluation

It would not be surprising if, by the time Temple Kehillah's scholar-in-residence weekend was over, neither Barbara nor Reva had much enthusiasm for conducting an evaluation of the event. Undoubtedly, the tasks of putting the weekend together were time-consuming and demanding; the planners also may have assumed that Dr. Fonferberg would ask people to assess what they had learned and how they might apply their new knowledge. But, as with most episodic adult learning events, evaluation gets overlooked or is designed as an afterthought. Time and again, program planners and policy makers regret the absence of program assessment and belatedly wish they had feedback about what worked, what needed improvement, what learners would next like to learn, and so on.

In most Jewish adult learning programs generally, evaluation is an underutilized process. Because so many Jewish organizations measure success in adult education in terms of "numbers," when Jewish professionals assess their programs they tend to focus on quantity rather than quality. Moreover, because resources are limited and time for program development is constrained, many rabbis and educators resist asking learners for feedback—fearing that they will not be able to meet the demands or expectations of their constituents. Ironically, it is the evaluation process that can provide both teachers and learners important perspective about how to make Jewish adult learning more effective and meaningful. Jewish professionals who build evaluation activities into their learning programs help both themselves and the learners to identify what is going well and what could be improved. Working together, teachers and learners can plan future learning activities that will ensure strong learner participation and satisfaction.

Because Jewish adult learners seek quality in their learning experiences, Jewish adult educators should take time to conduct evaluation activities *throughout* the Jewish adult learning process. As William Draves (1984) points out, "Teachers often don't think about evaluations until the end of the course . . . but the time to think about evaluation is before the class starts. . . . If you wait until the end of the course, it may be too late to do the kind of evaluation you want, or ask the kinds of questions you want answered" (p. 85). Draves encourages educators to think about several issues before a program begins and to ask themselves:

- What are the important aspects of my teaching I want evaluated?
- How do I want to do an evaluation—in conversation, as a group, with a questionnaire?
- When do I want to evaluate my teaching—as the class is progressing so that I can change it and make the class even better while I'm teaching it, or after the course is over?

Anticipating evaluation in this way pushes an educator to engage in the kind of reflective practice described in chapter 7. It also helps the individual to select strategies that will best support the achievement of his or her teaching objectives.

Evaluation *during* a course or workshop can be beneficial in a different way. Classroom assessment techniques such as those proposed by Wiggins and McTighe (1998) provide insight to what the students are learning; evaluative activities can be used to assess how the teacher is impacting the learners. Throughout a program, an educator can ask what learners like and dislike and how they feel their learning needs might be better served. Informal conversations with adults about their learning experience can also shed light about how they are responding to the teacher's pedagogical approach. William Draves urges adult educators to seek honest and positive feedback on their actions and behaviors, noting that the "adult learning situation is an excellent chance to get suggestions and ideas on helping yourself to improve your own image and behavior" (1984, pp. 86–87).

Evaluations can be conducted informally (in conversation or by e-mail) or in more structured ways. Structured questionnaires can include both "closed questions" (forced choices, such as yes/no and scaled responses) and "open-ended questions" (requesting written comments). Closed questions provide quick information, but often lack detail or suggestions. Not all learners are willing to devote the time involved with a more open format, but when teachers omit such questions they send the message that they don't want substantive feedback or suggestions for improvement. Accordingly, evaluative questionnaires should include both closed and open-ended questions.

Exhibit 8-14 displays several forms that Jewish professionals may want to adapt for evaluation of Jewish adult learning activities. There is no one-size-fits-all form that works with every group of learners or for every teacher. Teachers who genuinely wish to gain their learners' feedback will revise their evaluation forms over time, tailoring questions to specific learning situations.

EXHIBIT 8-14

Evaluation Forms

FOR EVALUATING FIRST SESSION
OR A SERIES OF SESSIONS

Form A

What is your overall rating of today's meeting for each of these items?
Circle the appropriate number.

1 = low; 5 = high

1. Physical arrangement and comfort	1 2 3 4 5
2. Choice of methods instructor used	1 2 3 4 5
3. Participation level	1 2 3 4 5
4. Group atmosphere	1 2 3 4 5
5. What was accomplished	1 2 3 4 5
6. Interest of participants	1 2 3 4 5

Comments:

Form B

1. The three most important things we talked about today were:

   a.

   b.

   c.

2. What I learned today was:

3. A new idea for me was:

4. I'm confused about:

5. I don't understand:

6. What this session meant to me was:

All forms in this exhibit are adapted from Jerold Apps, *Mastering the Teaching of Adults* (Malabar, Fla.: Krieger, 1991).

EXHIBIT 8-14 (continued)

END-OF-MEETING FORM
FOR CLASSES THAT MEET SEVERAL TIMES

Circle appropriate number
1 = standard not met, 5 = standard fully met

1. Objectives were met	1	2	3	4	5
2. Course was logically organized	1	2	3	4	5
3. Used time appropriately	1	2	3	4	5
4. Used students' experiences well	1	2	3	4	5
5. Used appropriate teaching methods	1	2	3	4	5
6. Communicated ideas and concepts clearly	1	2	3	4	5
7. Encouraged the free exchange of ideas	1	2	3	4	5
8. Instructor sensitive to student backgrounds and needs	1	2	3	4	5
9. Instructor demonstrated thorough and up-to-date knowledge	1	2	3	4	5
10. Course stimulating and thought provoking	1	2	3	4	5

Comments about myself

11. I improved my understanding of concepts and principles	1	2	3	4	5
12. I was inspired to learn more than required	1	2	3	4	5
13. I participated actively in class discussions and activities	1	2	3	4	5
14. I felt prepared	1	2	3	4	5

Comments about the course and instructor
Comments about likes/strengths/things to be continued:

Comments about dislikes/weaknesses/things to be changed:

Other comments about your experience in this course or special gains or values from the course:

EXHIBIT 8-14 (continued)

FORM FOR WORKSHOPS AND
ONE- OR TWO-SESSION CLASSES

When I came to this course, I had hoped . . .

Now that I have taken the course, I feel . . .

A practical thing from the course that I plan to use is . . .

A suggestion for improvement that I would make is . . .

FORM FOR ONE-SESSION GROUP DISCUSSION

Please circle your rating
1 = low
5 = high

1. How satisfied were you with this session?	1	2	3	4	5
2. To what extent did you feel comfortable with the group?	1	2	3	4	5
3. To what extent did you know the group members?	1	2	3	4	5
4. To what extent were your personal objectives met?	1	2	3	4	5
5. To what extent did you contribute to the discussion?	1	2	3	4	5
6. To what extent did the group stay on the announced topic?	1	2	3	4	5
7. I would rate the group leader	1	2	3	4	5

Suggestions:

Epilogue

Toward Using Skill, Ability, and Knowledge

And Moses said to the Israelites: See, Adonai *has singled out by name Bezalel, son of Uri son of Hur. . . . He has endowed him with a divine spirit of skill, ability, and knowledge . . . and has inspired him . . . to give directions. . . . Let . . . every skilled person whom* Adonai *has endowed with skill and ability to perform expertly all the tasks . . . undertake the task and carry it out.*
—*Exodus 35:30–34; 36:1–2*

Jewish adult learning journeys take many forms. As I described in chapter 1, my own journey began in the early 1990s when I was at a point of transition in my life and looked to Jewish learning as a way to understand more about my tradition and my relationship to Judaism. A turn in the road came when I began interviewing other adults about their learning experiences and discovered that little had been written about Jewish adult development and learning that could contextualize my research findings. I set out—using my "skill, ability, and knowledge"—to begin to correct this deficiency in the literature. Like Bezalel, I took on a challenge to offer some direction to others—in this case, to provide Jewish professionals with information and resources that would help them to become more effective in their work with Jewish adults. For several years, I conducted interviews with learners, consulted with Jewish educators, visited synagogues, and studied various adult Jewish learning programs, all of which helped me conceptualize both the framework for this book and the overview presented in Appendix 3.

A further turn in the road came in 2000, when I was invited by a small group of Jewish professionals to meet with them to discuss their work with adult Jewish learners. In the first of four meetings, each of the group members shared his or her "story" about Jewish learning and teaching, revealing a common theme that I had not anticipated: that even though each of these individuals was highly successful and well regarded as a teacher who helped

Jewish adults to grow, each felt blocked with respect to his or her *own* growth as a learner. Like many educators who are at risk for burnout, the group members said they were so busy "pouring out" ideas and information to others that they did not have time to replenish their own wells. They agreed that, at mid-career, in order to revitalize their teaching and nourish their souls, they needed—and yearned—to become learners again themselves.

Moved by their hunger for learning, I suggested to the group members that we use our time together to study texts about the educational process,[7] works I believed would help them to reflect both on their experience as educators and on their own Jewish lives and Jewish learning. At the end of the four meetings, the group agreed that learning together had been more nurturing than they had anticipated and proposed that we continue for another four sessions. Together we then studied texts on feminist pedagogy, distance learning, adult education, and Jewish education.[8] Over the period of a year, in addition to meeting with the group, I interviewed each person individually. From this sequence of conversations, I came to appreciate that *lifelong learning* is as important for Jewish professionals as it is for the people they teach. And, just as adult learners grow and thrive in learning situations that involve dialogue and community building, so too do Jewish professionals need opportunities to study with their peers on a regular basis. As one of the group members (a rabbi) commented in the fourth session:

> This is my first experience as a rabbi, aside from talking with colleagues in my own synagogue, of talking with other rabbis about what our work is. That there is a group of us sitting in a room and being very honest about what our work is—it's usually not done. I think about the loneliness of the profession and how I rarely see this much openness. It's been very comfortable in terms of hearing about our experiences together.

And another group member, an educator, responded:

> I'll just say ditto to that. I was thinking a lot about that last night and when coming this morning—thinking that this is rare, that it's easy to become insular and isolated. And to not have to struggle with these

---

7. *The Courage to Teach* by Parker Palmer; *Mentor: Guiding the Journey of Adult Learners* by Laurent Daloz; and *Becoming a Congregation of Learners* by Isa Aron.
8. *Women as Learners* by Elisabeth Hayes and Daniele Flannery; *Developing Adult Learners* by Kathleen Taylor, Catherine Marienau, and Morris Fiddler; *Mishneh Torah* by Maimonides; *Distance Training* by Deborah A. Schreiber and Zane L. Berge.

issues alone . . . it helps me in terms of my own development to have peers to share and learn with.

My involvement with this community of learners—albeit learners who were teachers themselves—opened my eyes to the needs Jewish professionals have for ongoing professional growth. As rabbis, cantors, educators, and communal workers take on the challenges of teaching greater numbers of Jewish adults, they will need opportunities to learn more about adulthood, adult learning, adult Jewish education, and themselves as Jewish adult educators.[9]

Arenas for Growth: What Jewish Professionals Need to Learn

My experience with the group described above, as well as my consultations with rabbis, educators, adult learning program coordinators, synagogue adult education chairpersons, and hundreds of Jewish adult learners themselves, have persuaded me that there are five "arenas" in which Jewish professionals who work with adults need to learn and grow.

1. **Learning about adult development and Jewish adult life.** The field of adult development provides an important framework for understanding the kinds of transitions, developmental tasks, and changes in personal meaning that mark the journey of adulthood. The more Jewish professionals take note of the many ways adults change and grow, the more alert they can become to the dynamics of adult Jewish growth. In order to authentically and sensitively meet Jewish adults who "knock on the door" of Jewish institutions, Jewish professionals need to learn from the emerging literature on Jewish identity and create programs that support individuals who seek to understand themselves as Jews.

2. **Learning about adults as learners and adult Jewish learners.** The literature on the characteristics of adult learners provides rich insight to what matters to adults when they engage in learning activities. As learners, adults strive to become independent, self-directing, and

---

9. This need is being recognized by a range of leaders in the contemporary Jewish community, including my colleagues at Hebrew Union College–Jewish Institute of Religion who have lent support to the establishment of the Institute for Teaching Jewish Adults, which will offer professional development seminars and resources to individuals who work with Jewish adults.

competent; they thrive in learning environments that help them to transform their perspective and to feel empowered to effect change in their lives. Jewish professionals need to understand the principles of adult learning in order to help Jewish adults move beyond the limitations of pediatric Judaism and to overcome personal "baggage" about their inadequate Jewish education or alienation from the Jewish community. They also need to recognize how diverse Jewish adult learners are and develop learning programs that accommodate the full spectrum of learning needs, styles, and preferences.

3. **Learning about teaching adults and teaching Jewish adults.** Effective adult education begins with the learner and utilizes teaching strategies that help learners find relevance and meaning in what they are learning. Such strategies build on learners' past experience, challenge old assumptions, encourage collaboration, and motivate the learner to acquire a sense of mastery and authority. To remain learner-centered, Jewish professionals need to understand the importance of *tzimtzum*—of creating space for Jewish adults to find their own voices as Jewish learners and Jewish knowers. They need to create learning experiences that show Jewish learners how to study Jewish texts, consult Jewish sources, and participate in ongoing Jewish discourse. In addition to helping people learn "how to learn," Jewish professionals need to help advanced Jewish adult learners develop the skills necessary for sharing what they have learned with others.

4. **Learning about oneself as a teacher.** Professional growth for educators requires reflection about one's practice. The more a teacher is willing to examine what occurs in his or her classroom, the assumptions that underlie curricular or classroom management decisions, and the ways that authority is used to create a successful learning environment, the more likely that teacher will be to make changes to ensure quality learning for the learners. Jewish professionals typically work in isolation and do not have much opportunity to get feedback on their work with adults. They need to create professional development opportunities that expose them to new ideas about education, encourage them to give and receive feedback with peers, and increase their awareness of how they interact with the adults they teach.

5. **Learning about one's own needs as a learner.** To stay "alive" as a teacher, one must have opportunities to revitalize through new learning. Lifelong learning sustains *both* learners and their teachers. Jewish professionals who stop learning put themselves at risk for burnout. They neglect their own love of learning and forget the Jewish admonition to study. Accordingly, it is crucial for Jewish professionals to take their own learning seriously. They must routinely build learning time into their schedules and request learning opportunities as part of their job contracts. When they are "renewed" by their learning experiences, they can serve as role models to others.

One Last Story

Although a central theme of this book has been "learner-centered learning," I learned an important lesson from Rabbi Eli Herscher of Stephen S. Wise Temple in Los Angeles. One day when I was at a meeting with Rabbi Herscher, he mentioned that he was "up against the deadline" for submitting brochure details for a class he would teach after the High Holy Days. This busy leader of the largest synagogue in the United States said that he was tired of his standard practice of teaching introductory material primarily to large classes; he wanted to offer a longer class for people who might be ready to study on a deeper and more systematic basis. But, he said, "I don't know what the 'hook' is: How do I make it attractive to get them in the door?"

The conversation shifted to the costs and benefits of reaching out to small "niche" groups of learners (especially when governing boards are impressed by *large* numbers), but then, almost as an afterthought, Rabbi Herscher mused, "You know, I love midrash, so it will probably be something with midrash. I have some time this summer to prepare. All I really need is to come up with the title and a couple of sentences." One of our colleagues replied, "Why not just call it 'Rabbi Herscher Loves Midrash' and say that you are going to share with them what got *you* 'in the door' of Jewish learning?" Rabbi Herscher looked startled—and bemused. "I could do that?" he asked. "I could actually begin with what I love and tell them how I got there? What an amazing idea!"

Beginning with "what one loves" and "how one got there" is what makes a teacher authentic and credible to learners. Although a central theme of this book has been "start with the learners," it would be shortsighted to ignore the strengths, talents, expertise, and passions that have brought each teacher to his or her work. When teachers start with their own love of learning and then enable others to see how what they have learned has given meaning and vitality to their lives, they create a *culture of learning* that is genuine, infectious, and lasting.

Kaddish D'Rabanan

It is my privilege to conclude this book by offering a blessing to Jewish professionals who, like Bezalel, design sacred spaces in which Jews can participate more fully in Judaism and Jewish life. Over the past fifteen years, the explosion of adult interest in Jewish learning could not have taken root if there had been no teachers to touch the minds and hearts of Jewish adults who thirst to learn. Again and again, gifted Jewish professionals have taken the initiative to make Jewish learning come alive in synagogues, Jewish Community Centers, community-based study programs, retreat centers, colleges, museums, travel-and-learn programs, and numerous other venues. They have diversified their offerings, honed their teaching strategies, developed curricular materials appropriate to the contemporary Jewish adult population, designed new learning centers and electronic networks, encouraged colleagues to become Jewish adult educators—all the while reaching out to people who never before imagined finding themselves welcome at the table of Jewish study. In forging ahead to create meaningful learning opportunities for Jewish adults, these rabbis and educators have "grown" hundreds of learners—cultivating their potential, feeding their hunger for knowledge, and supporting them in their aspirations to find a way to share what they have learned with others.

To those teachers, to their students, and to the students of their students, I extend heartfelt thanks. You have enriched the minds and spirits of Jewish adult learners and, through your teaching, modeling, wisdom, and support, have inspired them to live Torah and teach Torah.

May you be blessed throughout the journey of *your* Jewish life and Jewish learning.

Increasing Adult Learner Motivation*

Strategies for Establishing Inclusion	What Jewish Professionals Can Do
Allow for introductions.	• Have learners share their stories of Jewish learning, including how they learned what they know and Jewish learning in their families. • Tell your own Jewish learning stories.
Indicate your cooperative intentions to help adults learn.	• Invite learners to consult with you about their Jewish learning journeys. • Offer review sessions and audiotapes of lectures. • Create a class bulletin board on the Internet, and send tips to reinforce Jewish learning.
Share something of value with your adult learners.	• Describe your involvement with the subject matter. • Share credible intense experiences related to the learners or the material being learned. • Use humor.
Use collaborative and cooperative learning.	• Foster study partnerships (*chevruta*). • Encourage special interest learning projects. • Offer to partner with learners who have poor social skills or don't "fit in."
Clearly identify the learning objectives and goals for instruction.	• Put goals in writing and spend time reviewing your plans with the learners. • Adapt goals to learners' needs, as appropriate. • Show learners where your/their goals intersect.

* Based on Raymond Wlodkowski, *Increasing Adult Motivation to Learn* (San Francisco: Jossey-Bass, 1999).

Strategies for Establishing Inclusion	What Jewish Professionals Can Do
Emphasize the human purpose of what is being learned and its relationship to the learners' personal lives and contemporary situations.	• Relevance, relevance, relevance: help Jewish adults to see how what they are learning relates to their lives today.
Assess learners' current expectations and needs and their previous experience as it relates to present learning.	• Ask learners what they want to learn and how they best learn. • Offer private mechanisms (e-mail, appointments) for learners to share with you their needs, goals, and concerns. • Systematically "check in" with learners about their lives and learning.
Explicitly introduce important norms and participation guidelines.	• Remember that Jewish adult learners are volunteers and your classes are *not* "for credit" or mandated. • Respect learners' comfort zones about voicing opinions, reading aloud, self-disclosure, etc. • Ask students for "buy in" to in-class behavior norms. • Assert your role as the "limit setter."
Introduce the concept of "learning edges" to help learners accommodate more intense emotions during episodes of new learning.	• Acknowledge that some aspects of learning push Jewish adults to the edge of their own comfort. • Demonstrate respect for learners' boundaries, while also encouraging them to test themselves beyond the boundaries. • Help Jewish adults to identify new areas for intellectual and emotional growth.
Acknowledge different ways of knowing, different languages, and different levels of knowledge or skill to engender a safe learning environment.	• Encourage learners to serve as teachers or resources for one another, including you. • Ask learners to put ideas in their own language and convey meanings to one another.

Strategies for Developing Positive Attitudes	What Jewish Professionals Can Do
Ensure successful learning with mastery learning conditions.	• In addition to your primary instructional materials, provide alternative learning resources. • Set understandable standards and show what it takes to improve abilities or knowledge. • Avoid competition/protect learners' self-esteem. • Break content down into smaller units of learning, thus increasing learners' sense of accomplishment. • Give learners feedback about how to do better (formative evaluations).
Use assisted learning to scaffold complex learning.	• Give clues, information, prompts, reminders, and encouragement and then gradually help the learner to do more/think more. • Model skills that are to be learned and think learning processes "out loud." • Anticipate difficulties learners may encounter. • Regulate difficulty by combining demanding tasks with simpler tasks. • Use reciprocal teaching, rotating roles with the learner. • Provide a checklist so learners can self-monitor.
Encourage the learner.	• Give recognition for effort. • Minimize mistakes while learner is struggling. • Emphasize learning from mistakes. • Show faith in adult's capacity as a learner. • Work closely with the learner at the beginning of difficult tasks. • Affirm the "process" of learning and what it takes to learn new things.

Strategies for Developing Positive Attitudes	What Jewish Professionals Can Do
Promote learners' personal control of the context of learning.	• Help increase learners' sense of control by helping them to plan their Jewish learning journey. • Encourage learners to make choices about what, how, with whom, where, and when to learn something. • Help learners to identify personal strengths while learning. • Help learners to analyze potential blocks to progress in learning.
Use goal-setting and contracting methods.	• Discuss goals with learner. • Determine together how progress will be measured. • Preplan to consider and remove potential obstacles. • Identify resources. • Build in how learning will be assessed.

Strategies for Enhancing Meaning in Learning Activities	What Jewish Professionals Can Do
Provide frequent response opportunities to all learners on an equitable basis.	• Make sure all learners get an equitable chance to respond or perform. • Always dignify the learner's response. • When asking a question or announcing an opportunity to perform a task, wait three seconds or more before selecting a respondent.
Help learners realize their accountability for what they are learning.	• Show how all components of instruction are imperative for achievement of learning goals. • Use syllabi, outlines, models, or diagrams to show briefly but lucidly what you plan to teach. • Intersperse lectures with the *think-pair-share* process (learners reflect on ideas and then pair up with a partner and share reflections). • Round out reflective activities by soliciting comments, listing insights, taking questions.
Introduce, connect, and end learning activities attractively and clearly.	• Ask provocative opening questions. • Create anticipation about what lies ahead. • Relate the learning activity to pop culture or current events. • Use organizational aids such as handouts, outlines, models, and graphs that interrelate concepts, topics, key points, and essential information. • Make directions and instructions as clear as possible and then check for understanding. • In closing, review the basic concepts or skills achieved during the learning activity. • Allow for clarification at the end of the learning activity. • Request feedback, opinions, or evaluation.

Strategies for Enhancing Meaning in Learning Activities	What Jewish Professionals Can Do
Use critical questions to stimulate learner engagement and challenge.	• Help learners to distinguish between verifiable facts and value claims, determine credibility of sources, identify unstated assumptions and bias. • Ask thought-provoking questions that help learners to make connections between what they already know and new information. • Use real-world problems to engage critical thinking for problem-solving. • Use intriguing problems to make learners challenge old assumptions.

Strategies for Engendering Competence	What Jewish Professionals Can Do
Provide effective feedback.	• Ask what the learner would like feedback on. • Be sensitive to the learner's readiness for feedback. • Give feedback that is informational rather than controlling. • Give feedback that is personal and focuses on the learner's incremental improvement. • Show the learner how more effort or alternative approaches could contribute to their learning.
Use self-assessment methods to improve learning and to provide learners with the opportunity to construct relevant insights and connections.	• Help learners to understand themselves more comprehensively as Jewish learners, knowers, and participants in Jewish life. • Help learners weave relationships and meanings between their Jewish learning and their lives.
Effectively praise and reward learning.	• Give praise that is sincere, specific, sufficient, properly attributed for genuinely praiseworthy behavior. • Give praise in a manner that will be valued by the learner.
Provide positive closure at the end of significant units of learning.	• Achieve closure with celebrations, acknowledgments, and sharing.

Observation Guide for Culturally Responsive Teaching and Learning (Adult Version)

Margery B. Ginsberg

This guide is organized to identify elements that support intrinsic motivation. It is not an assessment tool but an instrument to promote dialogue about instruction and to affirm what is working to foster four motivational conditions.

Establishing Inclusion

How does the learning experience contribute to developing a community of learners who feel respected and connected to one another?

Norms are visible and understood by all:

- Norms are in place that help everyone feel that he or she belongs.
- Learners and instructor have opportunities to learn about each other.
- Learners and instructor have opportunities to learn about each other's unique backgrounds.
- Course agreements are negotiated.

Evidence:

All learners are equitably actively participating and interacting:

- Instructor directs attention equitably.
- Instructor interacts respectfully with all learners.
- Learners talk to and with partner or small group.
- Learners know what to do, especially when making choices.
- Learners help each other.

Evidence:

Developing a Positive Attitude

How does this learning experience offer meaningful choices and promote personal relevance?

Instructor works with learners to personalize the relevance of course content:

- Learners' experiences, concerns, and interests are used to develop course content.
- Learners' experiences, concerns, and interests are addressed in responses to questions.
- Learners' prior knowledge and learning experiences are explicitly linked to course content and questions.
- Instructor encourages learners to understand, develop, and express different points of view.
- Instructor encourages learners to clarify their interests and set goals.
- Instructor maintains flexibility in pursuit of emerging interests.

Evidence:

Instructor encourages learners to make real choices regarding such issues as:

- How to learn (multiple intelligences)
- What to learn
- Where to learn
- When a learning experience will be considered to be complete
- How learning will be assessed
- With whom to learn
- How to solve emerging problems

Evidence:

Enhancing Meaning

How does this learning experience engage participants in challenging learning?

The instructor encourages all learners to learn, apply, create, and communicate knowledge:

- Instructor helps learners activate prior knowledge and use it as a guide to learning.
- Instructor in concert with learners creates opportunities for inquiry, investigation, and projects.
- Instructor provides opportunities for learners to actively participate in challenging ways.
- Instructor asks higher-order questions of all learners throughout instruction.
- Instructor elicits high-quality responses from all learners.
- Instructor uses multiple *safety nets* to ensure learner success (for example, not grading all assignments, allowing learner to work with a partner, and so forth).

Evidence:

Engendering Competence

How does this learning experience create an understanding that learners are becoming more effective in learning what they value and perceive as authentic to their real-world experience?

There is information, consequence, or product that supports learners in valuing and identifying their learning:

- Instructor clearly communicates the purpose of the lesson.
- Instructor clearly communicates criteria for excellent outcomes.
- Instructor provides opportunities for a diversity of competencies to be demonstrated in a variety of ways.
- Instructor helps all learners identify accomplishments.

- Instructor offers options for assessment.
- Instructor provides opportunities for continual feedback for individual learning.
- Instructor provides opportunities for learners to make explicit connections between new and prior learning.
- Instructor provides opportunities for learners to make explicit connections between their learning and the real world.
- Instructor provides opportunities for learners to self-assess their learning and to adjust or reflect.
- Instructor provides opportunities for learners to self-assess their personal responsibility for contributing to the course or training.
- Instructor provides opportunities for learners to give each other feedback.

Evidence:

Jewish Lives, Jewish Learning: An Overview

Points about Adult Development	Points about Adult Learners	Points about Contemporary American Jewish identity
• There are developmental tasks that need to be completed throughout the life cycle. • Adult life is marked by periods of stability and periods of transition. • Hallmarks of midlife include a search for meaning and the desire to develop the underdeveloped parts of the self. • As adults mature, they find special meaning in passing on what they have learned to the "next generation." • Compared to earlier generations, adults today absorb more changes more often; they face more choices and grapple with decisions that require more flexible and adaptive responses. • To reduce cognitive disequilibrium, adults strive to forge new meanings about old ideas and test out these new meanings with other people. • At times of transition, adults look to new education to acquire new status, gain social support, and reduce stress.	• Adults are voluntary learners. • Adults bring experience to their learning and also value experiential learning; many seek application and immediacy rather than theory. • Adults are consumers who seek "quality" in their learning; they value credibility and authenticity in their teachers. • Adults bring different learning orientations: they may be goal oriented, activity oriented, learning oriented, or spirituality oriented. • Adults value both informational and transformative learning. • Transformative learning involves questioning old assumptions, reflection, and discourse. • Adults "develop" as learners through dialogue and by coming to see learning as lifelong. • When adults reframe their understanding of themselves as learners and knowers, they develop a more critical stance about their learning and their capacity to teach others.	• Most contemporary Jews come from the "the periphery to the center" (from life to Torah). • Many Jewish adults have a child's concept of Judaism and Jewish tradition; they see Jewish education as something "for children" (pediatric Judaism). • For most American Jews, Jewish identity is fluid, ebbing and flowing throughout a lifelong Jewish journey. • At midlife, Jewish adults often experience "paradoxical thinking" about their Jewish values. • Jewish adults value the "sovereign self" and want to voluntarily determine how Judaism fits into their lives. • Even moderately affiliated Jewish adults look more to family than synagogue for meaningful Jewish experience. • Jewish adults often feel a sense of tribal attachment to other Jews, but are selective about how and when they express group solidarity. • Jewish baby boomers are more assimilated than earlier generations and more universalistic in their social concerns.

Points about Adult Jewish Learners and Learning	"Quality" Jewish Educators...
• Many Jewish adults need to acquire positive Jewish memories and attachments with respect to Jewish learning. • Adult Jewish learners seek to make meaning of their Judaism and to understand how Jewish tradition can give meaning to their lives. • Jewish adults like getting an intellectual framework of Judaism —understanding where ideas and events "fit in." • Jewish adults value learning multiple perspectives, having opportunities for dialogue, and becoming part of an ongoing learning community. • Adult Jewish learner motivations for learning are diverse and change with experience. • Women are frequently overrepresented in adult Jewish learning programs. • Jewish adults utilize diverse communal, institutional, informal, and electronic learning opportunities and resources. • Jewish learning impacts Jewish generativity: passing on one's Jewish knowledge to others.	• Define Jewish learning broadly. • Assess the demographics, needs, and interests of learners. • Anticipate learner diversity and cultivate niche groups. • Offer programs that fit learners' availability and commitment level. • Provide informational, experiential, and transformative learning options. • Are credible and authentic. • Help learners learn how to learn. • Develop learners into teachers. • Look for mentoring opportunities. • Foster learners' collaboration and connection. • Solicit/utilize learners' feedback. • Reflect on practice. • Dialogue about practice with other professionals. • Revitalize through their own learning.

References

Ainsworth, Mary D. "The Development of Infant-Mother Attachment." In *Review of Child Development Research,* edited by B. M. Caldwell and H. N. Ricciuti, volume 3, pp. 1–94. Chicago: University of Chicago Press, 1973.

Antonucci, Toni C. "Social Supports and Social Relationships." In *Handbook of Aging and the Social Sciences,* 3rd ed., edited by Robert H. Binstock and Linda K. George, pp. 205–227. New York: Academic Press, 1990.

Apps, Jerold. *Mastering the Teaching of Adults.* Malabar, Fla.: Krieger, 1991.

Aron, Isa. *Becoming a Congregation of Learners.* Woodstock, Vt.: Jewish Lights, 2000.

Balinsky, Michael. *Preparing to Teach: Florence Melton Adult Mini-School Faculty Handbook.* Chicago: Florence Melton Adult Mini-School, 2001.

Bandura, Albert. "Self-Efficacy." In *Encyclopedia of Human Behavior.* San Diego: Academic Press, 1994.

Bee, Helen. *The Journey of Adulthood.* 3rd ed. Upper Saddle River, N.J.: Prentice Hall, 2000.

Belenky, Mary, Blythe Clinchy, Nancy Goldberger, and Jill Tarule. *Women's Ways of Knowing.* New York: Basic Books, 1986.

Blos, Peter. *On Adolescence.* New York: Free Press, 1962.

Borowitz, Eugene. "*Tzimtzum:* A Mystic Model for Contemporary Leadership," *Religious Education* 69, no. 6 (November/December 1974).

Brookfield, Stephen. *Understanding and Facilitating Adult Learning.* San Francisco: Jossey-Bass, 1986.

Brookfield, Stephen. *Developing Critical Thinkers.* San Francisco: Jossey-Bass, 1987.

Brookfield, Stephen. *The Skillful Teacher.* San Francisco: Jossey-Bass, 1990.

Brookfield, Stephen, and Stephen Preskill. *Discussion as a Way of Teaching: Tools and Techniques for Democratic Classrooms.* San Francisco: Jossey-Bass, 1999.

Buhrmester, Duane, and Wyndol Furman. "The Development of Companionship and Intimacy." *Child Development* 58 (1987): 1101–1113.

Caffarella, Rosemary. *Planning Programs for Adult Learners.* San Francisco: Jossey-Bass, 2002.

Clausen, John A. *American Lives: Looking Back at the Children of the Great Depression.* New York: Free Press, 1993.

Cohen, Steven M., and Aryeh Davidson. *Adult Jewish Learning in America: Current Patterns and Prospects for Growth.* New York: Heller/JCCA Research Center, 2001.

Cohen, Steven M., and Arnold Eisen. *The Jew Within: Self, Family, and Community in America.* Bloomington, Ind.: Indiana University Press, 2000.

Cowan, Rachel. "The New Spirituality in Jewish Life." *The 1994 Annual Report of the Nathan Cummings Foundation.* New York: Nathan Cummings Foundation, 1994.

Crain, William. *Theories of Human Development.* 3rd ed. Englewood Cliffs, N.J.: Prentice Hall, 1992.

Cranton, Patricia. *Understanding and Promoting Transformative Learning.* San Francisco: Jossey-Bass, 1994.

Crohn, Joel, Howard J. Markman, Susan L. Blumberg, and Janice R. Levine. *Fighting for Your Jewish Marriage.* San Francisco: Jossey-Bass, 2000.

Cross, K. Patricia. *Adults as Learners: Increasing Participation and Facilitating Learning.* San Francisco: Jossey-Bass, 1981.

Daloz, Laurent. *Mentor: Guiding the Journey of Adult Learners.* San Francisco: Jossey-Bass, 1999.

Davis, Barbara Gross. *Tools for Teaching,* San Francisco: Jossey-Bass, 2002.

Draves, William A. *How to Teach Adults.* Manhattan, Kans.: Learning Resources Network, 1984.

Eilberg, Amy. "Let Us Be Reflective, Present, during the Festival of Lights." *Jewish Bulletin of Northern California,* December 22, 2000; www.jewishsf.com/bk001222/torah.shtml

Elwell, Sue Levi. "Rosh Hashana Sermon, [1987]." In *Four Centuries of Jewish Women's Spirituality,* edited by Ellen M. Umansky and Dianne Ashton, pp. 269–273. Boston: Beacon Press, 1992.

English, Leona. *Mentoring the Religious Education of Adults.* Birmingham, Ala.: Religious Education Press, 1998.

Erikson, Erik. *Childhood and Society.* 2nd ed. New York: Norton, 1963.

Eshman, Robert. "The Searchers." *The Jewish Journal,* January 20–26, 1995, p. 10.

Flannery, Daniele. "Identity and Self-Esteem." In *Women as Learners: The Significance of Gender in Adult Learning,* edited by Elisabeth Hayes and Daniele Flannery, pp. 53–78. San Francisco: Jossey-Bass, 2000.

Fowler, James. *Stages of Faith: The Psychology of Human Development and the Quest for Meaning.* New York: HarperCollins, 1995.

Freire, Paolo. *Pedagogy of the Oppressed.* New York: Herder and Herder, 1971.

Friedman Lawrence J. *Identity's Architect: A Biography of Erik H. Erikson.* New York: Scribner, 1999.

Geller, Laura. "The Torah of Our Lives." In *Beginning Anew: A Woman's Companion to the High Holidays,* edited by Gail Twersky Reimer and Judith A. Kates, pp. 258–264. New York: Touchstone, 1997.

Goldman, Israel M. *Lifelong Learning among Jews.* New York: KTAV, 1975.

Gordis, Daniel. *God Was Not in the Fire: The Search for a Spiritual Judaism.* New York: Putnam, 1995.

Grant, Lisa, Diane Schuster, Meredith Woocher, and Steven M. Cohen. *Meaning, Connection, and Practice: Contemporary Issues in Adult Jewish Learning.* New York: JTS Press, in press.

Hammer, Barbara U. "Anti-Semitism as Trauma: A Theory of Jewish Communal Response." In *Jewish Women Speak Out: Expanding the Boundaries of Psychology,* edited by Kayla Weiner and Arinna Moon, pp. 199–220. Seattle: Canopy, 1995.

Hartman, David. *A Living Covenant.* New York: Free Press, 1985.

Hayes, Elisabeth and Daniele Flannery. *Women as Learners: The Significance of Gender in Adult Learning.* San Francisco: Jossey-Bass, 2000.

Heimlich, Joe and Emmalou Norland. *Developing Teaching Style in Adult Education.* San Francisco: Jossey-Bass, 1994.

Hendler, Lee Meyerhoff. *The Year Mom Got Religion: One Woman's Midlife Journey Into Judaism.* Woodstock, Vt.: Jewish Lights, 1998.

Herman, Simon. *Jewish Identity: A Social Psychological Perspective.* New Brunswick, N.J.: Transaction Books, 1989.

Hinchman, Lewis P., and Sandra K. Hinchman. *Memory, Identity, Community: The Idea of Narrative in the Human Sciences.* Albany: State University of New York Press, 1997.

Hoffman, Lawrence. "'*Al Chet Shechatanu* . . . for all the sins that we commit willingly or unintentionally . . .': Four Unintentional Sins of Synagogue Life." **www.uahc.org/living /letuslearn/515alchet.shtml/committ/**

Horowitz, Bethamie. "Connections and Journeys: New Findings on Jewish Identity Development." In *Beyond Continuity—Taking the Next Steps: A Handbook for Jewish Renaissance and Renewal.* New York: JESNA, 2000a.

Horowitz, Bethamie. *Connections and Journeys: Assessing Critical Opportunities for Enhancing Jewish Identity.* New York: UJA-Federation of New York, 2000b.

Houle, Cyril. *The Inquiring Mind.* Madison, Wisc.: University of Wisconsin Press, 1961.

Jordan, Judith V. "The Meaning of Mutuality." In *Women's Growth in Connection,* edited by Judith V. Jordan, Alexandra G. Kaplan, Jean Baker Miller, Irene P. Shiver, and Janet L. Surrey, pp. 81–96. New York: Guilford, 1991.

Jordan, Judith V., Alexandra G. Kaplan, Jean Baker Miller, Irene P. Shiver, and Janet L. Surrey. *Women's Growth in Connection.* New York: Guilford, 1991.

Kahn, Benjamin. "Introduction." In *Go and Study: Essays and Studies in Honor of Alfred Jospe,* edited by Raphael Jospe and Samuel Z. Fishman. Washington, D.C.: B'nai Brith Hillel Foundation, 1980.

Kegan, Robert. *In Over Our Heads: The Mental Demands of Modern Life.* Cambridge, Mass.: Harvard University Press, 1994.

Klein, Judith Weinstein. *Jewish Identity and Self-Esteem: Healing Wounds Through Ethnotherapy.* New York: American Jewish Committee, 1982.

Knowles, Malcolm S. *The Modern Practice of Adult Education: From Pedagogy to Andragogy.* 2nd ed. New York: Cambridge Books, 1982.

Knox, Alan B. *Helping Adults Learn.* San Francisco: Jossey-Bass, 1986.

Levinson, Daniel, and associates. *The Seasons of a Man's Life.* New York: Ballantine, 1978.

London, Perry, and Barry Chazan. *Psychology and Jewish Identity Education.* New York: American Jewish Committee, 1990.

Marcia, James. "Ego Identity Development." In *Handbook of Adolescent Psychology,* edited by Joseph Adelson. New York: Wiley, 1980.

Markus, Hazel, and Paula Nurius. "Possible Selves." *American Psychologist* 41 (1986): 954–969.

Maslow, Abraham. *Motivation and Personality.* 2nd ed. New York: Harper and Row, 1970.

McAdams, Dan P., Holly M. Hart, and Shadd Maruna. "The Anatomy of Generativity." In *Generativity and Adult Development,* edited by Dan McAdams and Ed de St. Aubin, pp. 7–43. Washington, D.C.: American Psychological Association, 1998.

McKenzie, Leon. "The Purposes and Scope of Adult Religious Education." In *Handbook of Adult Religious Education,* edited by Nancy T. Foltz pp. 7–24. Birmingham, Ala.: Religious Education Press, 1986.

Mezirow, Jack. "Learning to Think Like an Adult: Core Concepts of Transformation Theory." In *Learning as Transformation,* edited by Jack Mezirow and Associates, pp. 3–34. San Francisco: Jossey-Bass, 2000.

Miller, Jean Baker. "The Development of Women's Sense of Self." In *Women's Growth in Connection,* edited by Judith V. Jordan, Alexandra G. Kaplan, Jean Baker Miller, Irene P. Stiver, and Janet L. Surrey, pp. 11–26. New York: Guilford, 1991.

Narayan, Kirin. "'According to Their Feelings': Teaching and Healing with Stories." In *Stories Lives Tell: Narrative and Dialogue in Education,* edited by Carol Witherell and Nel Noddings, pp. 113–135. New York: Teachers College Press, 1991.

Palmer, Parker. *The Courage to Teach.* San Francisco: Jossey-Bass, 1998.

Parks, Sharon Daloz. *Big Questions, Worthy Dreams.* San Francisco: Jossey-Bass, 2000.

Piaget, Jean. *The Origins of Intelligence in Children.* New York: International Universities Press, 1952.

Randall, William. "Restorying a Life: Adult Education and Transformative Learning." In *Aging and Biography: Explorations in Adult Development,* edited by J. Birren, G. Kenyon, J.-E. Ruth, J. Schroots, and T. Svensson, pp. 224–247. New York: Springer, 1996.

Roof, Wade Clark. *A Generation of Seekers: The Spiritual Journeys of the Baby Boom Generation.* New York: HarperCollins, 1993.

Rosenzweig, Franz. *On Jewish Learning.* New York: Schocken, 1955.

Rosten, Leo. *The New Joys of Yiddish.* New York: Crown, 2000.

Salkin, Jeffrey K. *Searching for My Brothers: Jewish Men in a Gentile World.* New York: Putnam, 1999.

Schlossberg, Nancy. *Overwhelmed: Coping with Life's Ups and Downs.* Lexington, Mass.: Lexington Books, 1989.

Scholem, Gershom. *On the Possibility of Jewish Mysticism in Our Time.* Philadelphia: Jewish Publication Society, 1997.

Schreiber, Deborah A., and Lane L. Berge. *Distance Training.* San Francisco: Jossey-Bass, 1998.

Schuster, Diane Tickton. "Jewish Lives/Jewish Learning: From Life to Torah in Contemporary America." Paper presented at Annual Meeting of the Network for Research in Jewish Education, Palo Alto, California, June 1995.

Shrage, Barry. *Building a Community of Torah and Tzedek: A New Paradigm for the Jewish Community of the 21st Century.* Boston: Combined Jewish Philanthropies, 1996.

Siegel, Rachel Josefowitz. "Jewish Women's Bodies: Sexuality, Body Image, and Self-Esteem." In *Jewish Women Speak Out: Expanding the Boundaries of Psychology,* edited by Kayla Weiner and Arinna Moon, pp. 41–54. Seattle: Canopy, 1995.

Steinberg, Miriam. "Pursuing Justice to Better Ourselves and Better the World." *The Charlotte and Jack J. Spitzer B'nai B'rith Hillel Forum on Public Policy,* February 2001, www.hillel.org/Hillel/NewHille.nsf/fcb8259ca861ae57852567d30043ba26/541c15126 bfc090a85256a17006731b6?OpenDocument

Tarule, Jill. "Voices of Returning Women: Ways of Knowing." In *Addressing the Needs of Returning Women,* edited by Linda H. Lewis, pp. 19–34. San Francisco: Jossey-Bass, 1988.

Taylor, Kathleen, Catherine Marienau, and Morris Fiddler. *Developing Adult Learners.* San Francisco: Jossey-Bass, 2000.

Tough, Allen. *The Adult's Learning Project: A Fresh Approach to Theory and Practice in Adult Learning,* 2nd ed. Toronto: Ontario Institute for Studies in Education, 1979.

Union of American Hebrew Congregations. *Live Together, Learn Together.* New York: UAHC Press, 2000.

Vella, Jane. *Learning to Listen, Learning to Teach.* San Francisco: Jossey-Bass, 1994.

Westmeyer, Paul. *Effective Teaching in Adult and Higher Education.* Springfield, Ill.: Charles C. Thomas, 1988.

White, Robert W. "Motivation Reconsidered: The Concept of Competence." *Psychological Review* 66, no. 5 (1959): 297–333.

Wickett, R. E. Y. *Models of Adult Religious Education Practice.* Birmingham, Ala.: Religious Education Press, 1991.

Wiggins, Grant, and Jay McTighe. *Understanding by Design.* Alexandria, Va.: Association for Supervision and Curriculum Development, 1998.

Wlodkowski, Raymond. *Enhancing Adult Motivation to Learn.* San Francisco: Jossey-Bass, 1999.

Wuthnow, Robert. *Sharing the Journey: Support Groups and America's New Quest for Community.* New York: Free Press, 1994.

Yoffie, Eric. "Presidential Sermon," UAHC 64th Biennial Convention, Dallas, October 29–November 2, 1997.

Zachary, Lois. *The Mentor's Guide: Facilitating Effective Learning Relationships.* San Francisco: Jossey-Bass, 2000.

Zeldin, Michael, and Sara Lee, eds. *Touching the Future: Mentoring and the Jewish Professional.* Los Angeles: Hebrew Union College–Jewish Institute of Religion, 1995.

Index

Note: Exhibits are indicated by **bold** page numbers